THIS BOOK BELONGS TO

_____

Here's a **blank space**, baby.
Write your name.

THIS IS OUR SONG

TYLER CONROY

TAYLOR SWIFT

SIMON & SCHUSTER

London   New York   Toronto   Sydney   New Delhi

FOR TAYLOR

"I'm a fan of fans. You are absolutely wonderful to me.
I've got your back, just like you've had mine."
—*Taylor Swift, MySpace bio (2008)*

CONTENTS

This Is Our Introduction
Tyler Conroy   xi

PART ONE: THE EARLY YEARS

**Twelve-Year-Old Performs
at 76ers Game**
Jeremy Carroll   3

A review of *Taylor Swift*
Rick Bell   5

20 Questions with Taylor Swift
CMT.com   9

My Music, MySpace, My Life
Jon Caramanica   17

Prodigy: The Rise of Taylor Swift
Sasha Frere-Jones   25

A review of *Fearless*
Robert Christgau   31

**Taylor Swift: Growing into
Superstardom**
George Hatza   35

The Unabridged Taylor Swift
Austin Scaggs   42

**The Very Pink, Very Perfect Life
of Taylor Swift**
Vanessa Grigoriadis   55

The Tao of Tay
Taylor Swift   65

PART TWO: CROSSOVER

A review of *Speak Now*
Rob Sheffield   79

Princess Crossover
Chris Willman   81

A review of *Speak Now*
Robert Christgau   87

You Belong with Me
Lizzie Widdicombe   91

A review of *Red*
Robert Christgau   113

**If You Listen Closely, Taylor Swift
Is Kind of Like Leonard Cohen**
Brad Nelson   117

Taylor Swift in Wonderland
Brian Hiatt   127

Just Kidding, Love Sucks
Tavi Gevinson   141

Platinum Underdog
Jody Rosen   151

Taylor Swift: Girl Detective
Larissa Zageris and Kitty Curran   164

PART THREE: 1989 AND BEYOND

To Apple, Love Taylor
Taylor Swift   191

A review of *1989*
Rob Sheffield   193

Taylor Swift: "Sexy? Not on My Radar"
Hermione Hoby   197

A review of *1989*
Robert Christgau   207

Taylor Swift: A Socratic Dialogue
Jared Smith   210

**A Reasonable Conversation About
Taylor Swift's New Album,
Which Is the Best Album Ever**
Jane Hu and Jen Vafidis   217

**"Anything That Connects":
A Conversation with Taylor Swift**
Melissa Block   227

**On the Road with Best Friends
Taylor Swift and Karlie Kloss**
Jada Yuan   235

**No Blank Space, Baby: Taylor Swift
Is the Soul of Ryan Adams**
Ann Powers   245

**Taylor Swift on "Bad Blood,"
Kanye West, and How People
Interpret Her Lyrics**
Chuck Klosterman   251

I'm Sorry, Taylor Swift
Maggie Shipstead   265

**Taylor Swift As You've Never
Seen Her Before**
Jason Gay   273

Taylor Swift

FEARLESS

Speak Now

RED

1989

THIS IS OUR INTRODUCTION

AUGUST 2016 | TYLER CONROY

We'll never forget where we were the exact moment we found her. It might have been while we were listening to the radio, searching through MySpace or YouTube trying to pass the time, scream-singing with our friends in the car, or nursing a broken heart. We were young, nervous, free, and waiting for something great (at the same time). And then, there she was. She gave us words that taught us to celebrate and helped us to heal. In that instant, we knew we wanted this sparkly-dress-wearing, curly-haired girl in our lives forever. We never saw it coming, and we were never the same. She was a storyteller, a mind-reader, a believer, and a friend. She was one of us.

She was Taylor Swift.

Ten years ago, Taylor welcomed us into her world, and we welcomed her into ours, creating the greatest band of thieves in ripped-up jeans ever known: the Swifties. Ask us why we love her, and prepare to pull up a chair and give us an hour—at least—of your time. Everyone has a different reason, a different story. She was there for us when we needed her most. She wasn't afraid to talk about her feelings, and told us we shouldn't be either. She inspired us to play guitar and

write songs. She's invited us backstage, onto her tour bus, and into her home, stopping to say "Hi" and ask how we've been. She's sent us Christmas presents, MySpace messages, tweets, FaceTimed us, and even shown up at a wedding or

two. She's continually thanked us for knowing all of the words to her songs, for standing by her side. For a decade, she has given us so much, and we want to finally try to return the favor.

Which is why we're here.

This book is for all of us, from all of us. Like I said, every Swiftie has a story, and this book is meant to be a collection of them, told alongside the incredible journey of Taylor herself. With the help of thirteen fan ambassadors, we found the best writing, photography, and fan memories of her, starting with her appearance (as a twelve-year-old!) at a 76ers game and ending full circle with her return to her Pennsylvania hometown as a global superstar. To represent the different corners of the fandom, we wanted to make sure that we paid tribute in as many ways as possible. So, we dusted off our Taylor magazines, put her albums on repeat, looked through thousands of photos, relived our favorite moments, and got to work. Think of what you're now holding as the ultimate collection of liner notes, a record of Taylor's first ten years, filled with proof of how one person can (literally) change people's lives—and the world.

There are things you might know about Taylor in these pages, like how she got Apple to pay artists during their free music trial, or how her grandmother was a professional opera singer. There are other things you might not know, like how she wrote a full-length novel when she was FOURTEEN (!) or that her mom once visited a psychic and was

This College Just Created A Taylor Swift Musical!!! With Her Songs! Watch!!!

Hi Taylor!

What an incredible idea!

The Office of Residential Life at **Io** **College** in New Rochelle, NY had brazilliant idea to make a musical usi hit songs from none other than **Tay Swift**!

2014

1989 Roger.

I knew you were trouble when you walked in.

NO TRESPASSING

IT'S A LOVE STORY
AN ORIGINAL MUSICAL BY DALE MURPHY
MUSIC & LYRICS BY TAYLOR SWIFT

told that everyone would know her daughter's name (Andrea thought it meant that Taylor would be kidnapped). There are also personal stories and memories from our ambassadors that are sweet, funny, and really meaningful. Fourteen-year-old Emma Dugan dealt with bullies and making the right decisions by asking herself, "Would Taylor like me if I do this?"; Dan Gibson, twenty-four, wants her just to be happy, since that what she's made her fans; Zainub Amir, twenty, runs a Twitter account called @SimplySFans and Ashley Friedman, twenty-seven, hosts the SwiftCast, both bringing Swift love to the masses. These are just a few examples:

If we listed all the wonderful things our Swifties have said, we'd be here all day.

For some extra fun, there are crossword puzzles, coloring pages (designed by another of our ambassadors, Kelsey Quitschau, who has emerged as the book's artist-in-residence), a collection of our favorite Taylor quotes we've dubbed *The Tao of Tay*, gorgeous fan art, and even an excerpt of the Nancy Drew–inspired spoof, *Taylor Swift: Girl Detective*, straight from Tumblr. While all of these things come together to show how we have seen and loved Taylor over the years, the longer pieces of journalism from publications like *Vogue*, *The New Yorker*, *The Believer*,

GQ, and *The Reading Eagle* (Taylor's hometown paper) show how the *world* has seen her grow. They range from album reviews and professional profiles, like Jada Yuan's, to personal reflections, like Tavi Gevinson's. To honor the level of Taylor's influence on musical culture, we've included some of the most influential figures in cultural criticism, from Sasha Frere-Jones and Robert Christgau to Ann Powers and Rob Sheffield. The book was titled by a fan (Tenay Barker, a college student in Nacogdoches, Texas) and its cover design was created by one as well (Shanna Canarini, a recent graduate of the American Academy of Art).

TAYLOR SWIFT
THE RED TOUR

MARCH 28, 2013
PRUDENTIAL CENTER
NEWARK, NJ

In short, we just want to follow Taylor's advice and "capture it, remember it." Seeing it all here in one place—and finally being able to share it with you!—is one of the most amazing feelings in the world.

Before I leave you to it, though, I should introduce myself properly. What kind of Swiftie would I be if I didn't tell you my Taylor story, after all?

Hi. Nice to meet you! I'm Tyler Conroy.

My love of all things Swift hit me like a big tour bus—almost literally. It was the summer of 2008 and I was finally going to see Taylor in real life for the first time. I'd became a huge fan after hearing "Tim McGraw" at a family party. As a coun-

try fan raised in Conway, Massachusetts (a town known for its hills and cows), I was instantly awestruck by the song, the sound, and the lyrics. I remember going home, downloading the entire album, and just sitting there, listening and thinking how unbelievable it was that someone so young had created something so amazing. But back to the concert! It was in Hartford, Connecticut, and she was opening for Rascal Flatts. I was walking toward the venue, crossing the street with my nose in my phone (DON'T DO IT, KIDS), when I heard my friend scream, "TYLER! WATCH OUT!" I whipped around just in time, and as the giant white bus sped past

me, I noticed a silver silhouette of a girl with a guitar printed on the back. "THAT WAS TAYLOR SWIFT!" I screamed. Later, as she took the stage, I danced and sang, and made a hand heart that she returned, smiling at me.

Everything had changed.

For the next eight years, I've been a devoted Swiftie, soaking up everything I could from Taylor and her music. *Fearless* rescued me when I was being kicked into lockers and bullied by other kids, and taught me how to pick myself up and be the best version of myself, regardless of what people said or thought. Taking the album's message to heart, I learned how to play the guitar and started writing music of my own. One day, I uploaded a video of myself singing a parody of "Hey Stephen" called "Hey Taylor." Not even a month later, I was backstage at Gillette Stadium, getting a kiss on the cheek from Taylor herself. She'd seen the video and loved it. (I would eventually meet her two more times, at Club Red and at her New York apartment for the launch of 1989.) *Speak Now* inspired me to find my voice and tell the truth about who I was, and helped me to feel like I was finally, truly living for the first time. *Red* taught me all I needed to know about relationships and heartbreak. *1989* reminded me to have fun and just shake it off. Looking back now, I realize that what made all of those songs and their creator so important to me was not only knowing she understood; it was knowing she *cared*.

And with that, I'd like to say, THANK YOU, TAYLOR. On behalf of all the people who will read this book, who have been fans forever and the ones who have yet to discover you and your beautiful music, thank you for being fearless. Thank you for your confidence, your assurance, and your hope. Thank you for embracing the good and the bad, for speaking from your heart and letting the world listen, for letting us know that we'll forget the name of the person who broke our heart at fifteen and find someone better—that we'll find ourselves, too. For teaching us that if we put enough good into the world, good things will happen and good people will stand by us, and for creating this community that wants nothing more than to see you—and each other—happy. Because of you, we'll never stop dreaming, writing, and singing at the top of our lungs.

This is your story. This is our song. ◆

PART ONE

THE EARLY YEARS

I was from a small town, and nobody really expects you to leave, especially before you graduate. That doesn't happen. I actually went back a couple months ago and played a sold-out show in my hometown, and it was amazing; ever since all this stuff started happening, the people in Pennsylvania have been the most supportive people I've ever known. But I wouldn't change a thing about growing up and not exactly fitting in. If I had been popular, I probably wouldn't have wanted to leave.

TWELVE-YEAR-OLD PERFORMS AT 76ERS GAME

Taylor Swift of Wyomissing Hills was invited to sing the national anthem

READING EAGLE, **APRIL 19, 2002** | JEREMY CARROLL

Taylor A. Swift, twelve, of Wyomissing Hills thought her ten-year-old brother, Austin K., might have been playing an April Fools' Day joke on her when he told her the Philadelphia 76ers invited her to sing the national anthem at an upcoming home basketball game.

But Austin was telling the truth, relaying the information from their father, Scott K., who phoned with the thrilling day-after-Easter news.

"My mom and I were just jumping up and down we were so excited," said Taylor, who sang the anthem just before the tip-off of the Sixers game against the Detroit Pistons on April 5.

"I just really love doing that sort of thing," she said. "It is an adrenaline rush for me."

Swift, a sixth grader at West Reading Elementary Center, sang the national anthem at a Reading Phillies game several years ago.

Last month she did another rendition at a basketball game at Wyomissing High School in which the Harlem Wizards played against the Wyomissing Heroes, made up of school faculty and other members of the community.

It was her first performance at the Wizards' game that gave her the chance to sing at a much larger venue, Philadelphia's First Union Center, where 20,754 fans came to see the Sixers and Pistons play.

Scott Swift sent in a video of his daughter singing the anthem to the 76ers, hoping the team would recognize her talent.

Sixers manager of game operations Kathy Drysdale, who said she gets hundreds of videotapes from performers interested in singing the anthem at one of the team's exhibition games or forty-one regular season home games, sat up and took notice of Swift.

"She has this fantastic voice that catches everyone's attention," Drysdale said. "Her voice is so strong and powerful at twelve years old. You look at her and think, 'Did that come out of her mouth?'"

Swift left for Philadelphia right after school on April 5 with her parents, brother, and a friend of her brother. They encountered lots of traffic and wound up making it to the arena just in time for her sound check at five.

Shortly after their arrival, team officials presented Taylor, Austin, and Austin's friend with duffel bags full of 76ers merchandise, including basketballs, jerseys, and hats. Taylor also received a jersey signed by some of the Sixers players.

After getting ready in a private dressing room, Swift was escorted by a security guard onto the court, which was adorned with a red carpet.

Her mother, Andrea F., admitted she was very nervous leading up to the anthem.

"They had a small number of cameras all focused right around her and she was up on the big screen," Andrea said. "It's very, very scary as a mom to see your child out there."

Taylor was much more relaxed about the whole thing, experiencing few butterflies even as the lights were dimmed just moments before her performance.

"I was just practicing the first note over and over in my head," she said.

Swift, who sang the final words of the anthem in the midst of deafening cheers from the crowd, said the whole experience was a big thrill.

"All of these NBA players and all of these other people were looking at me," she said. "It was really a wonderful feeling."

Swift has been performing practically all of her life in local theater productions.

Next Friday and Saturday she will perform in Wyomissing High School's production of *The Sound of Music.*

Swift, whose maternal grandmother, Marjorie Finlay, of Wyomissing Park, is a retired opera singer, has been pursuing a country music singing career.

The aspiring singing star, who also plays electric guitar, performed with the Pat Garrett Band at last year's Bloomsburg Fair and has cut a country CD.

Late last month the Swifts traveled to Nashville, where they distributed the CD to record companies in the hope of landing a recording deal.

When she is not busy performing, Swift enjoys spending time with her friends. ♦

A REVIEW OF *TAYLOR SWIFT*

FALL 2006 RICK BELL

Despite a grown-up major-label debut, it appears Taylor Swift is okay with just being a kid sometimes. Swift, a native of Pennsylvania's farm country, is all of sixteen. She keeps up with friends and fans on MySpace, bored-teenager doodles meander through the liner notes, and the album, which includes her coming-of-age debut single "Tim McGraw," has an iPod feel with as much pop as country among the eleven cuts.

Yet Swift, thanks in part to unknown producer Nathan Chapman, deftly blends a Cyndi Thomson–meets–Hilary Duff sound anchored in Swift's smart songwriting while employing a heady list of studio musicians. Chapman is a budding talent as well, playing about every instrument imaginable while handling the production chores. Swift wrote or cowrote all the cuts, but credits her coauthors—primarily Liz Rose, who pitched in on seven songs, including "Tim McGraw"—for lending direction and focus.

Swift's best efforts come on her deeply personal, self-penned songs, particularly "The Outside" and "Our Song," which she sings with stirring conviction.

It's an impressive debut that, while she pines about lost love and Tim McGraw, will likely have others singing the praises of Taylor Swift.

Taylor Swift

by Tony Orbach, edited by Ben Tausig

ACROSS

1 Grouchy types
6 Actress Reid of the *Sharknado* movies
10 Letters on a party invitation
14 Hard-hit baseball
15 Unwelcome smell
16 Olympic fencing sword
17 Assume the role of
18 Taylor Swift single named for Faith Hill's husband, who recorded her "favorite song"
20 Competes in a slalom race, say
21 "My country, 'tis of ___ . . ."
22 Train track
23 Taylor Swift breakup song in which she will "strike a match on all my wasted time"
26 Once ___ lifetime
27 Build on
29 Made into grain-sized pieces
32 Contented sound from a cat
35 What a commoner might call a king
37 Progressive Insurance ad character played by comedian Stephanie Courtney
38 Taylor Swift's album-closing tune that is "the slamming screen door, sneakin' out late, tapping on your window"
41 Sergeant or corporal: Abbr.
42 Heidi of *Project Runway*
44 Prod into action
45 Church instrument
47 Hair tangle
49 Sheep's greeting
50 Taylor Swift song in which she hopes "your life leads you back to my door"
57 College bigwig below the provost
58 Toddler's song, perhaps
59 Back of the neck
60 Taylor Swift song in which there is "a rainy ending given to a perfect day"
62 Treat badly
63 Cowboy's suffix with buck
64 Car horn beep
65 Solitary person
66 *Roseanne* star
67 Film protagonist Skywalker
68 Tries to flatten, as a fly

DOWN

1 Manila envelope fastener
2 Talk show host ___ Lake
3 Single bit of silliness
4 "Fight for Your Right" band the ___ Boys
5 Twelfth graders: Abbr.

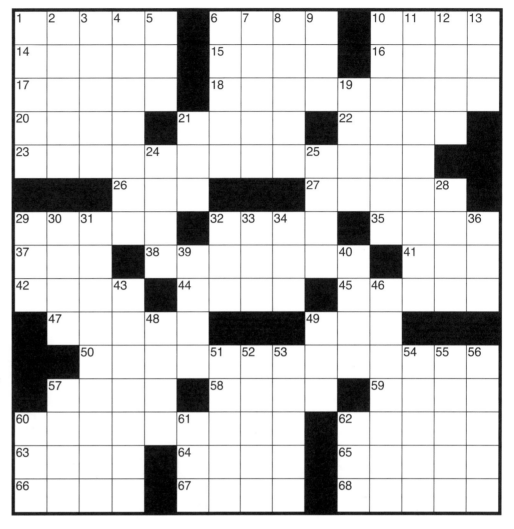

6 "Take Me Out ___ Ball Game"
7 On ___ (trying to lose weight)
8 Juliet's love
9 Body part on which Taylor Swift wrote lyrics during her Speak Now tour
10 "Give My ___ to Broadway"
11 Competing in the 100-meter, say
12 Cutlet meat
13 Bench in a church
19 Gunk
21 ___ la la (nonsense song syllables)
24 Computer editing command
25 Farm building in which Taylor Swift's "Crazier" video is set
28 Killer whale
29 ___ Stadium (D.C. United's home field)
30 Misfortunes
31 Summer camp boss
32 Paid player
33 Team ___ (Olympic basketball powerhouse)

34 Fishing pole
36 Extremely long time
39 Especially unpleasant, like some breakups
40 The best ever, for short
43 Bullfighter
46 LGBT flag symbol
48 ___ temperature (was feverish)
49 Tour vehicle for Taylor Swift
51 Blue ___ (hit song for both Roy Orbison and Linda Ronstadt)
52 Purchase for a Kindle
53 Sharp, as an angle
54 Flora's counterpart
55 Unexpected sports outcome
56 Lascivious looks
57 Nickelodeon's ___ *the Explorer*
60 Big city transportation option
61 Letters on a Cardinals cap
62 Politicians Gore and Franken

20 QUESTIONS with Taylor Swift

CMT.COM, NOVEMBER 2007

Taylor Swift hasn't graduated from high school yet, but she's already smart enough to know the secret to success in country music.

"I think the first thing you should know is that nobody in country music 'made it' the same way," says the seventeen-year-old singer-songwriter who won the coveted Horizon Award at last week's CMA Awards. "It's all different. There's no blueprint for success, and sometimes you just have to work at it. You should make sure that you know who you are as an artist and make sure it's nothing like everyone else. It's good to be inspired by other artists, but you should always make sure that you've got your own niche."

Answering these questions from fans, she talks about learning dance moves from Kellie Pickler, the song that inspired "Tim McGraw," and why she's going to skip college.

1. Who influenced you and why did you choose to make country music?

I was influenced early on by all of the great female country artists of the '90s and all of the cool music they were putting out. Like Shania, Faith, the Dixie Chicks. It was such great music, and it completely drew me in to country music.

2. If you could record a duet with any country music star, who would it be?

I think Kenny Chesney or Garth Brooks would be the coolest duet partners. I look up to them so much for their work ethics. I was lucky enough to open up for Kenny on some shows this summer, and watching him work was so inspiring. He and Garth just represent true artists to me, and any project I could work with one of them would be an honor.

3. If you could tour with all women, which artists or bands of any genre would you like to go on the road with you?

Wow, out of all genres I would pick Rihanna and Brandi Carlile. You say "random." I say "interesting."

4. When you are not touring, what do you like to do for fun?

My best friend, Abigail, and I like to drive past our ex-boyfriends' houses.

5. What do you remember the most about the night you filmed Brad Paisley's video, "Online"?

I remember looking over at Kellie the whole time, trying to copy her dance moves. I'll admit it: That girl can dance!

6. It's so fun to see you come out onstage singing an Eminem cover and your version of Beyoncé's "Irreplaceable" rocks. Any plans to do a duet with a rap artist on an upcoming album?

Ha ha! I don't know! I'm not planning anything like that right now, but I think the coolest thing in the world would be to do something with Jay-Z. When I was twelve, I sang the national anthem at a 76ers game in Philly. Jay-Z was sitting courtside and gave me a high five after I sang. I bragged about that for like a year straight. I love doing cover songs that nobody expects. When I went to live shows, I always loved stuff like that. I like it when something you wouldn't expect to happen onstage happens—musically or visually. I think Sugarland does a great job of incorporating different surprises into their shows.

"I write songs like diary entries.

Tim McGraw

but in a box
beneath my bed
is a letter that
you've never
read,

from three
summers back.
TS

Picture to Burn

So watch me
strike a match
on all my wasted time.
TS

I have to do it to stay sane."

7. I love to sing but have a big problem with stage fright. Do you have any advice for me to conquer this problem?

I think everyone has that problem when they first start singing. In my opinion, the only way to conquer stage fright is to get up onstage and play. Every time you play another show, it gets better and better. I started singing in front of crowds when I was ten, and it was a little scary at first. Anything you've just started doing is going to be scary. Once, somebody told me to picture the audience in their un-derpants. Do *not* picture the audience in their underpants. That does not work. At all.

8. How has your homeschooling experience helped or hindered your musical development?

My homeschooling has been a great experience. I feel like I've had the best senior year possible. It's awesome that I've been able to stay on the same path to graduating that I would've been on if I'd stayed in high school. I'm going to graduate this year, and I'm so excited about that. My ed-ucation was always a big deal to me, and I'm so glad homeschooling allowed me to keep it up.

9. Do you feel like you miss the so-called normal life of a teenager?

I don't, really. Of course, you're always going to wonder about the road not taken, the dorm not taken, and the sorority not taken. But if I wasn't doing this, I would've missed out on the best moments I've ever known and the most wonderful life that I still can't believe I get to live. I'm still friends with the same people I was friends with in high school, and I feel like I haven't changed as a person.

10. Do you plan on attending college?

Right now, I'm pursuing my career. I always thought that I would go to college, most definitely. But then I really thought about it and assessed the situation, and I can't leave this life. Going to college would mean saying goodbye to my music career, and I just can't do that. There just wouldn't be enough time in the day to be on tour, do interviews, meet and greets, TV appearances, and everything else that I need to do and go to college. Maybe later on in life I'll end up taking a few classes or doing it online. But right now, it just isn't where I need to be.

11. I absolutely love your outfits. Where do you shop?

Thank you! I love to shop. One of the things I love about doing this is that you can shop for every season, because you know that sooner or later you're going to be in every part of the country and in every type of weather. I love Forever 21 and BCBG. Those are probably my favorite stores.

12. I know you wear dresses a lot, so I was wondering if you would ever want to have your own dress line. I would definitely buy them.

I love dresses, and I've definitely thought about designing them someday. I just want to make sure that I wait until the time is perfect and I can do it right. My stylist, Sandi Spika, makes my dresses for award shows and videos. We have so much fun planning the next big dress to make.

I think it would be great to work with her on some cool dresses for a line.

13. What kind of TV shows and movies do you like to watch?

I love *CSI: Las Vegas* and *Grey's Anatomy*. I've come to the conclusion that the guy I end up with will remind me of the character Denny Duquette from *Grey's*. Ha ha. My favorite movie is *Love Actually*. It's got the cutest ending.

> "Do *not* picture the audience in their **underpants**. That does not work. At all."

14. Is the song "Tim McGraw" about a specific Tim McGraw song you danced to?

It's called "Can't Tell Me Nothin'"—and it's my favorite Tim song.

15. What do you do for inspiration when you sit down to write a song and it seems that nothing wants to come out?

That happens all the time. What I do is just put the guitar down and wait for something to hit me. You can never push songwriting. It happens or it doesn't.

16. Do you also want to write songs for other artists?

Yes! Kellie Pickler and I wrote a song together when we were out on the road, and it was so cool jumping into someone else's feelings for a minute and writing from their perspective. It was like I was writing my very first song. Exhilarating.

17. You are such an inspiration and role model to all girls of any age, and I think that's awesome! How do you manage to stay away from all the bad things superstars seem to be getting pulled into these days?

I think it all comes down to who you surround yourself with and how strong your morals are. Before I make a decision, I stop and think about the ten-year-old girl I saw last night at my concert in the front row. I think about her mom. I think about how they bought my CD, thinking that I'm a good role model. Then I think about how they would feel if I did something to let them down. I can't imagine a greater pain than letting one of those mothers down. I honestly can't.

18. If you were driving cross-country and could only bring one CD, what would it be?

Def Leppard. *Pyromania*.

19. From performing in front of thousands of fans to daily interviews and signing autographs, how do you keep up your energy?

I'm seventeen. I think that helps a lot. I'm lucky to have been able to do all of this at a young age. Also, I'm just so consumed by it. I'm just so fascinated by every aspect of this. Whether it's radio or videos or concerts, I never want to stop getting excited. I hope I never do.

20. Do you have any pets?

I have a cat named Indi (who hates everyone in my family except for me) and two Dobermans. They're really sweet, but if you break in, they will eat you. ♦

LIVIA JAHN

STUDENT, 15, INDIANA

My first memory of Taylor is from Valentine's Day 2007. I was five and my grandma bought me her first album. It was raining so I stayed inside, played Barbies, and viciously headbanged to "Our Song." Ten years later, not much has changed.

Taylor is always starting conversations for me. Whenever I wear her merchandise people come up to me and say things like, "Hey! You like Taylor Swift?" After that it's like an endless array of "Yeah! Once I made a foxtail out of a bath rug for her concert." "You did not!" "Oh yes I did."

She's willing to change and yet stay true to her roots. Most people look at change as something horrible. But she has always made it her own. I find that really inspiring.

I cry every time I hear "Never Grow Up." I think it's because I have a younger brother who I see grow up every day. It's a big sister's job to make sure no one ever breaks his heart.

My ultimate dream is to bake with Taylor. That would give us enough time to talk about stuff going on in our lives.

My dad thinks it's funny when I refer to Taylor as "Taylor." He says it sounds like we're best friends and says no one will know who I'm talking about. But what other Taylor would I be talking about?

There are so many things that make Taylor different from all the other artists out there. For starters she's willing to go the extra mile for her fans. She invites us into her home. She talks to us online. She makes us a part of something bigger than ourselves.

I hope that Taylor writes an autobiography someday.

Taylor stars in every dream I have. It's funny because sometimes I'll meet her in a pretty realistic setting but other times she'll be the grocery clerk or something odd. Then for a couple of weeks I'll be paranoid that I'm going to see her bagging groceries in the store.

One thing that everyone could learn from Taylor is how to take hurtful things and turn them into something beautiful. She constantly has people saying things behind her back, and she's always been able to make the best out of it.

> "One thing that everyone could learn from Taylor is how to **take hurtful things** and turn them into something beautiful."

The first time I saw Taylor live was when I was in fourth grade at the *Speak Now* tour. My friend and I got on the big screen with our hand hearts. We thought it was the coolest thing ever. I remember being really scared when she was on the floating balcony.

Taylor inspired me to learn to play the piano. I had always loved music, but piano opened up a huge world of ideas for me. It's one of those instruments that can nourish happiness and relieve pain.

If I ever meet Taylor I'll probably tell her how grateful I am for her. Not only for her powerful songs, but also for her beautiful personality, which has taught me to do what I love and keep going. I'd also shed some tears because I've only met her in dreams.

MY MUSIC, MYSPACE, MY LIFE

THE NEW YORK TIMES, **NOVEMBER 2008** | JON CARAMANICA

Chattanooga, Tennessee

By now Taylor Swift knows how to work all the different digital cameras, all the different camera phones. When surrounded by a group of fans clamoring for pictures, as she was here on a Saturday night in mid-October after a sold-out show at the McKenzie Arena, she warmly appropriated the camera of each one, struck a cute pose, snapped the picture, and then handed it back, usually followed by a hug. All in all it was a fair trade: intimacy for control.

"Intimidation isn't what I'm going for," Ms. Swift, eighteen, said earlier in the day in the Zen-like tour bus she and her mother, Andrea, designed, from the leather on the sofas to the faux peacock feathers on the bathroom wall. "I don't have big security guards," she said as Fox News played mutely on the television. "I don't have an entourage. I try to write lyrics about what's happening to me and leave out the part that I live in hotel rooms and tour buses. It's the relatability factor. If you're trying too

hard to be the girl next door, you're not going to be."

Thus far Ms. Swift, who spends much of her free time updating her MySpace page and editing personal videos to upload to the internet, has not had a tough time finding the right balance. She has quickly established herself as the most remarkable country music breakthrough artist of the decade. In part that's because she is one of Nashville's most exciting songwriters, with a chirpy, exuberant voice. But mainly Ms. Swift's career has been noteworthy for what happens once the songs are finished. She has aggressively used online social networks to stay connected with her young audience in a way that, while typical for rock and hip-hop artists, is proving to be revolutionary in country music. As she vigilantly narrates her own story and erases barriers between her and her fans, she is helping country reach a new audience.

Ms. Swift's second album, *Fearless* (Big Machine), will be released Tuesday, and like her self-titled 2006 debut, it's full

of charming, clean-scrubbed songs about teenage love and heartbreak. Ms. Swift writes from her own experiences, names intact, giving her songs an almost radical intimacy, especially in a pop world of plasticized come-ons and impersonal brush-offs.

She has placed the concerns of young women at the center of her songs, subject matter that generally has been anathema in the more mature world of country singers. Most important, though, she very much sees country music as part of the larger pop panorama. A huge success on country radio, she has also found homes on pop stations and at MTV, including a gig hosting the MTV Video Music Awards preshow in September, an unheard-of slot for a country singer. This week an entire episode of *The Ellen DeGeneres Show* will be devoted to her album release party. Put more plainly, she has proved that there's no reason a country singer can't be a pop star too.

Just four years ago, when Ms. Swift and her family moved from Wyomissing, Pennsylvania, to Hendersonville, a Nashville suburb, this seemed an impossible proposition. It had been more than a decade since a teenager last made a true impact in town, but that singer, LeAnn Rimes, had been praised for sounding grown-up; Ms. Swift's music was unabashedly youthful. When Scott Borchetta, president of Big Machine Records, would talk to Nashville insiders about his teenage signee, "people would look at me cross-eyed," he said. "I would feel like they were deleting me from their Blackberrys as I was telling them."

But Ms. Swift had been carefully honing her sound for a few years already. After a trip to Nashville when she was eleven, she began writing songs and learning to play guitar in earnest. (She now often plays a Swarovski crystal–encrusted one.) By the time her family moved, in the summer before her freshman year of high school, she had already been singing at coffee shops and minor league baseball games.

Ms. Swift first signed a publishing deal with Sony/ATV Music Publishing, the youngest person the company had ever signed. Every day after school she would truck off to one of Nashville's many studios on Music Row for writing appointments.

"I knew every writer I wrote with was pretty much going to think, 'I'm going to write a song for a fourteen-year-old today,'" Ms. Swift said. "So I would come into each meeting with five to ten ideas that were solid. I wanted them to look at me as a person they were writing with, not a little kid."

It was during this time that Ms. Swift honed her songwriting strength: looking in the mirror. Relationships and their failures, the fodder for so much teenage pop, are her primary texts. "I have an obsession with knowing the answers to things," she said. "When I don't know what happened, it just bothers me, gets under my skin, and I need to write about it. For years."

Her mother, Andrea, said: "She simply has to write songs. It's how she filters life." (Andrea, who was previously a stay-at-home mom, now travels with her daughter; Ms. Swift's father, Scott, is a stockbroker.)

And so, around the play-by-play details

> She has proved that there's no reason a country singer can't be a **pop star** too.

of broken hearts and romantic dreams, Ms. Swift's sound began to coalesce. She has an ear for the indelible chorus—"She's one of those writers who won't run away from a hook," Mr. Borchetta said—but her music is appropriately loose. There are obvious country flourishes in the arrangements, but mainly her vocals, excitable and airy and hardly twangy at all, take center stage.

Whether anyone would accept Ms. Swift's sound was an open question. "We felt it wasn't likely that country radio would embrace it unless we had a story," Mr. Borchetta said, so Ms. Swift made a series of biographical shorts to air on the GAC (Great American Country) cable network. Then came "Tim McGraw," Ms. Swift's canny first single, named after the country superstar. (In the lyrics Mr. McGraw is the singer of a special song she and a boy share.) "We put that out deliberately, so people would ask, who's this new artist with a song called 'Tim McGraw'?" said Mr. Borchetta, who likened its reception to that of "a grenade in a still pond."

Released in late 2006, Ms. Swift's debut album sold a modest 39,000 copies in its first week, but as Ms. Swift gained attention and released more singles, it did not stop selling. It has now moved well over three million copies. Last year Ms. Swift won the Country Music Association's Horizon Award for best new artist, and this year she is nominated for female vocalist of the year. She will also perform at the ceremony, which is Wednesday.

"From the moment 'Tim McGraw' hit the channel, she began to amass an audience that traditional Nashville didn't know or didn't believe existed, and that is young women, specifically teens," said Brian Philips, executive vice president and general manager of CMT (Country Music Television). "It's as if Taylor has kind of willed herself into being."

She has willed herself beyond the country music world too. After landing at No. 2 on the *Billboard* Hot Country Singles chart, "Teardrops on My Guitar," the third single on her first album, became a crossover hit, peaking at No. 13 on the Hot 100. "In a lot of cities the pop stations will take a chance because there's been exposure in that market on the country station," said Sharon Dastur, program director of the New York Top 40 station Z100 (WHTZ-FM), which played the song in a medium-level rotation last year after it had been broken at Top 40 stations in more country-friendly markets like Greenville, South Carolina; Wichita, Kansas; and Austin, Texas.

Ms. Swift is not without forebears. In the past fifteen years female country stars like Faith Hill, Shania Twain, Lee Ann Womack, and the Dixie Chicks have all experienced some degree of pop success. And Ms. Swift's ability to straddle both country and pop was facilitated by the recent crossover success of Carrie Underwood, the *American Idol* winner.

Monte Lipman, president and chief executive of Universal Republic Records, which joined with Big Machine to work Ms. Swift's records to pop radio, said: "We don't want to alienate country radio at all because we've found pop success. Scott is always super-serving the country marketplace first, and we work for him."

Mr. Borchetta said that country radio would always be the top priority. "They're always going to get the singles first, always going to be first in line at the meet and greets," he said. "We overthink everything. One thing we can't do is chase the moving target of pop radio. It could be all emo next year, all urban next year."

No one much complains when a rapper or indie rocker crosses over to the pop charts, but a country singer perceived as trying to go pop can still raise eyebrows. Nashville remains a fiercely hermetic town and is unusually protective, or possessive, of its own.

"I'm not about to snub the people who brought me to the party," said Ms. Swift, who when she speaks of her plan to manage her crossover fame sounds like a well-seasoned executive. "We went back

and studied other cases where it had failed every way that it can fail, and we tried to avoid those things."

Ms. Swift is, by all accounts, an extremely good-natured micromanager. "She's a very competitive person, and she's always got her game face on," said the country singer Kellie Pickler, one of Ms. Swift's closest friends. "And she's a really smart businesswoman, smarter than a lot of forty-year-olds I know."

Right before the show in Chattanooga, as she does before every performance, Ms. Swift loaded up her wrists with bracelets that she would later toss out to fans, allowing them to take home a small piece of her. And after she finished singing "Should've Said No," about a boy who cheated on her, she dropped to her knees and bent forward, holding her head still as fans in the front rows patted it concernedly. It was a scarily intimate moment but essential to her self-presentation that there is no barrier between her and her songs, and their listeners, the consumers. That insistence informs every aspect of her work.

It has also led to the decimation of her privacy. "Every single one of the guys that I've written songs about has been tracked down on MySpace by my fans," she said, a little giddy. "I had the opportunity to be more general on this record, but I chose not to. I like to have the last word."

That may become less tenable, though, as Ms. Swift's personal life makes its way into the tabloids, as it lately has in regards to her never-confirmed romance with Joe Jonas, the would-be rake of the Jonas Brothers. On this subject, at least, Ms. Swift is uncharacteristically mum: "He's not in my life anymore, and

I have absolutely nothing to say about or to him."

At least until the next album, maybe, which Ms. Swift insists will detail her life just as thoroughly as the first two. "When I knew something was going on in someone's personal life and they didn't address it in their music, I was always very confused by that," Ms. Swift said. "I owe it to people from letting them in from day one."

But eventually, if things continue as they are, walls will have to be erected. Jakks Pacific has just released a line of Taylor Swift dolls, making her even more of an abstract idol and less of a real person. She is also the face of the l.e.i. clothing brand, carried exclusively at Walmart, one of what is certain to be many endorsements to come. And next year she will be spending time in England, Japan, and Australia in hopes of facilitating Taylor Swift, the global brand, a move that few country acts have been able to pull off.

That she's likely to become only less accessible is a problem that Ms. Swift is, naturally, very attuned to. "All I can do," she said, "is put up a MySpace video where I don't have any makeup on and am wearing a periodic table of the elements T-shirt."

That and continue to make connections, one person at a time. The night before Chattanooga, Ms. Swift was at Sommet Center in Nashville, opening a charity gig for Rascal Flatts. After emptying her wrist during "Tim McGraw," she took in the sold-out crowd. "I am so proud to live in Nashville, Tennessee," she said, "and I hope to run into you at the grocery store." ♦

MIKAYLA SCANLAN-CUBBEGE

STUDENT, 18, CALIFORNIA

I will probably never meet Taylor, but if I do I will most likely forget how to function.

"Fifteen" will always be relevant. No matter how old I get, I don't think I'll ever stop requiring the reminder to "look before you fall."

I made up my mind the second I heard "You Are in Love" that it will be my wedding song. It's a piece of music that tells the story of what genuine love must be like, love that some people spend their whole lives trying to find.

I don't trust people who can choose a favorite album. I mean, what is wrong with them?

I will probably always be salty about the fact that there was never a *Red* tour live DVD. I mean, the disrespect! It's ghastly.

I regret not being able to see Taylor on the *Fearless* tour. The rain during "Should've Said No" was the coolest thing ever and I watch that particular performance on YouTube at least five times a week.

Taylor has helped me realize that time can heal most wounds.

I'm eighteen now and there isn't a day that's gone by in the past ten years that I haven't quietly thanked my younger self for choosing Taylor. Little me got at least one thing right.

I admire that Taylor is simultaneously strong and emotional. Watching her confidence blossom over the past couple years has been incredible. It's like she's finally been able to see the human being that all of us have seen for so long.

I'm scared that growing up means growing away from Taylor and the people who I've been lucky enough to meet because of her.

I still find it unbelievable that Taylor wrote the entirety of *Speak Now* by herself. I mean, a teenager wrote that.

I love it when Taylor smiles with her teeth.

It makes me really happy that Taylor is in a good place in her life. I realize I don't know her personally, but I feel sad when she's sad and happy when she's happy. She's made me a happier and better person in a million different ways and I will forever continue to love her unconditionally.

> "There isn't a day that's gone by in the past ten years that I haven't quietly thanked my younger self for choosing Taylor. **Little me got at least one thing right.**"

I ♥ Taylor
and
The Agency!

I ♥ TAY TAY

Tonight feels like a Perfect night

I ♥ TAYLOR SWIFT

PRODIGY

The Rise of Taylor Swift

THE NEW YORKER, NOVEMBER 2008 | SASHA FRERE-JONES

Taylor Swift, a slender, pale eighteen-year-old with curly blond hair that hangs in long tresses, is one of the biggest young stars in popular music. I recently caught her at an arena in St. Paul, where she opened for the country trio Rascal Flatts. Before the show, she chatted calmly with her mother, Andrea. "So the hockey team is the Wild or the Wilds?" Taylor asked a stagehand as she prepared her between-song patter. A few minutes later, the crowd cheered as she came onstage in a sleeveless, calf-length gold-sequinned dress, and the cheering continued throughout her performance. It became obvious that she and Rascal Flatts had equal claims on the room. Strutting across stage platforms, performing a percussion duet on garbage cans, and switching gears without pause—her voice, all the while, light and breathy and without affectation—she returned the crowd's energy with the professionalism she has shown since the age of fourteen, when she was signed as a songwriter to Sony/ATV Music Publishing, in Nashville.

The music industry's collapse may have seemed like a dress rehearsal for the current financial meltdown, but there are still stars in the business, and there is an interesting trend in both number and gender: the popular groups are male—Nickelback, Coldplay, the Eagles. The solo stars now, though, are more likely to be women: Alicia Keys, Carrie Underwood, Beyoncé, Rihanna, and Taylor Swift (who probably won't need that surname for long). Her self-titled debut album, released when she was sixteen, has been on the charts for two years. It is triple platinum and still rests, impressively, at No. 31 on the *Billboard* 200. Swift wrote or co-wrote every song on the album, one when she was twelve. Her second album, *Fearless*, will be released on November 11, and has already delivered two singles to the upper reaches of the charts: "Fearless" is at No. 9 on the *Billboard* Hot 100, and "Love Story" is at No. 14. Short samples of both songs were available for streaming on Swift's MySpace page weeks before they hit radio, and that page has garnered more than ninety million plays. After her St. Paul show, she changed into sweatpants, curled up inside a silk comforter on her tour-bus couch, and checked her page for new comments from fans, which she answers herself. (She was soon distracted by her iPod Touch.)

One aspect of Swift's story is timeless, and could have happened during any decade in the last century. Her talent as a songwriter and singer was obvious enough to her parents that they moved their family from Wyomissing, Pennsylvania, to Hendersonville, Tennessee, when she was thirteen. Though prodigies are always surprising, the surprise is only in degree, not category; what is surprising about Swift is her indifference to category or genre. She is considered part of Nashville's country-pop tradition only because she writes narrative songs with melodic clarity and dramatic shape—Nashville's stock-in-trade. But such songs also crop up in R&B and rap and rock. It is evidence of her ear that she not only identifies with songs in other genres but performs them, even though Nashville is a musically conservative place. It is only superficially jarring that Swift, the "country" artist, has covered Eminem's "Lose Yourself" and Beyoncé's "Irreplaceable" in concert. Both are fat-free, unerring pieces of songwriting. Swift is not an agent of revolution; she, much like Beyoncé, is a preternatu-

rally skilled student of established values. Her precociousness isn't about her chart success, but lies in the quality of her work, how fully she's absorbed the lessons of her elders and how little she seems to care which radio format will eventually claim her. Change the beat and the instruments around the voice, and her songs could work anywhere.

You could also give a Swift composition like "Our Song" to someone twenty years older and it could work just fine. The concerns of kids aren't necessarily juvenile—just their reactions. Bridging this gap is the trick of pop music; when people sing "Love Me Do" to themselves on their way to a date ten years on the other side of their second divorce, it's a sign that a young songwriter has got to a universal truth. This kind of precocious wisdom is embedded in the work of songwriters like Hank Williams, Prince, Elvis Costello, and Randy Newman. People who aren't old enough to have lived the songs they've written nevertheless know how the song embodying that life should go.

"Our Song" was not Swift's first hit, but it was the first to stop me in my tracks. It's a breezy recounting of frustration, streaked with simple phrases so conversational that on first hearing they fly by without registering. For example: "He's got a one-hand feel on the steering wheel, the other on my heart." Not one hand here and another there; first comes a "one-hand feel," and then the asymmetrical "hand"—on someone else's heart, not his own. The song's tension is that Swift and her man don't have a song to call their own; its genius is that they never pick one—their romance is the song, and both characters get a chance to narrate. Swift, the writer, also gets to transubstantiate; their song is their life as she describes it. He says, "Our song is the slamming screen door, sneakin' out late, tapping on your window." She says, "Our song is the way he laughs, the first date, man, I didn't kiss him, when I should have." There may be two characters, but there's only one songwriter, and this time the writer is keeping pretty august com-

pany: "And when I got home, before I said amen, asking God if he could play it again." Life is their song, a lark in a car, with the Deity himself cowriting.

Swift's new release is one of the few albums I can imagine selling truly astonishing numbers in today's timid, parched market. While Swift's debut was a happy shock, driven by several unexpectedly good songs, *Fearless* is a streamlined machine without a bad track, appropriate for all ages and demographics. Cynics may be able to resist it, precisely because the marks are all hit so deliberately. "The Best Day" will dissolve anyone with children, and might become the official Mother's Day song. (It's sung to her mom.) The album's finest effort, "Fifteen," will feature in yearbook quotes for years.

In that song, Swift has unpacked the emotional math of being fifteen. The mood is undecided, switching among remorse, reflection, and an understanding that belongs as much to adults as it does to the tweens who will be performing renditions on YouTube the day the album is released. "'Cause when you're fifteen and somebody tells you they love you, you're gonna believe them" is the first line of the chorus, and it sounds much more like the comforting words of a parent than like the quixotic pride of a young romantic. When the redheaded best friend, Abigail, is disappointed by a boy, Swift drops back, underplaying a sorrow that probably felt like surgery without anesthesia: "Abigail gave everything she had to a boy who changed his mind, and we both cried." In weaker hands, this song would be littered with broken hearts; Swift's boy just "changed his mind." In twenty years, when Swift has a songbook as long as her hair, "Fifteen" will sound no different. Will Swift sing to her daughter then the way she sings to her mother now? ◆

A REVIEW OF *FEARLESS*

2008 ROBERT CHRISTGAU

"You have to believe in love stories and prince charmings and happily ever after," declares the eighteen-year-old Nashville careerist. You can tell me that's worse than icky if you like; I believe in two of the three (prince charmings, no), and I think it's kind of icky myself. But I'm moved nevertheless by what can pass for a concept album about the romantic life of an uncommonly-to-impossibly strong and gifted teenage girl, starting on the first day of high school and gradually shedding naïveté without approaching misery or neurosis. Partly it's the tunes. Partly it's the musical restraint of a strain of Nashville bigpop that avoids muscle-flexing rockism. Partly it's the diaristic realism she imparts to her idealized tales. And partly it's how much she loves her mom. Swift sets the bar too high. But as role models go, she's pretty sweet.   **A–**

ACROSS

1 Toothpaste stopper, e.g.
4 *The Cosby Show* son
8 Snail mail need
13 In the past
14 Slippery sea creatures
15 Panda's diet
16 *Name of a blog about Taylor Swift's mascara?
18 Electronic musician that kind of looks like he was separated from Taylor Swift at birth
19 Aged
20 Land of leprechauns
22 October gem
25 *Taylor Swift lines about painful memories?
31 Maya of *SNL*
33 Soften
34 Kanye West has a big one
35 Priory of ___ (*The Da Vinci Code* organization)
37 Garb at many frat parties
38 *Houses where Taylor Swift enjoys her noon meals?
42 Landlocked African land
45 Volcanic flow
46 Bitter beer
49 Introduction
53 Adjective that describes Taylor Swift's "Thug Story"
55 *What Taylor Swift would be if her radiator failed in the middle of winter?
57 Thing held in a Taylor Swift song
58 Dunham of Taylor Swift's squad
59 Jean-____ Picard of *Star Trek: TNG*
61 Bring down
65 Taylor Swift's second album, and what the answers to the starred clues are, collectively
70 *Dirty Dancing* star
71 Baby goats
72 King Kong, e.g.
73 It holds water
74 Author Seton
75 Like foods in some celebrity diets

DOWN

1 "___ I Go With You?"
2 Taylor Swift's is 26, as of this puzzle's writing
3 Sound of a smack
4 Inform
5 Breakdancing move requiring good balance
6 Chicago trains
7 Milo of *The Verdict*
8 "Help! We're trapped!"
9 "Stop, I'm going to throw up . . ."
10 *Modern Family* airer
11 Pronoun used by Miss Piggy
12 Islands finger food
15 Big name in root beer
17 Alone
21 Radio host Glass
22 Mined metal
23 Flat-faced dog
24 *Much ___ About Nothing*
26 Dipping sauce for strawberries, perhaps: Abbr.
27 Exposes a secret of
28 Subject of meditation
29 Chicken alternative, in an unanswerable question
30 Mediterranean ___
32 The Tigers of the NCAA
36 Stanley Cup org.
38 Steal
39 Speed
40 Sales rep who offers facials
41 Beaver structure
42 Letters on a dashboard
43 "You ___ in Love"
44 Michele of *Scream Queens*
46 Words spoken at an altar
47 Indy 500 service area
48 It's worth one or eleven, in blackjack
50 On fire
51 *Zorba the Greek* setting
52 Long, long time
54 Letter-bottom abbr.
56 *The Metamorphosis* author
60 Constellation animal
61 Really slow internet connection, often: Abbr.
62 Lamb's mother
63 Bestest
64 "You break my heart in the blink of an ___"
66 German article
67 Musical ability, as it were
68 Day ___
69 Repair, as clothes

TAYLOR SWIFT

Growing into Superstardom

READING EAGLE, DECEMBER 2008 | GEORGE HATZA

The headlines read like something one would see in an old Barbra Streisand movie, those newspapers spinning wildly toward the viewer when, to the world's surprise, a star is born:

"Swift's Sales Soar," screams *Daily Variety*. "Taylor Swift, at eighteen, poised to be pop superstar," whoops the Associated Press. "Prodigy!" howls the *New Yorker*, for a moment forgetting its legendary austerity.

Usurping half the lead page of the Sunday *New York Times* Arts & Leisure section, the world's most famous newspaper declares: "My Music, MySpace, My Life: Taylor Swift expands country music's audience by stressing young love and personal connections."

Oh, and let's not forget *Rolling Stone*'s four-star review for the eighteen-year-old Wyomissing native's sophomore album, *Fearless* (Big Machine Records), No. 1 on *Billboard*'s country chart, with a handful of tunes in various locations on *Billboard*'s Top 10s.

Not bad. Not bad at all.

Both of her albums (*Taylor Swift* and *Fearless*) remain on the *Billboard* chart. Her MySpace page boasts nearly as many hits as McDonald's does hamburger sales. And forget about the downloads. Zillions.

So when Taylor spoke during a recent telephone interview, the once gawky teenager (and Abercrombie & Fitch model) was between rehearsals for the Grammy

Awards nominations TV special, which she cohosted Wednesday night with LL Cool J. Moreover, she was in the middle of getting her hair and makeup done.

"This will be interesting," she said with a laugh—actually, more like a giggle, referring to being fussed over while simultaneously talking seriously about her music.

Taylor will turn nineteen on Saturday, and already she's a superstar. The trophies are beginning to clutter whatever sort of mantel she has in the Hendersonville, Tennessee, home she shares with her father, Scott; her mother, Andrea; and her younger brother, Austin.

So how did this all begin, this explosive rise to fame and fortune? How does an eighteen—well, almost nineteen-year-old—handle that kind of attention without turning into Britney Spears or Lindsay Lohan?

"The words," Taylor said. "I love words. I love to write. Being an artist is what I love."

If Taylor—passionate and savvy—is anything, she's grounded. The "words" to which she refers are more than just lyrics to bouncy country melodies. They have deep, emotional meaning for her. They emanate from the chill of rejection and romantic loss and the pain of being thought strange when she was a middle-schooler in Wyomissing.

"I didn't have friends," she said. "No one talked to me. I used to go to the Wyndcroft School [nationally recognized for

academic excellence] in Pottstown, and when I moved to Wyomissing, I didn't know anybody."

But she got through the day knowing that when she went home, she would turn to her diary, write poems and songs. She would work through the pain. And she still is, if you take the time to listen closely to her songs, to the words, in "Our Song," "Teardrops on My Guitar," "Tell Me Why," and "Fifteen," to name a few.

As a young child, she said she would leave a Disney movie, and rather than talk about what she saw she would sing all the songs, nailing all the words. Music was then, and still is, the love of her life.

Her grandmother Marjorie Finlay was an opera singer, so she comes by her talent honestly.

"I can remember her singing, the thrill of it," she said. "She was one of my first inspirations."

Others include teachers at Wyndcroft and country performers Patsy Cline, LeAnn Rimes, Shania Twain, and the Dixie Chicks.

"When I was nine or ten, I used to get all the lead roles because I was the tallest person," she said. "But my interest in music soon drew me to country music. I was infatuated with the sound, with the storytelling. I could relate to it. I can't really tell you why. With me, it was just instinctual."

From her earliest memories, she recalls thinking in musical terms, in rhyme and melody. Her interest in poetry honed her skills with language. And soon, the two merged into song: words married to music about the real world, at least Taylor's world.

It was what she claims informed her music when she attended Wyomissing.

"The people around me provided all the inspiration I needed," she said. "Everything I wrote [at that time] came from that experience, what I observed happening around me."

To this day, that remains true. It is, experts agree, what sets her apart from her peers. Her music emanates from what she feels. Today, it's boys and, uh, boys. Also it's family and, oh yes, boys. However, what will it be in twenty years?

Young girls are her biggest fans. They understand her music, what she's saying about youth and romance. These kids also have technical skills. They know MySpace and Facebook and YouTube and all the other networking places where tweens and teens trade horror stories about the opposite sex.

What comes later?

Perhaps acting?

"I've had offers for roles on sitcoms," she said. "But it has to be the right one.

So far, nothing has been. But I do enjoy acting on my videos."

When Taylor manages some all-too-rare downtime, she spends it with her friend Abigail, who emerges as a character in the song "Fifteen." The pair dis boys and bake and drive around Nashville talking about, you guessed it, boys.

"Actually, most of all I enjoy editing my videos for MySpace," she confided. "It actually relaxes me."

Her connection to Pennsylvania has diminished, she admitted. There is no family here. Her father, a stockbroker, still has clients who live in the area. And her closest friend when she was growing up, Britany Maack, still has roots here. They keep in touch while Britany's at college.

"Hendersonville is home because I live there and I work there," she said. "But when I come back to Pennsylvania and see the crowds and the landscape, it's such a rush. It just feels like home."

> "I write songs about my life. When my life **changes**, so will my music."

These days, however, Taylor is hanging out with Kellie Pickler, the country singer and former *American Idol* contestant, whom Taylor clearly adores.

"She's like a sister," she said. "People say we're such opposites, but that's what makes us such good friends. She's incredibly blunt. I love that about her. If some guy has said or done something to me she doesn't like, she'll grab my cell phone and say, 'I'm deleting his number.'"

As critics debate whether Taylor's music is pop or country, the issue already has been decided by the singer-songwriter.

"I write songs the way I hear them in my head," Taylor said. "Call it what you want, but country is where I'm proud to be. Sure, the crossover success is wonderful."

Indeed it is. It has helped to sell more CDs and downloads, expanded her fan base, and put her on the cover of every

mance. Yet others have found it sweetly understated, working in ironic counterpoint to her shrewd, often biting lyrics.

So does she think of herself more as a singer or a songwriter? She doesn't hesitate.

"I love lyrics more than notes," she admitted. "A song is a favorite song not because the singer can hit and hold a high note but because of the words, their meaning. Sure, you have to incorporate a great melody. But I'm proud of those lyrics. And I'm lucky that I have a label that lets me sing and write all the songs on my records. Don't get me wrong; I'm thankful I get to be a singer."

So backing up to an earlier question: What comes later? If she's writing about boys and, uh, boys today, what will she be writing about in the future if her career is to have longevity?

"I write songs about my life," she said with Pickleresque bluntness. "When my life changes, so will my music. It's as simple as that. I tell stories." ♦

major magazine in the country. The level of her success even has shocked her.

"What surprised me over the past year is that I thought I'd already made it," she said. "That I was in an amazing place where I would be thrilled to stay. I thought, 'I don't need to be any bigger than this to be happy.' But then it just blew up! I'd be lying if I said I had this all planned. I honestly don't know how it happened. It's such a blessing."

When asked what she would choose if she could change anything about her life at this moment, she responded following a long silence: "Look, even the things I would change"—she remains markedly unspecific—"well, there's probably a reason for my going through it. I have to trust that. Otherwise, that's just added stress."

She has taken a few knocks from some critics about her singing voice—that it can be thin and unexpressive in a live perfor-

KELSEY QUITSCHAU

TEACHER, 24, ILLINOIS

My first memory of Taylor is listening to her self-titled album every morning on the way to high school with my sisters and every afternoon home.

She made me realize that I wasn't alone in the things I was feeling.

The song that made me realize she's a genius was "Tim McGraw." I mean, just listen to it.

The album I find myself going back to the most is *Fearless.* Let me give you eighteen reasons why: "Fearless." "Fifteen." "Love Story." "Hey Stephen." "White Horse." "You Belong with Me." "Breathe." "Tell Me Why." "You're Not Sorry." "The Way I Loved You." "Forever & Always." "The Best Day." "Change." "Jump Then Fall." "Untouchable." "Come in with the Rain." "Superstar." "The Other Side of the Door."

My favorite song is probably "Fearless." It's played over and over in the back of my head for years and means so many different things to me. It's about love and falling hard, falling freely. It's about being brave and about finding myself. It's about being vulnerable. About letting go. It encompasses so many different feelings. Happy feelings. Like you just want to be trapped in the moments of "Fearless" for the rest of your life.

She sang "Fearless" as her surprise song on the B stage in Chicago during the *Red* tour. I always regretted not going to see the *Fearless* tour and kept thinking that there was no way she would just so happen to sing it that night. But she did. I think she only sang it four times throughout the tour, and being able to experience that is a moment I'll never forget. I'll never be able to sing the line any other way: "in Chicago now, capture it, remember it."

I have a friend who loves "Breathe" but I can never listen to it because how can anyone ever listen to that song without feeling like their heart is breaking into a million tiny pieces? *cue ugly crying*

My high school students think I'm insane because I know so many Taylor Swift facts that they think I stalk her. My life-size Taylor cutout also stares at them every day in class.

I have spent hours upon hours creating lyric art and creative interpretations of Taylor's songs. It started as something personal, a way to reconnect with my passion for art while I was living alone, but it turned into so much more. I started posting my pieces online and it became a way to connect with fans all over the world. I even brought huge stacks with me to the three *1989* tour shows I went to and passed them out to different fans. Taylor's lyrics mean so much to all of us and it has been really special to make things other fans love too.

I was so excited when Taylor followed me on Tumblr!!!!!!!!!!!!!!!!!!!!!!!!!!!!!!!!!!!!!!!

One thing that Taylor doesn't seem to understand about life is that it's too short to not release "Holy Ground" as a single. Like, come on, girl.

I can't wait till Taylor's forty and Meredith is somehow still truckin', glaring at her from every corner.

If I ever meet Taylor I'll probably cry shamelessly, thank her for being so wonderful, ask when she's planning on releasing "Sweet Tea and God's Graces," show her my lyric art, faint, forget my name, cry some more, and be sure to wear my sick beet costume from the *1989* tour. I might also ask for a few pictures. And ask if she could go back out on the *Fearless* tour one more time so I can go.

I ♡ 1989

This night is sparkling don't you let it go

TAYLOR SWIFT

1989

THIS SICK BEET

DANCE TO THIS BEET FOREVERMORE

T S

89

WE FOUND WONDERLAND you & I got lost in it.

SWIFT

IT'S LIKE I GOT THIS MUSIC IN MY MIND SAYING IT'S GONNA BE ALRIGHT

T.S.

The Unabridged
TAYLOR SWIFT

ROLLING STONE, **NOVEMBER 2008** | AUSTIN SCAGGS

What's up, Taylor?

I am in Nashville and I just left a meeting with a guy who does a lot of video editing for the promotional stuff that we do, like for my MySpace. I have to edit all the videos and sometimes I just go over and learn new tricks and go over footage. We're also collecting a bunch of stuff for an *E! True Hollywood Story* thing that they're doing. Lots of video footage stuff going on right now.

Everywhere you turn there must be a video camera in your face?

It seems like it, and if it's not somebody putting a video camera in my face, it's me putting a video camera in other people's faces. I'm working on a video blog right now. I was at CMT's Alan Jackson "Giants" taping last night, and I got every single artist who was there to say that my album comes out November 11th. I'm going to put them all together and put it on my MySpace and it's going to be fun. I have Hank Williams Jr., Brad Paisley, George Jones, George Strait, Miranda Lambert, Martina McBride, Dierks Bently. All the artists I love were there, and I got them all to say, "Taylor's album comes out November 11th—go get it." I was so paparazzi, it's not even funny.

Cool. Do you have any superstitions about 11/11?

No, it's just the same number twice, so I figure it'll be easier to remember than other numbers. It's just kind of repetitive.

Let's talk about music. Let's start from the beginning. I know your mother was listening to a lot of Def Leppard when you were in the womb.

My mom was obsessed with Def Leppard. I ended up liking country music, and I think we're just a random family when it comes to musical tastes.

And your grandmother was an opera singer?

She was actually a recording star in Puerto Rico when my mom was growing up. My mom was always stuck sitting backstage somewhere or sitting in a front row, watching a performance her entire childhood. She thought that when her mom stopped performing she was relieved of those duties, but all I wanted to do was sing, ever since I was born, so she's always been backstage.

How did your grandma become a star in Puerto Rico?

My grandparents were American, but my grandfather took a job building oil rigs over in Vietnam, so they were overseas all the time. Wherever my grandfather would go for his engineering job, my grandmother would go and perform and sing opera. She was in all these musicals in Singapore and all these gorgeous places where my mom grew up. My mom has these amazing stories of growing up overseas, and then she moved to America when she was about ten.

She moved to Pennsylvania?

She moved to Texas. My mom grew up in Texas and my dad was a Pennsylvania boy.

So what kind of opera was your grandmother performing?

She was in *The Bartered Bride*, *The Barber of Seville*, and musicals like *West Side Story*. I have these gorgeous, glamorous pictures of her all in black and white. She was just so beautiful.

Let's talk about Def Leppard a little bit. Obviously it was the thrill of a lifetime for you to perform with those guys, but I'm wondering if you could tell me what it was like for your mom to meet them?

She was so starstruck, and so was my entire band and I, because before we go on-stage we all listen to Def Leppard music and jump around and get ready. There was this moment where Rick Allen was testing his drum kit and they set up their instruments and everything first, and we were all sitting around watching, my band, my mom, and I. You know the signature drum hit for "Pour Some Sugar on Me" the first time you hear it.

It's absolutely unmistakable. The first time he hit it, my band and I just erupted and were just looking at each other like, "This is not happening, you've got to be kidding me."

Let's embarrass your mom—what was your mom doing?

My mom was turning red, and had my camera the whole time and filmed everything. I was like, "Mom, please don't miss any of this." So she had the digital camera in Joe Elliot's face the entire time, and I had the camera in their faces, and I was like walking around interviewing them. A lot of the time, if I'm at an event with other celebrities, I want to get it on film. I'm like the biggest super-fan there, so I'll be interviewing people and I'm doing videos with them and then I put them up on my MySpace.

> "When I play a song, **I want people to feel like they're experiencing exactly what I went through** when I wrote the song as I'm singing it for them."

You should get a job with *Rolling Stone* interviewing people, come on.

I would love to. I'm all about video editing more than anything else. I love how if you put music behind a moving image it pops and it comes to life. That's my favorite thing about that.

Being around Joe Elliot and realizing that these people sold over sixty million records in their careers, I thought that they would be divas. I thought that they would be snobby. I thought that they would only want to sing certain things and would only let me sing certain things. When I walked in, I very timidly

and politely asked Joe Elliot if I could sing one of the lines in "Hysteria." He goes, "Honey, I've been singing that for twenty-five years—you sing whatever you want." I was able to sing all my favorite songs, and I could not believe it when Joe Elliot was singing "Picture to Burn."

Yeah, that's awesome. I wanted to talk to you about singing the national anthem at the World Series. How many times have you done the national anthem in your lifetime?

I would say I've sung the national anthem hundreds of times. When I was eleven years old, it occurred to me that the national anthem was the best way to get in front of a large group of people if you don't have a record deal. So, I started singing the national anthem anywhere I possibly could—76ers games, the U.S. Open, and I would just send my tapes out everywhere. I would sing the national anthem at garden club meetings. I didn't care. I figured out that if you could sing that one song, you could get in front of twenty thousand people without even having a record deal. So I've sung that song many, many, many, many times and it still gives me chills, you know, when I get to sing it at an event like the World Series. Whoever thought that that was going to happen?

And the Phillies ended up winning.

And the Phillies won! Oh my God. I was watching and my dad and I were sitting there crying, especially during the last throw of the game and the catcher caught the ball and .2 seconds later he's running to the pitcher and just tackles him. It was just the sweetest thing and just watching all the instant replays of all the people's reactions. I love it when people are so excited about success. I love it when people freak out when they win something, and it's crazy, because I actually used to sing the national anthem for the Reading Phillies, which is their minor league team, and a lot of the members of the Philadelphia Phillies now were on that minor league team when I sang that anthem years and years and years ago.

Like who, for instance?

Pat Burrell. There were two or three others, I was told, that were on the same team. So that was kind of an interesting coincidence.

Is the national anthem hard to sing?

For me, the national anthem is not as challenging range-wise, because I've been doing it for so long. The challenge for me is the utter silence that comes over forty thousand people in a baseball stadium and you're the only one singing it. Even though I've sung it hundreds of times, it still gets you a little bit that you're the only one singing and all those people are just focused on the song that you're singing. It's a really surreal moment for me. I love to play guitar with it, because I think sometimes the national anthem can become a singing competition. I think that the national anthem, in my opinion, is better just as a song. I think playing guitar with it just sort of puts the music back into it.

Is there a certain line in the song that's harder to hit than the other ones, where you buckle up?

No. It's the utter silence, the silent beginning in the "Oh, say, can you see by the dawn's early light"—that's when everybody's watching, and when I get to the high notes at the end, "And the rockets' red glare," I know I'm fine. From that point out it's free sailing, but it's all about not letting my nerves kick in.

You were on a karaoke circuit growing up—what does that mean?

I wanted to sing in front of people, and I didn't have a band, and I was ten or eleven, so the first thing that I started doing was musicals. I was in a children's company and I got all the leads because I was tall and I could play adults. That was my first taste of performing in front of people.

You did *Grease* . . . what other stuff did you do?

Yeah, I played Sandy in *Grease*; I played Kim in *Bye, Bye Birdie*; I played Maria in *The Sound of Music*, and I was twelve. What I started realizing was that, even more than the musicals, I looked forward to the cast parties afterward because there was a karaoke machine set up at every party. That's when I got to sing country music. I got to sing Dixie Chicks songs and Shania Twain songs and Faith Hill songs and one day, somebody turned to my mom and said, "You know, she really ought to be singing country music." It kind of occurred to all of us at the same time that that's what I needed to be doing.

I would go through the phone book

and look for places where I could sing karaoke. There was this broken-down roadhouse where you could go and sing karaoke competitions, and the owner of the roadhouse also owned the amphitheater across the street. He had all these traditional country acts come to the amphitheater, like George Jones and Loretta Lynn and Charlie Daniels. If you won the karaoke contest, you got to open up for them. You got to play at like 10 a.m. when George Jones would go on at like 8 p.m. I would go there every single week until I won, and I got the chance to open up for Charlie Daniels. That was something that was just really exciting to me when I was like eleven.

What was the roadhouse called?

Pat Garrett.

Pat Garrett.

Oh yeah. Strausstown, Pennsylvania.

Cool, so talk about finding country music.

LeAnn Rimes was my first impression of country music. I got her first album when I was six. I just really loved how she could be making music and having a career at such a young age.

I think the thing that cemented it in my mind and made me fall in love with country music was seeing three great examples of what females could bring to country music—I saw that Shania Twain brought this independence and this crossover appeal; I saw that Faith Hill brought this classic old-school glamour and beauty and grace; and I saw that the Dixie Chicks brought this complete "we don't care what

you think" quirkiness, and I loved what all of those women were able to do and what they were able to bring to country music.

I thought, "You know, if Nashville is the town that lets you be yourself and do things like that, and be different, then that's where I need to be." And country music absolutely became everything to me. I started obsessing over George Strait records and Kenny Chesney, and going back and looking through Loretta Lynn and Dolly Parton. It was such a big deal to me that those women stood for things in country music.

> "I never want anyone leaving my concert feeling like I didn't appreciate them coming in with **everything that I have.**"

Throughout most of your career you've been an opening act. It seems like now is the turning point where you're about to take over.

Oh wow, thank you. I'm very fascinated with the music industry, the touring industry, and the business end of things, so I've paid attention to other careers, the timing and decisions that were made in other careers. I've seen it happen where you have a successful first record, and they throw you out as a headliner way too early and it doesn't work. You never want to have to go backwards. I don't have an ego issue. I'm cool being an opening act. I'd rather be an opening act longer than I should, than headline too early. So, now we're headlining. I'm

starting to headline this summer and I'm really excited about that because I feel like I waited so long, that I want it so bad, and I can't wait. I'm going to throw everything I have into this headlining tour. I feel like we're in a place where I can really put together a great tour.

What are you most excited about offering your fans in this capacity, where you're the headliner, and it's your stage?

I've been on tour with every single one of my heroes and I've seen what they do live. Some things have blown me away, and I've taken away some things that I really want to incorporate. But there are some things that I haven't seen done, and I want to do them. For my concerts, I really don't want people to be seeing the same thing for more than two songs in a row. For my headlining shows, when I actually am allowed to have my own stage and my own production, I've already drawn up the stage plan and what I want it to look like. It's going to look nothing like the headlining tours that I've supported in the past two years. I feel like there's drama that I've always been attracted to—sort of a theatrical type, dramatic performance that I feel is sometimes missing when you see shows these days. I never want people to think that they're just seeing a show where I'm playing song, after song, after song. When I play a song, I want people to feel like they're experiencing exactly what I went through when I wrote the song as I'm singing it for them. There are setups that I really want to create. There are visuals that I'm really excited about, and I can't wait for you to come out and see a show.

Is it going to be like the *Romeo and Juliet* bit and stuff like that?

I really want some costume changes. I'm going to create a bunch of video content specifically for the concert. I would love, when I'm singing "Love Story," to be dressed up in the video outfit, make people feel like they're experiencing something really unique. If they want to hear the record, they'll listen to it. You know? They'll put in the CD or they'll listen to their iPod. But if they want to come out to a concert, I feel like it should be something completely different.

Do you ever write songs that aren't about boys?

Yes. I do. I have a few on this record that are about other things. I have a song called "Fifteen" that reminisces about my freshman year and a song called "Change" that was actually featured on the Olympics. And there's a song called "The Best Day" that I wrote about my mom and my childhood. It was really cool to go back to that place and reflect. I wrote some of the lyrics in the song, sort of in a childlike kind of language, which was really fun for me as a writer to stretch that way. But I really like writing songs about boys. I like writing songs about relationships. And when someone breaks up with me, I like to write about it, because I feel like I have the last word.

You don't have any problem naming names in your songs, do you?

I have no issue with naming names. I think that it's sort of fun for me to know that when the album comes out, there are going to be people who are going hear about it. My per-

sonal goal for my songs is to be so detailed that the guy the song is written about knows. It's so detailed, it's so personal, that he knows it's written about him. I think it's just a fun thing for me. I don't know why I like it so much. It's kind of exciting to put a song on the album that you know is going to personally affect you when it comes out.

Or affect somebody else?

Mostly that it will affect somebody else. That's the fun part.

What are your favorite country songs that—not necessarily where you're dissing somebody, but just those great country lines like, "Take your tongue out of my mouth cause I'm kissing your ass goodbye."

Loretta Lynn, "Fist City"—have you heard that?

Sure . . .

She says, "I'll grab you by the hair on your head, and I'll lift you off the ground. I'm not saying my baby's a saint, 'cause he ain't." Isn't that a cool line?

Yup.

"But he won't cat around with a kitty." That's so amazing.

Obviously you have a song called "Change," and we've been hearing a lot about that, a lot about change in the presidential election, and I'm wondering if you're a Pennsylvania Democrat or a Pennsylvania Republican.

You know, I just try and stick to my specialty and my specialty is music, and writ-

ing songs. I voted yesterday, but I don't think it's my job to try and influence people which way they should vote, because it's a very personal thing. All the way through the line—I waited an hour and a half to vote—I was wavering back and forth whose ideas I liked better, and who really represented what I believed in. I kept going back over articles I'd read, and trying to figure out who to vote for. When I got in the voting booth, I just said to myself, "All of my best decisions have been based on my gut instinct. Who's the president of the United States?" And I pushed a name and I voted.

Really?

Honestly, I think it's good to be well versed on the election and who believes in what. Sometimes I think you can oversaturate yourself with facts, and in a lot of cases, it sounds cliché, but you should really just do what you feel.

Your record is called *Fearless*. And you've definitely shown, in your musical career, a fearless attitude. But what are you scared of?

Well, thank you for saying that. I think what I'm scared of, honestly, is anything happening to my family, or anything happening to my fans. The hardest that I've cried in my life is when I've been told that I've had fans that have had something tragic happen to them, and lost fans. That's a really, really big fear of mine. I've sat there in the bus with the family of an eighteen-year-old who got in a car wreck and died his senior year, who had my CD cover taped to the dash of his car. That kind of loss—that's what scares me. I've had an amazing run at this. If it were to go away, I would hate it, but I can't say that that's my biggest fear.

What artists do you know nothing about—that you might be embarrassed to know nothing about? I mean, you must have older guys in your band who say, "Oh, you don't know this song, you don't know that song?" Like the Rolling Stones or Bob Dylan or something?

I'm pretty well versed on that, but the stuff that my band is obsessed with, like the hair metal—I've just always been so focused on Def Leppard that I never explored too much more of the hair metal bands. I wish I knew a little more about them. Just so that I could keep up, you know, in the conversation about the hair metal bands. That seems to be the topic of choice for my band.

I'm just wondering if you've found something recently that you've really fallen in love with, maybe outside of the country realm.

There's a song that I really love, and I haven't heard the whole record. But, there's a song called "After Tonight" by Justin Nozuka and the song is completely acoustic until the chorus. It's got a really cool rootsy sound to it. You should listen to it. It's really great—like Jack Johnson with a different twist. I really like that.

Are you a Jack Johnson fan?

I'm a huge Jack Johnson fan. My ringtone is "Taylor" by Jack Johnson. I just ignore the fact that the song is about a—it's about a prostitute or is it a stripper? But I will take ownership because it has my name in it. And you know what, also—I think, and this is a really poppy choice, but I think it's really cool that

Jesse McCartney is R&B now. I think it's a really cool direction for him. I just recently listened to the whole record, and I was like, "You know what? I didn't really understand it at first, but now I get it." I love the new single, and I think that's a really good place for him to be. I think it's really good for his voice. He did a T-Pain cover recently and killed it live, so I have a newfound respect for him and his vocal abilities, and the way his career has gone. Also, I'm really into Katy Perry. The whole record is great. There's a song called "Thinking of You" that I'm really, really obsessed with. I'm also obsessed with Sinéad O'Connor's "Nothing Compares 2 U." I have that song on repeat right now. And I love it.

That's something that you just discovered or . . .

It's something that stuck with me. I discovered it last year, and I feel like there's a timeless thing that that song has. It's just really awesome. It's just one of those songs where you know that when it was written, like five thousand songwriters just put their pen down and went, "All right. I tried." The way that it is and the way that it's sung, I think it's a brilliant song.

Does your guitar have a name? Did you name your guitar?

I know that the techs have named them different things and there's one that's completely covered in crystals, so they call that "Sparks" or "Sparkles." I have a Koa guitar. It's either the Koa or the sparkly guitar that I use or the black electric, so usually we'll just say, Koa, Sparkles, or Black Electric.

How many songs have you written?

It's got to be about five hundred. I absolutely can't stop writing songs. It's funny because sometimes you'll hear artists

talking about how they have to hurry up and write this next record and it's like, I can't stop writing. I can't turn it off. I go through situations and I go through experiences and I go through life and I need to write it. I need to write it down. It's like breathing. It's kind of interesting because whenever I've gone in to record albums, I mean, we're going through like a hundred songs and trying to pick the best one.

That's a good problem to have.

I'm really grateful that I haven't had any major writing blocks or anything like that. I just like to write my life. I just did an Alan Jackson painting last night and I realized

something about him that I've always loved—you know who he is and you know who he stands for and you know what he believes in because his main goal is that he's always written about his life, and he hasn't really strived for the vocal acrobatics. He hasn't tried to be anything but a guy who sings about his life. I realized last night, that's my goal. That's all I want to do.

I know that you have covered Eminem and I'm wondering if you notice a connection between country and hip-hop, lyrically.

I feel like country and hip-hop are two of the most honest genres because we just like

to sing about our lifestyle. We like to sing about the things that go on in our daily activities and we're proud of the way we live and we're proud of the things that we stand for. I feel like that pride is something that both country and hip-hop share. I've always been fascinated by hip-hop. I've always just really taken a keen interest in the rhyming of it all. Poetry was the first thing that ever fascinated me about words and about writing. Poetry is what turned me into a songwriter. I found out that if you get the right amount of words and the right syncopation and you get the right rhymes at the end, you can make words bounce off of a page. So hip-hop has always been something that I looked at and thought, "Wow, that really

is an incredible art form." I think Eminem does it unbelievably well.

You read a lot of poetry growing up?

I would read the Shel Silverstein poems, Dr. Seuss, and I noticed early on that poetry was something that just stuck in my head and I was replaying those rhymes and trying to think of my own. In English, the only thing I wanted to do was poetry and all the other kids were like, "Oh, man. We have to write poems again?" and I would have a three-page-long poem. I won a national poetry contest when I was in fourth grade for a poem called "Monster in My Closet."

Wow.

Yeah, that's big-time.

You've been winning awards your whole life! That's crazy. What award do you want to win the most?

I want an American Music Award really bad. Really bad! They're so shiny!

More than a Grammy or a Moon Man?

I mean, a Grammy would be wonderful. That would certainly make me cry upon my name being announced, but the American Music Awards are very shiny and they are fan-voted and that's where I base most of my pride in awards. My award shelf has got a lot of CMT Music Awards on it. Those are the ones that I'm most fond of because the fans went online and voted. I love industry awards. I love my ACM. I give my TMA award a hug every now and then. That's all well and good, but I think the fan-voted awards have always been my favorite.

Tell me about the first song you wrote. I believe it was called "Lucky You."

Oh yeah, and there are some great versions of that online. You can hear my chipmunk twelve-year-old voice singing that song. I'm pretty sure it got leaked on the internet because some fans were telling me that they heard it and I was like, "Oh no!" But that's a song that I wrote . . . it was one of the first finished songs. It was made of three chords because those are the only chords I knew at the time.

It's a G, an A, and a D, or something like that?

It's a G and a D and a C, then back to D. The song was about a girl who didn't fit in and she didn't care and she was different

than everyone else. I think there's a long chorus of me singing "Do do do do do do do do do do." It's very young and I look back and it's kind of interesting to hear those kind of story lines and the lyrics that I used to write compared to the lyrics that I write now.

So you've come a long way?

I would hope.

Do you think in songwriting and just about anything else in life that practice makes perfect?

I think sometimes practice makes perfect. But I think sometimes you look back on the things that you wrote when you were twelve and you were like, "Wow, I couldn't have thought of that now." I think that it's all case by case. I'm more proud of the music on this record than I am with the music on the first record, but you never know if that's just me being a songwriter who likes the last thing that I wrote the best. In retrospect, I've been going over all these videos for some of the bio specials that have been asking for video content and I've been looking over the videos of stuff that I wrote when I was twelve and there are songs that I've found myself relating to. It's kind of interesting to hear the lyrics I was writing back then. But I'm definitely really proud of the stuff that I've been writing lately.

What's the most bizarre, craziest thing you've seen looking out into a crowd?

There's always the frat boy who has got my name painted on his chest, which is always awesome. One of my favorite moments of the night is when I'm in the middle of my acoustic set and I'm in a really poignant moment and I'm trying to be serious and you hear the group of guys with Southern accents going, "Marry me!" It's really good to have that in my life because it just makes me happy. I find that there are people out in the crowd of all ages. I've got a group of seven-year-olds that their moms all took them to the show, there's a group of six forty-year-olds all wearing tiaras and holding scepters and singing "Love Story." I really don't have just one age group.

So the guys don't knock you off your game when they're screaming at you from the crowd?

No. Dolly Parton had the best response to that kind of thing. Some guy screamed from the crowd, "I love you, Dolly!" and she goes, "I thought I told you to stay in the truck!" I'm going to start saying that.

Have you ever met a guy while on-stage? Like a boyfriend?

One time, like a year and a half ago, I was doing a show at a college and I was signing autographs afterward and there was a guy that I saw from across this field and I noticed that he looked just like Denny from *Grey's Anatomy*. I was so obsessed with Denny from *Grey's Anatomy* and he died and he was my favorite and I have this weird obsession with that character. So this guy and I made eye contact from across this field and I had a line of people that were waiting to get autographs and he waited at the end of the line and came through the line. We made small talk and I was talking to him and he held out a picture for me to sign and I just grabbed his hand and wrote my number down.

Are you serious?

I'm not kidding. That's the one time that I've done anything bold like that in my entire life. But he looked so much like Denny, come on!

I don't even know who Denny is. I'm sorry.

Okay, well he was the best character that ever existed on *Grey's Anatomy*. He was the one for Izzie. She would've been happy forever if he hadn't died, but he died tragically of a heart condition.

Oh, I shouldn't be laughing but it's so funny.

He was so sweet, and he was played by Jeffrey Dean Morgan (who is my favorite actor). He's tragic. He always plays people who die because he's a wonderful actor and you don't want to see him die so he always does.

So what happened with that relationship? The guy called you, then what?

Oh, I didn't follow through. I think I was like, "Get a hold of yourself! You just wrote your number on a stranger's hand. Get yourself together."

Let me ask you, finally we have this whole Taylor Nation thing going on, about your run-ins with your fans, I'm sure you've encountered fans that have been like, gasping for breath, passing out, crying hysterically. Give me a good story about that.

I get a lot of criers, and I love criers because I like emotional people. Some artists are very uncomfortable when people cry but I happen to think it's the cutest

thing on the planet when someone meets me and starts crying. Sometimes I get gropers though. Like, I hug everyone that comes through my meet-and-greet line, and sometimes they don't let go.

I saw some photos on your website of you meeting fans, and you really get into it.

Yeah, well I love to hug them and I love to thank them for coming. I was a fan, I went to concerts, and I went through meet-and-greet lines and I know what it's like to walk away and think that you didn't really make an impression on your favorite artist and that you were kind of just in a line. I never want anyone leaving my concert feeling like I didn't appreciate them coming with everything that I have. I like to hug them and I like to talk to them and I like to have conversations with them and I like to look at them in the eye. Sometimes there's one that doesn't let go, really tight grip . . .

Is there like a three-second rule or something?

No, there's no three-second rule. I think when it gets above ten to fifteen seconds, then it's a little excessive. I, in general, love hugs and I love huggers. I think I've been really lucky because I haven't had that many crazy people at all. The craziest fan gift I got was one time this guy gave me this giant turtle shell with my face painted on it.

So, to make an impression, you should look like Jeffrey Dean Morgan, cry a lot, and you're all good, right?

Sometimes they show me their freshly tattooed arms or midriffs that have my signature there for life. That's always an interesting moment for me. ◆

THE VERY PINK, VERY PERFECT LIFE
of Taylor Swift

ROLLING STONE, MARCH 2009 | VANESSA GRIGORIADIS

On a bright Sunday afternoon in Los Angeles, Taylor Swift is on good behavior, as usual. In high school, she had a 4.0 average; when she was homeschooled during her junior and senior years, she finished both years of course work in twelve months. She has never changed her hair color, won't engage in any remotely dangerous type of physical activity, and bites her nails to the quick. At nineteen years old, she says she has never had a cigarette. She says she has never had a drop of alcohol. "I have no interest in drinking," she says, her blue eyes focused and intent beneath kohl liner and liberally applied eye shadow. "I always want to be responsible for the things I say and do." Then she adds, "Also, I would have a problem lying to my parents about that."

Swift has gotten far playing Little Miss Perfect—not only was her second album, *Fearless*, at No. 1 for eight weeks this winter, but she's enjoyed numerous perks, like a ten-day stay at the West Coast home of her childhood idols, Faith Hill and Tim McGraw, which is where she is today. The couple, who befriended Swift in Nashville, offered the use of their house while she is in L.A. appearing on an episode of her favorite show, *CSI*. The fact that Swift's first hit single is called "Tim McGraw"—a wistful, gimmicky ballad about a separated couple who recall each other by their favorite McGraw song—is a clue to her feelings about them. "I love Tim and Faith," she says, dashing about the house, which is utterly enormous, filled with gilt crosses and life-size Grecian statues, and worth about $14 million (Eddie Murphy is a neighbor, in a house "the size of a country," says Swift). "I think I like the bright colors in here better than the lighter ones," she says, critiquing the rooms, which seem to go on endlessly, like galleries in a museum. "I don't know. I go back and forth. You know when you walk into a furniture store, and you're like, 'Oh, that's how I'm going to decorate my house,' and then the next one you're like, 'No, *that's* going to be the way I decorate my house'?" She giggles. "I think when I do it, I'm going to be so indecisive."

Swift lives at home with her parents in a suburb outside of Nashville, in a big house overlooking a lake. The family was wealthy before she became a star—both of Swift's parents have had careers in finance, which makes them particularly good advisers, and they aren't interested in their daughter's cash. One of them usually travels with her, and her father, a kind and friendly stockbroker, has just arrived, a stack of business documents in tow. Swift seems to have three gears—giggly and dorky; worrying about boys and pouring that emotion into song; and insanely driven, hyper self-controlled perfectionism—and, as she embarks on a wholesome afternoon activity, the third aspect of her personality comes into play. In Hill and McGraw's white-marble kitchen, she attacks the task of baking mocha chocolate-chip cookies with a single-mindedness rarely seen outside a graduate-level chemistry class, measuring and sifting and whipping with sharp, expert movements, while her father keeps up a patter about her career.

It takes superhuman strength for a teenager to listen to her father talk at length about her personal life, and even Swift—the goodiest goody-goody in the nation—struggles to remain polite. She's constantly worried about saying something that could be construed as offensive to her fans, and even swats away a question about her political preferences before conceding that she supports the president: "I've never seen this country so happy about a political decision in my entire time of being alive," she says. "I'm so glad this was my first election." Her eyes dart around like a cornered cat as her dad runs on about the tour bus on which she travels with her mom: "We call it the 'Estrogen Express,'" he says. "That's not what we call it," counters Swift. Then her dad talks about the treadmill he got for her, because she didn't want to deal with signing autographs at the gym. "That's not why!" yelps Swift. "I just don't want to look nasty and sweaty when people are taking pictures of me."

But these are momentary distractions in an otherwise pleasant afternoon. Within forty-five minutes, Swift produces two dozen perfect, chewy cookies, which she offers around with a glass bottle of milk. Suddenly, she squints at the jar and shrieks a little: *eggnog.* She scours the fridge but comes up empty-handed, irritated by the foolishness of her mother, whom she surmises was shopping absent-mindedly. This cannot be. Snack time is ruined. Then she blinks rapidly and composes herself.

"I didn't do that," she says, shaking her head firmly. "Mom did that."

Swift likes to do everything the right way, and most of the time that means she likes to do everything herself. She may be a five-foot-eleven-inch blonde, but she does not have the carefree soul that usually goes along with that physiognomy, and her back is starting to hunch a little from stress. Swift writes or cowrites all of her songs: she's been a working songwriter since the age of thirteen, when she landed a development deal with RCA Records. "Taylor earned the respect of the big writers in Nashville," says Big & Rich's John Rich, a hot Nashville producer. "You can

hear great pop sensibilities in her writing as well as great storytelling, which is the trademark of old-school country song-crafting." At fourteen, Swift walked away from RCA's offer of another one-year contract—"I didn't want to be somewhere where they were sure that they kind of wanted me maybe," she deadpans—and put herself on the open market. She received interest from major labels but held out for Scott Borchetta, a well-regarded executive at Universal who left the company to start his own label, Big Machine Records. "I base a lot of decisions on my gut, and going with an independent label was a good one," she says. "I thought, 'What's a once-in-a-lifetime opportunity? What's been done a million times?'" Says Borchetta, "Taylor and I made an aggressive deal on the back end." He chuckles. "I've written her some very big checks," he says.

Swift has sold six million of her first and second albums, making her the best-selling artist of 2008. Now she is preparing to launch her first headlining arena tour of fifty-two cities in April (a date at the Staples Center in L.A. sold out in two minutes). She's benefited from a broad demographic appeal: The "Taylor Nation" ranges from country to indie-music fans to the Disney generation, particularly the good girls. Her impeccably crafted songs easily translate to pop radio, and Swift is clearly taken with the notion of crossing over, though she's nervous about alienating her core audience. "You can't forget who brought you to the party, and that's country radio," she insists. She's very savvy: it was her decision to sing "Fifteen," her song about the innocence of that age, with Miley Cyrus at the Grammys. "I think it's cool, because when she was fifteen she had a lot

of things going on," says Swift. "Lessons learned." (This is how savvy she is: when she was starting out in music, she used her spare time to paint canvases—"I'm interested in Jackson Pollock's kind of art, where art is beautiful but it's nothing and yet it's incredible"—which she then sent to country-radio managers as gifts.)

For all her high-minded business acumen, as an artist Swift is primarily interested in the emotional life of fifteen-year-olds: the time of dances and dates with guys you don't like, humiliating crying jags about guys who don't like you, and those few transcendent experiences when a girl's and a boy's feelings finally line up. You can't go anywhere without your best friend. You still tell your mom everything. Real sexuality hasn't kicked in yet. Swift won't reveal anything on that topic herself. "I feel like whatever you say about whether you do or don't, it makes people picture you naked," she says, self-assuredly. "And as much as possible, I'm going to avoid that. It's self-preservation, really."

Self-preservation is one of Swift's favorite phrases, and she uses it in reference to both her professional and personal lives. She wants to have a long career, not get tossed away like most teen stars. "I've not seen many people work as hard as Taylor," says Kellie Pickler, a good friend. "She's a very competitive girl, and those people go far." Along with the Jonas Brothers and a gaggle of young Disney stars like her pals Miley Cyrus, Selena Gomez, and Demi Lovato, she's part of a backlash against the pantyless TMZ culture of earlier this decade, which proved to be a career-killer for Lindsay Lohan and her clique. Swift admits that she was fascinated by girls like Paris Hilton when she was younger—in a rare moment of prurience, she notes that her high school football team was named the Commandos, then laughs wryly—but says that she never thought the gossip about these women was true. "You should never judge a person until you know the full story," she explains, matter-of-factly.

Swift is certain she would never let herself get caught up in such shenanigans. "When you lose someone's trust, it's lost, and there are a lot of people out there who are counting on me right now," Swift says. She cocks her head. "Rebellion is what you make of it," she says. "When you've been on a tour bus for two months straight, and then you get in your car and drive wherever you want, that can feel rebellious."

If this is Swift's game face, it must be tattooed on, because it never drops during hours of press on a recent weekday in New York, a day that includes mind-numbing patter on SiriusXM and Clear Channel, a voice-over for a new style show on MTV, and a sickeningly saccharine luncheon for her l.e.i. sundress line sold at Walmart. It's a tour de force: Swift engages easily with the teen-fashion journalists following her around, bantering about blow-dryers and bachelorette parties; then, she's gracious to the misshapen radio hosts, calling everyone by their names and administering warm hugs by the dozen. But there's a moment, at the Walmart luncheon, when she gets a little testy with a young fan—Swift asks the fan where she's from, and when the girl answers, "New Jersey," Swift makes fun of her accent—but this is literally the only sin against a human she commits during a ten-hour day in which she's barely fed, never stops smiling, and signs hundreds of autographs with a pink Sharpie pen.

This politesse is part of Swift's character, a way of treating others taught by her loving family. Her parents intentionally raised their kids in the country, on a Christmas-tree farm with a grape arbor and seven horses, in eastern Pennsylvania, while Swift's father commuted to work. "I had the most magical childhood, running free and going anywhere I wanted to in my head," says Swift. But her parents also prized success in the real world: they even gave her an androgynous name, on the assumption that she would later climb the corporate ladder. "My mom thought it was cool that if you got a business card that said 'Taylor' you wouldn't know if it was a guy or a girl," says Swift. "She wanted me to be a businessperson in a business world."

"In school, **I loved reading *To Kill a Mockingbird***, and I'm very interested in any writing from a child's perspective."

Swift rode horses competitively as a child, but her main hobby was making up fairy tales and singing the songs from Disney movies by heart. At six, she discovered a LeAnn Rimes record, which she began to listen to compulsively. "All I wanted to hear from then on was country," she says. "I loved the amazing female country artists of the '90s—Faith, Shania, the Dixie Chicks—each with an incredible sound and standing for incredible things." She began to act in a children's musical theater company but found that she preferred the cast parties, which featured a karaoke machine, to the stage. "Singing country music on that karaoke machine was my favorite thing in the world," she says. As is the Swiftian way, even at eleven she was determined to "pursue other venues" where she

could perform, and soon found the Pat Garrett roadhouse, which had a weekly karaoke contest. "I sang every single week for a year and a half until I won," she says. Her prize: opening for Charlie Daniels at 10:30 a.m.; he played at eight thirty at night.

Newly emboldened, Swift began to perform the national anthem at local sports games, and even landed a gig with her favorite team, the Philadelphia 76ers. But tragedy soon befell our young songstress. It seems that her classmates did not agree that country music was cool. "Anything that makes you different in middle school makes you weird," she says. "My friends turned into the girls who would stand in the corner and make fun of me." She was abandoned at the lunch table. She was accused of possessing frizzy hair. She tried to fit in by joining teams but proved to be horrible at every sport. Then redemption came in the form of a twelve-string guitar. "When I picked up the guitar, I could not stop," she says. "I would literally play until my fingers bled—my mom had to tape them up, and you can imagine how popular that made me: 'Look at her fingers, so weird.'" She takes a deep breath. "But for the first time, I could sit in class and those girls could say anything they wanted about me, because after school I was going to go home and write a song about it."

This is Swift's tale of triumph, and she likes to tell it a lot when she's interviewed. It sounds canned, in a way—who hasn't been made fun of in middle school?—but she's managed to keep the feelings raw, and access to them is part of her appeal. The sun is starting to set as Swift heads downtown, near the World Trade Center site, to play a live acoustic set on the radio station Z100 for about fifty "Caller

100s"—a group that happens to be almost exclusively plain, primly dressed girls between twelve and seventeen. The fans listen raptly as Swift chats about bad-hair days and ex-boyfriends. They hold up their camera phones, sometimes with a Sidekick in the other hand. Swift keeps insisting that they sing along with her, and at first they're shy, but soon the scene resembles a teenage-girl "Kumbaya" session, all the alienation and hurt that they feel in their real lives melting away, replaced by a deep sense of peace. "Taylor is so down-to-earth," gushes Darlane Shala, a ninth grader from Manhattan. "She's just such a good person."

Afterward, Swift takes more photos with the girls and looks at her fan letters. The girls write about feeling like outsiders, about getting ostracized by girlfriends over misunderstandings with boys, about hating girls who make fun of other girls and not understanding why some people enjoy being so cruel. "When I first discovered your music a few years ago, something in me opened up," says a meticulously crafted two-page letter from a high school sophomore, who included a picture of herself at the beach. "I had been feeling upset, and you told me that I'm not alone," she continues. "Your lyrics mean the world to me, and I swear they are the narration of my life." She adds that Swift has given her a path for the future: "I wish more than anything that I could change a teenager's perspective," she writes, "the way you have done for me."

This is Swift's primary hope for her music: she wants to help adolescent girls everywhere feel better about themselves, and in the process heal her younger self. "In school, I loved reading *To Kill a Mockingbird*, and I'm very interested in any writing from a child's perspective," she says. At high school in Henderson, Tennessee, a suburb of Nashville—her parents agreed to move when she landed her RCA contract, at the beginning of her freshman year—Swift's interest in country music was obviously considered normal, but she still wasn't popular. She may be pretty now, and she eventually might have abused the power that comes with being a beautiful senior girl, but when she left high school, at sixteen, she was still a gangly sophomore. "There were queen bees and attendants, and I was maybe the friend of one of the attendants," she says. "I was the girl who didn't get invited to parties, but if I did happen to go, you know, no one would throw a bottle at my head."

In a way, Swift's emotional state seems to be stuck at the time when she left school. She says that she has only a half-dozen friends now—"and that's a lot for me"—and she talks constantly about her best friend, Abigail, a competitive swimmer and freshman at Kansas State, with a new nose ring and a new pet snake, doubtless having many experiences that Swift may not be ready for. In fact, Swift is a very young nineteen-year-old. "I feel like Miley, Selena, and Demi are my age," she says at one point, acknowledging the fast-paced lives of her Los Angeles–based contemporaries. "It's crazy, I always forget that they're sixteen."

And in her love life, Swift admits to being mighty inexperienced. She says that she's had her heart broken, but she's not sure if she's ever really been in love. She had a boyfriend her freshman year, a senior hockey player: "We weren't an It couple," she drawls. But there really haven't been many guys since then except for Joe Jonas, who famously broke up with her over the phone for another girl. Swift wrote a song on her second album, called "Forever & Always," about Jonas, then filmed a MySpace video with a Joe Jonas doll, during which she remarks, "This one even comes with a phone so it can break up with other dolls!" Jonas later insinuated that she hung up on him. "I did not hang up on him," she says now, then mouths, "Omigod."

The illogic of love is unsettling to Swift, who has a hard time understanding it with her supremely rational mind. Music, for her, is a way of expressing feelings that are largely repressed or absent. She maintains that marriage is something she would "only do if I find the person I absolutely can't live without" and "it's not my ultimate goal in life." In fact, the first two singles on *Fearless*—"Love Story" and "White Horse"—are about a guy that she considered dating but never even kissed. Many of her songs are not about her own personal experiences with love—about half are inspired by her friends' relationships. "I'm fascinated by love rather than the principle of 'Oh, does this guy like me?'" she says. "I love love. I love studying it and watching it. I love thinking about how we treat each other, and the crazy way that one person can feel one thing and another can feel totally different," she says. "It just doesn't take much for me to be inspired to write a song about a person, but I'm much more likely to write that song than do anything about it. You know, self-preservation."

A couple of weeks ago, Swift started four days of rehearsal at a studio on the outskirts of Nashville for her upcoming tour. She picks the alfalfa sprouts out of a sandwich—Swift avoids vegetables, hates sushi, and in general gravitates away from anything healthy—and straps on her guitar, strumming as she gives her tour

manager instructions on the set list. As much as she engages in good-natured banter with her band, she's clearly in charge of this show: with a faintly sex-kitten stage presence—punctuated by many pumps of her very long arms in the air—she cues fiddle licks, restages a number, and shuffles the orchestration in a mash-up. Then she stops. "Omigod." She giggles. "For 'Love Story,' the stage is going to become a church, and I'm going to get into a white dress." She bites her lip. "There's so many cool sets," she says later. "We're going to have a giant castle!"

After rehearsal, she returns to her parents' home, which is set on a promontory over Old Hickory Lake. "In the summer, people fish off the dock," says Swift, then deadpans, "More people now. Apparently, there are more fish now." The mantel of their living room is crammed with bulky glass awards, and posters of Swift line the hallways; a large sitting room is devoted to racks of clothes that Swift has worn in performance or public, with a sign affixed that reads, PLEASE GO THROUGH: KEEP OR GIVE TO GOODWILL. Her younger brother, Austin, a sixteen-year-old lacrosse player and academic overachiever, has moved into a room on the garage level, doubtless to have some space away from the Taylor Nation, but Swift still lives in her childhood bedroom.

It's a small room, decorated almost exclusively in pink and purple. Her closet is itty-bitty, with clothes organized in neat rows above her shoes and a drawer of padded bras. Any sign of her life as a superstar has been scrubbed, with the exception of a postcard from Reba McEntire. She rifles around in her armoire—careful not to show its contents, which she considers too messy for guests—and pulls out a cardboard box of colored wax, which she used to seal envelopes. "I wrote my Valentine's Day cards yesterday," she says, holding up a thick stack. "It's not going to be a big shindig for me. I didn't have that one person." She smiles. "So I had to write thirty."

It's almost 8 p.m., and Swift is planning to work on her set lists for a few hours tonight, but first she needs a Frappuccino. She hasn't started her car, a champagne-colored Lexus, in a couple of months—her brother has to jump-start it—and when she finally pulls out onto the road, she seems a little less perfect. She's an unsure, semi-reckless driver, hitting the brake too hard, pointing the car this way and that at various intersections like she's tacking a boat. She screams, "Five-oh!" as she spots a cop, then pulls into a drive-through Starbucks. "I've been in three accidents, but none of them were my fault," she wails.

Soon she comes to a stop, pointing to an expanse of lawn. "This summer, the guy from the 'Fifteen' song came back into Abigail's life," she says. "He got me to bring her here, and while we were on the way he texted her, 'We need to talk.'" When they arrived, the guy was standing in the center of this field in a big heart made of candles, holding a bunch of roses. "It was so romantic," she says, smiling dreamily. "I love that kind of stuff." Then she starts pulling away. "You know, I totally burned a CD for him to play that night, because he wouldn't have known Abigail's favorite songs otherwise," she says, tapping the steering wheel. "And as usual, I had to clean up the mess the next day." She sighs. "But that's okay," she says. "I didn't mind." ♦

MALLORY ARNOLD

STUDENT, 19, NEVADA

The first time I realized my obsession with Taylor's music I was nine years old and had "Should've Said No" stuck in my head. I'd never loved another song so much, and in that moment, I knew I'd be a fan for life.

If it wasn't for Taylor, my room and my wardrobe would be empty.

She was the reason I learned how to play the guitar and the piano. My favorite song to play is "Ours" because I can play it with both instruments.

I turned my dad into a Swiftie. He appreciates Taylor's music as much as I do, and he loves to blast her music whether I'm with him or not.

My dad and I have a tradition of counting the "Swift" trucks whenever we go on road trips. We started in 2013 when we were on our way to Los Angeles to see Taylor perform at the Staples Center. Every time we see one, we yell "Swift!"

I loved when she came to the middle of the Staples Center and played "Enchanted." Not only do I love that song, but it was the very first song I learned on the guitar and of course I was wearing my Wonderstruck Enchanted perfume that night.

I had a dream where Taylor and I were on the same airplane. She let me hold Olivia and Meredith while we chatted.

When I finally meet Taylor I will probably lose my mind and speak uncomprehendingly fast because there's so much I want to tell her and ask her.

I love the way Taylor can laugh at herself.

My favorite unreleased songs are "Never Mind," "Diary of Me," "Better Off," and "One Thing." I think they would have made great additions to her albums.

If I could change one thing about Taylor's concerts it would be to add at least two Las Vegas stops for each tour.

I love how Taylor is close to her mother and I'm glad that I have a similar relationship with my own mom. "The Best Day" really encourages me to never take my parents for granted.

Taylor makes me believe that anything's possible. Her story of going from record label to record label and then writing her own songs to set herself apart is so inspirational. It shows that you can accomplish anything if you work hard and persist.

"Taylor makes me believe that anything's possible."

The
TAO
of
TAY

Ten Years of Wisdom
on Life, Love, and Learning
to Dance in the Rain

— ON LIFE —

"No matter what happens in life, be
good to people. Being good to people is
a wonderful legacy to leave behind."

"If I had to give my younger self some advice, it would be that you
have to laugh at things. You have to laugh at things that scare you,
things that intimidate you, and things that hurt you. You have to laugh
when you're humiliated, when you're rejected. Maybe not immediately,
but at a certain point you have to be able to turn whatever bad
experience you've had into a funny dinner party joke."

"Life can be unexpected, but that's
what makes it beautiful."

"Karma is real."

"I wouldn't change anything. I would repeat
the same regrets, the same mistakes, the same
wonderful, beautiful, accidental triumphs."

"Real life is a funny thing, you know. I think most of us fear
reaching the end of our life and looking back regretting the
moments we didn't speak up. When we didn't say 'I love you.'
When we should have said 'I'm sorry.' I don't think you
should wait. I think you should speak now."

"I've found growing up can mean a lot of things.
For me, it doesn't mean I should become somebody
completely new and stop loving the things I used to
love. It means I've added more things on my list."

"Live your life like you're eighty
looking back on your teenage years."

"In life, you learn lessons. And sometimes
you learn them the hard way. Sometimes
you learn them too late."

"The thing about life is, every time you learn a lesson, another is
waiting right at the corner. You never know everything."

"All of my favorite people—people I really trust—
none of them were cool in their younger years."

"The lesson I've learned the most often in life
is that you're always going to know more in
the future than you know now."

"Silence speaks so much louder than screaming tantrums.
Never give anyone an excuse to say that you're crazy."

"I'm intimidated by the fear of being average."

"Be that strong girl that everyone knew would make it through the worst; be that fearless girl, the one who would dare to do anything; be that independent girl who didn't need a man; be that girl who never backed down."

"Never believe anyone who tells you that you don't deserve what you want."

"You just have to have faith in the fact that everything is a process."

"You have people come into your life shockingly and surprisingly. You have losses that you never thought you'd experience. You have rejection and you have to learn how to deal with that and how to get up the next day and go on with it."

"There's beauty in the ups and downs. The only thing we know is that what we're experiencing is going to change into something else."

"Life isn't how to survive the storm, it's about how to dance in the rain."

"I wish you a lifetime of moments too beautiful to capture on film."

— ON BEING YOURSELF —

"If you're lucky enough to be different
from everyone, don't change."

"I'm trying to become a new version of the
person I've been my whole life."

"I never want to change so much that
people can't recognize me."

"If you go too far down the rabbit hole of what people think about
you, it can change everything about who you are."

"Don't ever regret being honest. Period."

"Be yourself, chase your dreams,
and just never say never.
That's the best advice I could
ever give to someone."

"Beauty is sincerity. There are so many ways,
different ways, someone can be beautiful."

"I don't think I was born to be in the
club. Just to throw that out there."

"Just be yourself. There is no one better."

"If they don't like you
for being yourself,
be yourself even more."

"What I've learned is not to change who
you are, because eventually you're going
to run out of new things to become."

— ON LOVE —

"I have rules for a lot of areas in my life.
Love is not going to be one of them."

"Just because something is over doesn't mean it wasn't incredibly
beautiful. Because another lesson I've learned is not all stories have a
happy ending and you have to learn to deal with that."

"I think the perfection of love is when it's not perfect."

"It's the most maddening, beautiful,
magical, horrible, painful, wonderful,
joyous thing in the world, love."

"In life and love, you learn that there
comes a time to let go and move on."

"When you grow up and experience
different kinds of relationships or love, you
realize it's not always black-and-white."

"It's a song about saying goodbye to somebody,
but it never blames anybody. Sometimes that's the most
difficult part. When it's nobody's fault."

"I approach love differently now that
I know it's hard for it to work out."

"I realized there's this idea of happily ever after which in real
life doesn't happen. There's no riding off into the sunset,
because the camera always keeps rolling in real life."

"Here's what I've learned about deal-breakers.
If you have enough natural chemistry with
someone, you overlook every single thing that
you said would break the deal."

"Love is the wild card."

"There are two different categories of love. The first
category is called a fairytale. The second category of love is
called just another lesson."

"Real love still happens sometimes. It's not just something we make up when we're nine. I have to believe that. You do too."

"Don't worry. You may think you'll never get over it. But you also thought it would last forever."

"A heartbroken person is unlike any other person. Their times moves at a completely different pace than ours. It's this mental, physical, emotional ache—and feeling so conflicted. Nothing distracts you from it. Then time passes, and the more you live your life and create new habits, you get used to not having a text message every morning. . . . And then all of a sudden one day you're in London and you realize you've been in the same place as your ex for two weeks and you're fine. And you hope he's fine."

– ON MUSIC –

"I think I fell in love with words before I fell in love with music."

"I can write a song about making eye contact with someone from across the room in three seconds. I don't need a relationship to have good material."

"A lot of my cues are taken from what I know my fans want. And those cues are taken from having a really close relationship with them online and hearing what they have to say. Their feedback's really important."

"There's really no feeling quite like writing a song
about someone who's really mean to you and
someone who completely hates you and makes your
life miserable and then winning a Grammy for it."

"I write songs to help me understand life a little more. I write
songs to get past things that cause me pain. And I write songs
because sometimes life makes more sense to me when it's being
sung in a chorus. And when I can write in a verse."

"For me, genres are a way of
categorizing music. But it doesn't
have to define you. It doesn't
have to limit you."

"I've always felt music is the only way to give an instantaneous
moment the feel of slow motion. To romanticize it and glorify
it and give it a soundtrack and a rhythm."

"Words can break someone into a million pieces, but they can
also put them back together. I hope you use yours for good,
because the only words you'll regret more than the ones left
unsaid are the ones you use to intentionally hurt someone."

"Sometimes the lines in a song are lines you wish you could
text-message somebody in real life."

"As a writer you have to be open to everything, and that includes pain, rejection, self-doubt, fear. I deal with that enough on my own."

"People haven't always been there for me, but music always has."

— ON BEING FEARLESS —

"To me, fearless is not the absence of fear. It's not being completely unafraid. To me, fearless is having fears. Fearless is having doubts. Lots of them. To me, fearless is living in spite of those things that scare you to death."

"It's being terrified but you jump anyway."

"Fearless is getting back up and fighting for what you want over and over again, even though every time you've tried before, you've lost."

"There are two ways you can go with pain: You can let it destroy you or you can use it as fuel to drive you."

"Keeping your emotions all locked up is something that's unfair to you. When you clearly know how you feel, you should say it."

"It isn't history that makes heroes, it is heroes that make history."

"Giving up doesn't always mean you're weak. Sometimes
it just means that you're strong enough to let go."

— ON SUCCESS —

"It's possible to get to the top without stomping on others."

"There are girls out there who are determining their thoughts and
dreams and opinions about who they want to be. If I have a small part
in that, I take it seriously. A lot of moms come up to me at the grocery
store and say, 'Thank you for being a role model for my daughter.' "

"I've wanted one thing for my whole life and I'm not going to be that
girl who wants one thing her whole life then gets it and complains."

"There's no blueprint for success, and
sometimes you just have to work at it."

"You have to be happy with who you are and the choices you
make. If you don't like yourself, you'll never be truly happy."

"Other women who are killing it should motivate you, thrill you,
challenge you and inspire you rather than threaten you and make
you feel like you're immediately being compared to them."

"The world doesn't owe you anything.
You have to work for everything you get
and you have to appreciate every bit of
success the world gives you."

"I'm beginning to think that you don't find happiness
from living your life looking ahead or back, that you
find it when you look around."

"The only thing I compare myself to is
me two years ago, or me one year ago."

"I have this really high
priority on happiness and
finding something to be
happy about."

"You can be accidentally successful for three or four years.
Accidents happen. But careers take hard work."

"My mom went to a psychic when I was twelve
years old and was told, 'The whole world
will know your daughter's name.' But my mom
thought that meant I was going to be kidnapped."

PART TWO

CROSSOVER

I just kept going back to "Speak Now," because I think it's a metaphor for so many things we go through in life, that moment where it's almost too late, and you've gotta either say what it is you are feeling or deal with the consequences forever. I think I've developed, as many people do, this sense of "Don't say the wrong thing, or else people will point at you and laugh." In your personal life, that can lead to being guarded and not making what you feel clear in the moments that you're feeling it. For me, it's never really fearing saying what's on my mind in my music, but sometimes having a problem with it in life. Sometimes you lose the moment.

A REVIEW OF *SPEAK NOW*

ROLLING STONE, NOVEMBER 2010

★ ★ ★ ★ ☆

ROB SHEFFIELD

People like to fixate on Taylor Swift's youth, as if to say, yeah, she's pretty good for her age. But that just begs a question: Where are all the older people who are supposedly making better pop records than Taylor Swift? There aren't any. In a mere four years, the twenty-year-old Nashville firecracker has put her name on three dozen or so of the smartest songs released by anyone in pop, rock, or country.

Swift's third album, *Speak Now*, is roughly twice as good as 2008's *Fearless*, which was roughly twice as good as her 2006 debut. These fourteen tunes chronicle the hopes and dreams of boy-crazy small-town Everygirls, and Swift wrote them all by herself. (She also coproduced *Speak Now* with Nathan Chapman, who oversaw Swift's first two albums.) Swift might be a clever Nashville pro who knows all the hit-making tricks, but she's also a high-strung, hyper-romantic gal with a melodramatic streak the size of the Atchafalaya Swamp. So she's in a class by herself when it comes to turning all that romantic turmoil into great songs. At this point, she's like the new Morrissey, except with even more eyeliner.

Swift takes a step into adulthood with *Speak Now* — she clearly aspires to the divorced-mom market where country stars do most of their business, slipping more grown-up details into her love stories. It's tame by country-radio standards, but it's still weird to hear T-Sweezy sing lines like "There's a drawer of my things at your place." Sometimes you can even tell what chick flicks Swift has been watching from the song titles: "Dear John," "The Story of Us," "Enchanted."

In up-tempo tunes like "Mine" and "Sparks Fly," or ballads like "Back to December" and "Enchanted," Swift's voice is unaffected enough to mask how masterful she has become as a singer; she lowers her voice for the payoff lines in the classic mode of a shy girl trying to talk tough. Check the way she tosses off the "You made a rebel of a careless man's careful daughter" part in "Mine." Anyone else would have built the whole song around that, yet for Swift it's just another brilliant throwaway detail. There's a minimum of country schmaltz on *Speak Now* — Swift likes her tempos fast and her choruses rock-size. In "Enchanted," she even cops the Prince trick of duetting with her own filtered voice.

As for the boys she tangles with on *Speak Now*, they're her usual type. "You're an expert at sorry / And keeping lines blurry / And never impressed / By me acing your tests" — get used to that guy, Taylor, you'll be meeting a lot of him. Her advice to these dudes for holding on to her? "Just keep on keeping your eyes on me," she sings in "Sparks Fly." And yet we can already tell this guy's going to be long forgotten by the next song.

Speak Now peaks with "Long Live," a ridiculously over-the-top prom anthem with all the epic girl-group swoon of the Ronettes or the Shirelles, plus a guitar hook from Def Leppard's "Hysteria." Swift belts about how getting crowned king and queen is the most excellent event that could ever happen. It's the sort of prom song that could only come from an artist who chose to spend her high school years on a tour bus. Yet when Swift sings it, damn if you don't believe every word.

PRINCESS CROSSOVER

NEW YORK, **OCTOBER 2010** | CHRIS WILLMAN

ris Kristofferson is a man besotted. Tonight, he is the oldest performer at an L.A. benefit concert for Nashville's Country Music Hall of Fame, and since the seventy-four-year-old legend is known for suffering neither fools nor fads gladly, you might expect him to be hanging back with relative contemporaries like Emmylou Harris and Vince Gill. Instead, his still-babyish-blue eyes are twinkling over a pop-crossover superstar who's his junior by a half-century plus change. Backstage, as they exchange courtesies before the sold-out show, Taylor Swift plays an unlikely Bobby McGee to Kristofferson's Me.

"I just know you are going to have the most wonderful career, and most wonderful life," Kristofferson is telling her. He praises the precocity of her songwriting. In return, she gushes over his mad skills. "I could not ask for a better role model," she says. "Now who's the silver-tongued devil?" Kristofferson quips. I ask if he thinks Swift has a shot at making the Country Music Hall of Fame someday. "She's already in the Hall of Fame!" he bellows back, taking almost chivalrous offense; it's as if being decades away

from eligibility is, to his mind, a laughable formality.

At least there's *something* for Taylor Swift to aspire to! She doesn't reach drinking age until December, but her list of accomplishments is already staggering. (Among them: youngest person to win Album of the Year at the Grammys; Entertainer of the Year at the Country Music Awards; top-selling recording artist of 2008 and 2009; most legally downloaded artist of all time; an *SNL* hosting gig that seems to be the most-rerun episode ever.) And she might just knock off another one this month with the release of her third album, *Speak Now*, on October 25. Number crunchers are already predicting that Swift could be the last pop star in history to move a million units in a week. More challenging, perhaps, will be convincing that unconvinced half of a polarized public that she's a confessional singer-songwriter in the classic vein and not just a teen-pop blip.

As the third volume of Swift's soon-to-be-encyclopedic public diary, *Speak Now* may or may not be her *Tapestry* or *Blue*, but it is definitely not her *Can't Be Tamed*. The title song, inspired by the impending nuptials of a friend, imagines

a *Graduate*-like scenario in which Swift busts up an ex's wedding. It's "You Belong with Me" redux, but bumped from high school bleachers to wedding-chapel pews. In titling the album, Swift says, "I just kept going back to 'Speak Now,' because I think it's a metaphor for so many things we go through in life, that moment where it's almost too late, and you've gotta either say what it is you are feeling or deal with the consequences forever." Given that the singer's whole image is based on her willingness to lyrically identify ignorant boys by their Christian names, has learning to speak her mind really been a problem before now? "I think I've developed, as many people do, this sense of 'Don't say the wrong thing, or else people will point at you and laugh,'" says Swift of her "emotionally intense" last two years. "In your personal life, that can lead to being guarded and not making what you feel clear in the moments that you're feeling it. For me, it's never really fearing saying what's on my mind in my music, but sometimes having a problem with it in life. Sometimes you lose the moment." And sometimes you get it back in time to spin that great afterthought into quintuple and sextuple platinum.

Country music has always had uneasy relationships with its pop-cross-over stars, and there's a history of giants who've had dual citizenship—from John Denver and Olivia Newton-John to the Dixie Chicks and Shania Twain (whose *Come On Over* is Swift's favorite country album)—only to find one foothold or the other inevitably slip away. Swift won the CMA's Entertainer of the Year last year, but wasn't even nominated this year, which could count as a "We're keeping an eye on you, MTV girl" warning shot from Nashville. But if anyone can come close to being all things to all industries, genres, and fan bases, it's Swift, who's been unusually careful to nurture her Music Row roots. It doesn't hurt that she stayed in Tennessee after moving out of her parents' house in Hendersonville and into her own condo in Nashville, custom-built to her specifications. (Its living room has a pond with thirteen fish, her lucky number.) And she continues to cheerfully make rounds that would have been beneath a Natalie Maines—like gladly showing up for Hall of Fame benefits long after most everyone stopped appending "country star" to her name.

When Swift takes the stage with the other performers for the acoustic "guitar pull" format at the September 23 benefit, the next-most-fresh-faced singer on the bill is Vince Gill, who is a third of a century older than she is. "We were smart enough to invite the kid," Gill tells the sold-out hall, immediately addressing the disparity. "We dig her because she sold all the tickets." Over the next two hours, Swift more than holds her own, singing well-crafted hits with confidence (and without the help of Auto-Tune, which she has been accused of using) in a format that emphasizes her deceptively simple lyrical acuity.

But there's a thematic difference that becomes almost comical at certain points. The older performers seem intent on pulling out their most despairing material. Emmylou Harris sings an ode to melancholy she wrote in her forties, noting that she has survived into her sixties. Gill sings about the death of his homeless brother. And Swift, perhaps aware that she doesn't have too many songs about depression and mortality in her catalogue, points out that almost all of her thwarted-romance songs begin with "So, there was this guy . . ."

Back in her dressing room, Swift nearly hyperventilates as she tells her mom, Andrea, about her mutual lovefest with Kristofferson. "I felt like I was going to pass out! He said so many nice things about my songwriting . . . I can't even remember everything he said; I blacked out a little bit." The Swift you see on awards shows who looks honestly agape every time she wins something? That's for real, and she has moments like that just about every week. Of course, there are those lying in Schadenfreude-fueled wait, too. As she tells a certain rap superstar in a new song, "Life is a tough crowd."

So there was this guy. "I think a lot of people expected me to write a song about him. But for me it was important to write a song to him," says Swift about Kanye West, who infamously stole her Best Female Video moment at MTV's VMAs in 2009 (which in turn inspired the president of the United States to call West a "jackass"). "Innocent"—the song prompted by The Interruption, which she debuted at this year's VMAs—is a tricky piece of songcraft: Some viewers took it as deeply sympathetic toward West, others as patronizing in its sympathy. But

"Innocent" clearly provides a turning point in which Swift gets the upper hand by casting herself in a mature, even maternal light. The music video for the new album's first single, "Mine," may portray her growing up and having children, but "Innocent" is where she really plays mother to a baby.

What's not clear from the song is how the MTV incident affected her own sense of innocence. "How it affected me," she says, then pauses. "It doesn't really add anything good if I start victimizing myself and complaining about things. Because I'm proud of that performance at the VMAs last year, where my fans helped me get through it. And there was a lot that went down backstage that I will always be thankful for, and the fans in the subway [where she sang "You Belong with Me" shortly after The Interruption] know exactly what happened that night. I feel everything. I've never had this thick skin that can't be . . . It's not like I am bulletproof in any sense of the word."

Kristofferson and Twain notwithstanding, there are no real models for Swift's career path in the end. A handful of other singer-songwriters have made great records before exiting their teens, from Laura Nyro to Fiona Apple, but none made great records so explicitly *about* their teens. In captivatingly nailing everything that is awesome and awful about coming of age—"in real time," as she puts it—her nearest antecedent might be '60s-era Brian Wilson, the one true adolescent auteur before she came along. But he stayed in the sandbox, and she can't.

Swift does have one great truth on her side in easing from teen apologist to grown-up troubadour: adult life is just like high school. To that end, her new song "The Story of Us" (about a recent near-run-in with, most likely, ex-boyfriend Taylor Lautner) proves that show business is nothing but a glorified prom. "It was at an awards show"—presumably the People's Choice Awards—"and there had been this falling-out between me and this guy," says Swift. "I think both of us had so much that we wanted to say, but we're sitting six seats away from each other, just fighting this silent war of 'I don't care that you're here.' I remember getting home and sitting at the kitchen table and saying to my mom, 'It was like I was standing alone in a crowded room.' That's when my eyes glazed over and I got distracted and walked away to write. My mom is used to me doing that." ♦

TAYLOR COMPTON

STUDENT, 18, GEORGIA

I grew up in a small town in Georgia, and the fact that her first single said "Georgia stars" was like fate. I was probably ten at the time. I just assumed that Taylor was from Georgia. I felt very betrayed when I found out she was from Pennsylvania. Obviously, I've moved on.

Everybody has a Taylor Swift song that takes them back to a really vulnerable time in their lives. For me it's "Fifteen." We all have our own Abigail and the boy who changed his mind.

Having the same name as her is amazing. Anytime one of my friends says something like "I really wish Taylor would like this post" on social media I immediately like it and say, "There you go!"

What looks good on Taylor doesn't always look good on me. Trust me.

I've always been really afraid of cats. They're just so sneaky. But I've got to admit Meredith and Olivia make me question my fears.

There is a Taylor Swift lyric for every moment in your life. I once spent an entire year only captioning my Instagram pictures with her lyrics with no difficulty. *And I was single.* Shout-out to the people who say she only writes about love. Theory disproved.

Country Taylor is glitter and fire and everything good in the world. Who can resist singing that their ex is a "redneck heartbreak who's really bad at lying"?

> "There is a Taylor Swift lyric for **every moment** in your life."

Taylor made me fall in love with playing the guitar. I really believe she's helped a generation of girls turn to writing and music to express their feelings, including me.

My brother's best friend is named Drew, so hearing his name in "Teardrops on My Guitar" really wigged me out as a ten-year-old. To this day I can't sing along to it. It's too strange.

Taylor's shown us that you don't have to be a good dancer to dance. Having fun is what's important.

But dancing to "You Belong with Me" in the shower is dangerous. Let's just say I know someone who slipped and sliced open her toe on the drain. Let's just say it really hurt.

There's so much good music in the world. Taylor hasn't only brought me her amazing music, she's also shared so much great music by other artists.

The best people in life love Taylor Swift. I've met so many beautiful people through being a fan. Everyone in my life thinks I'm insane, but it's definitely a good insane. They know that if a Taylor song comes on in public they are in for a good embarrassment and that when Taylor wins a new Grammy it means they get to spend the rest of the night watching me happy cry.

A REVIEW OF *SPEAK NOW*

2010 ROBERT CHRISTGAU

The fourteen songs last upward of sixty-seven minutes, some 4:45 apiece; they're overlong and overworked. And I believe what I read about their origins in the romantic and other feelings of America's Ingenue for identifiable major and minor celebrities, which may thrill her fan base but means approximately nothing to me. Even in their overwork, however, they evince an effort that bears a remarkable resemblance to care—that is, to caring in the best, broadest, and most emotional sense. I even like the one about Kanye West—including when I remember that it's about Kanye West, which usually I don't.   **A–**

Speak Now

by Finn Vigeland, edited by Ben Tausig

ACROSS

1 Nintendo console that sounds like a pronoun
4 Fill with joy
9 Big name in telling time
15 Unwelcome picnic guest
16 Actress Sophia from 3-Down
17 Kidman of *Rabbit Hole*
18 *Speak Now* single about falling for someone who you maybe shouldn't
20 Even (with)
21 *A Writer's Life* memoirist Gay ___
22 *Speak Now* song rumored to be about Swift's ex Jonas
24 Shamrock land
25 "What if ___ milk is just regular milk introducing itself in Spanish?"
27 "___ a girl!"
28 Source of fresh veggies: Abbr.
30 Place with a platform
32 Body of water under the Golden Gate Bridge
33 Excel units
34 More intense
36 Heavenly glows
37 *Speak Now* song rumored to be about Swift's ex Lautner
41 Matt Lauer's show, casually
42 Dreamy guy
43 Frozen dew
44 Friends, in slang
46 Rehab attendees
50 Heart chart, for short
51 Identify, as a photo on Facebook
52 Chicken ___ King
53 Greenish-blue color
54 *Speak Now* song rumored to be about Swift's ex Mayer
57 *Toy Story* canine
59 Martial arts master
60 Track from *Speak Now* about meeting someone new
62 Small pouch
63 Ploys
64 Genre related to punk
65 Actress Milano who claims she inspired the look of Ariel in *The Little Mermaid*
66 Cloud nine
67 Rule, briefly

DOWN

1 Squanders
2 To an extent
3 Roma's country
4 "Benevolent" order
5 Gets the short end of the stick
6 Yip relative
7 London tube?
8 Irish singer with an Oscar-nominated song in *The Lord of the Rings*
9 Stuck up
10 Flirts ocularly
11 Trendy fruit juice berry
12 Accomplishment that gets you on the video game leaderboard
13 Socioeconomic conflict
14 Pronoun that's the title of a 2013 Joaquin Phoenix film
19 Budget deal?
23 "Chandelier" singer with an oversized wig
26 "Hold ___ your hat!"
29 Ignorant person
31 Revolting
32 Born and ___
33 Gloats
35 Cheese in a red coat
36 In the thick of
37 Aspiring writer's goal
38 Workplace on *Mad Men*
39 Santa's gift for the naughty
40 Punctuation marks longer than hyphens
41 Word disregarded in alphabetization
44 Burrito alternative
45 Fourth word of the *Star Wars* crawl
47 Shaq's position
48 "I volunteer!"
49 Devious guy
51 Plantings in some street medians
52 Negate, as a marriage
55 Gives a *Jeopardy!* response
56 Sage or basil
58 Fair maiden
59 Relaxing place
61 CBS police procedural franchise

YOU BELONG WITH ME

THE NEW YORKER, OCTOBER 2011 | LIZZIE WIDDICOMBE

One afternoon this spring, the twenty-one-year-old country pop star Taylor Swift was in the back seat of a black Escalade going up Madison Avenue, on her way to the annual Costume Institute Gala at the Metropolitan Museum. Swift is known for sparkly, beaded dresses that make her look like a flapper, but she had adopted a more polished look for the ball: a gauzy, black-and-peach dress by the designer J. Mendel spilled its train around her feet; her hair was up; her lips were dark red and her eyes were smoky. Swift was sending text messages. None of the car's other passengers—her bodyguard, Greg, a burly former Washington, DC, cop; her publicist, Paula Erickson, a tall blond woman in a black blazer—spoke. The only sound came from Swift's iPhone, which emitted an occasional *ding!*

After a minute, Swift looked up from her phone. "It's so fun!" she said, talking about the ball. "One of my best friends"— the actress Emma Stone—"is here tonight. So that'll be really fun, because the past two times I've been at this party I haven't had any of my close friends." She exhaled loudly. *"Whew!"*

Swift is sometimes called a twenty-one-year-old 2.0—the girl next door, but with a superior talent set. She has an Oprah-like gift for emotional expressiveness. While many young stars have a programmed, slightly robotic affect, she radiates unjaded sincerity no matter how contrived the situation—press junkets, awards shows, meet and greets. (Both Winfrey and Swift made appearances at a recent Target sales conference, where Swift performed a funny song she'd written for the company, called "Red Shirt Khaki Pants.") As the car turned onto Fifth Avenue, Swift recalled making a midnight trip, last fall, to buy her most recent album, the triple-platinum *Speak Now*, at a Starbucks in Times Square. She said, in a solemn whisper, "I was so stoked about it, because it's been one of my goals—I always go into Starbucks, and I wished that they would sell my album." I found it hard to believe that she could feel enthusiastic about a sales opportunity at Starbucks, but Swift was insistent. "You go to Starbucks and there's only, like, two CDs for sale," she said. "And I felt like that would be a really big deal if they wanted to sell one of *my* CDs."

The limestone hulk of the Metropolitan Museum came into view. There was a tent in front of the entrance, covering a red carpet, and across the street a mob of screaming spectators stood behind a barricade. The car door opened, and Swift got out to chants of "Tay-*lor!* Tay-*lor!*" Easing herself onto the sidewalk, she proceeded to the base of the stairs, and struck a pose before a phalanx of cameras: a sultry, fierce expression, one hand on her hip, her eyes narrowed, her head cocked back. She seemed to age ten years.

Swift has the pretty, but not aggressively sexy, look of a 1930s movie siren. She is tall and gangly, with porcelain skin, long butterscotch hair that seems crimped, as if from a time before curling irons, and smallish eyes that often look as if they were squinting. She loves to wear makeup, but it tends to resemble stage makeup: red lipstick, thick mascara. In a world of Lohans and Winehouses, Swift is often cited as a role model, a designation she takes seriously. "It's a compliment on your character," she told me. "It's based on the decisions that you make in your life." She is in the midst of her second world tour, and every show begins with a moment in which she stands silently at the lip of the stage and listens to her fans scream. She tilts her head from side to side and appears to blink back tears—the expression, which is projected onto a pair of Jumbotron screens, is part Bambi, part Baby June.

Swift's aura of innocence is not an act, exactly, but it can occasionally belie the scale of her success. She is often described using royal terminology—as a pop princess or, as the *Washington Post* put it recently, the "poet laureate of puberty." In the past five years, she has sold more than twenty million albums—more than any other musician. And, in an era of illegal downloading, fans buy her music online, too. Swift has sold more than twenty-five million digital tracks, surpassing any other country singer, and she holds the Guinness World Record for the fastest-selling digital album, for *Speak Now*. *Forbes* ranked her as last year's seventh-biggest-earning celebrity, with an annual income of $45 million—a figure that encompasses endorsements, products (this month, she releases a perfume with Elizabeth Arden, which is estimated to generate $50 million during its first year of sales), and tickets. Her concerts, which pack both stadiums and arenas, regularly bring in some $750,000 a night. These feats are all the more impressive because Swift writes her own material—a rarity for a country singer, but especially unusual for a teen star.

That Swift is a country star at all might come as a surprise to the casual music fan, who probably knows her as a generic teen queen, supplying background music for slumber parties and shoppers at Forever 21. On her first album, which was released in 2006, when she was sixteen, Swift sings with a twangy Southern accent, and makes references to God and pickup trucks. But

---

Onstage, she shapes her fingers into a **heart**— "I did it at a concert one time, and people screamed, so I just kept doing it."

she veered deeper into pop territory with her second record, *Fearless*, which won four Grammys in 2010. It is a collection of guitar-driven hits with a slick, commercial sheen. The typical Taylor Swift song is gentle but full of insistent hooks; it features Swift's delicate voice, singing about love in all its variations—or, as she told me, "Love, and unrequited love, and love that didn't last, or love that you wish had lasted, or love that never even got started."

The setting, on her first two albums, is high school, but the lyrics are layered with dreamy images that could have come from the romantic imagination of a much younger child—princes, fairy tales, kissing in the rain. One of her hits, "Love Story," recasts the tale of Romeo and Juliet in a small town, with a happy ending: "Marry me, Juliet, you'll never have to be alone!" Others are wistful, and sometimes theatrically sad. In "Forever & Always," Swift sings about a failed relationship: "It rains in your bedroom / everything is wrong! / It rains when you're here and it rains when you're gone!" It's easy to imagine a chorus of young voices belting out the words from the back seat of the minivan.

But Swift has also won the approval of people in the music industry, from Neil Young ("I like Taylor Swift. I like listening to her") to Dolly Parton ("Taylor Swift is the greatest thing that's ever happened to country music") to the rock critic Robert Christgau, who said of her previous album, "The level of craft made the narrowness of focus forgivable." She has won virtually every industry prize—an ACM Award for Entertainer of the Year, a CMT Award for Video of the Year, and a Grammy for Album of the Year—and she has been nominated for six categories at the upcoming CMA Awards, more than any other solo artist. Her work has received almost uniformly positive reviews, although most of them portray her more as a skilled

technician than as a Dylanesque vision-
ary. "Swift is a songwriting savant with an
intuitive gift for verse-chorus-bridge ar-
chitecture that . . . calls to mind Swedish
pop gods Dr. Luke and Max Martin," Jody
Rosen wrote in *Rolling Stone*. "If she ever
tires of stardom, she could retire to Swe-
den and make a fine living churning out
hits for Kelly Clarkson and Katy Perry."

Like Parton, Swift writes autobio-
graphical songs, a technique that, in the
Internet era, is a clever marketing device.
After *Speak Now* was released, last fall,
Swift became known for writing about
her celebrity boyfriends: the *Twilight*
actor Taylor Lautner, the Disney star
Joe Jonas, the singer John Mayer. "Dear
John" includes the line "Don't you think
I was too young to be messed with?"
(Mayer was thirty-two when they dated.)
After the album's release, public scrutiny
of her love life blossomed into something
like a stalker school of literary criticism.
One blogger analyzed the lyric "I ran off
the plane that July ninth," and figured out
that the song was about Jonas: "She flew
to Dallas on July 9, 2008, to sit in the audience for a Jonas Brothers show." In its
first week, *Speak Now* sold more than a
million copies.

Swift is tolerant of her fans' interest in
her love life, as she is of gawkers who approach her on the street. "It's human nature!" she told me. While she doesn't talk
about dating in interviews, she helps am-
ateur sleuths along, using capital letters
to spell out coded messages throughout
the lyrics in her liner notes that indicate
which boyfriend the song is about. Swift
has an affinity for codes and symbols.
Onstage, she shapes her fingers into a
heart—"I did it at a concert one time,
and people screamed, so I just kept doing
it," she said—and appears with her lucky
number, 13, written on her right hand

in Sharpie. More recently, she has been scrawling lyrics, such as U2's "One life, you got to do what you should," on her left arm; deciphering the references has become another fan activity. Swift's ability to hold her audience's interest reflects, in part, a keen understanding of what fuels fan obsession in the first place: a desire for intimacy between singer and listener. She told me that the best musical experience is "hearing a song by somebody singing about their life, and it resembles yours so much that it makes you feel comforted." Her website includes video journals and diary-like posts to her online message board, which Swift does not outsource. Her fans, who call themselves Swifties,

respond with passionate testimonials—"i would drink her bathwater"—and confessions about their own crushes: "Jake. Jake. Jake. Jake. I can't say it enough. I just love the sound of his name."

On the red carpet at the Met, Swift stood still before the cameras. Then she walked up the stairs, letting Erickson usher her through a series of TV interviews. She addressed each reporter, "Hey! I'm Taylor. Nice to meet you." Paparazzi swarmed for a better angle. "Miss Swift, right here!" one shouted. When a civilian wandered into their sight lines, a photographer bellowed, "Please! Step away from the beauties!"

As other guests arrived—the brown-haired *Twilight* star Ashley Greene, Harvey Weinstein—the crowd formed a bottleneck. Swift neared the top of the stairs and froze. She grabbed Erickson's sleeve in a panic: "Am I supposed to talk to him or not?" Standing by the door was the rapper Kanye West.

To some, Swift is best known for an episode at the 2009 MTV Video Music Awards. As she began to deliver a heartfelt acceptance speech for Best Female Video—"I always dreamed about what it would be like to maybe win one of these"—West, in sunglasses and jeans, strode onto the stage and grabbed the microphone from her hands. Hunched over, he announced, "Yo, Taylor, I'm really happy for you, I'mma let you finish, but Beyoncé"—another nominee—"had one of the best videos of all time!" The moment, which had started out like a coronation, turned into something closer to a public shaming. Swift's happy expression dissolved into shocked dismay as West handed the microphone back to her and walked off-stage. Her mouth dropped open, and she seemed to sway a bit. She eventually left the stage without speaking. (Later that night, Beyoncé invited her back onstage to finish her speech.)

The event—replayed endlessly on television and online—ended in mortification for West. He unleashed an apologetic rant on his website ("I'M SOOOOO SORRY TO TAYLOR SWIFT AND HER FANS") and eventually took a year off to recover. President Obama called him "a jackass." Swift will say only that the fallout was "handled very privately," but she added, "I think that you learn a lot of lessons as you're growing up, and one of them has to be human compassion." Her last album includes a mournful song called "Innocent," which is, presumably, about West.

It concludes, "Who you are is not what you did / You're still an innocent." It's a nice thought, although the tone is a bit grave: listening to it, you could get the impression that she is forgiving him for armed robbery.

If the Kanye West incident did not reflect badly on Swift, it did forecast some backlash about her ascent. Critics have always gone after her voice, which sounds warbly and sweet on albums but has sometimes been off pitch in concert. A few months later, at the 2010 Grammy Awards, she gave a disastrous live performance in which she harmonized off-key with Stevie Nicks. Although she won Album of the Year that night, her singing prompted a flurry of comments along the lines of one made by the *Family Guy* creator, Seth MacFarlane, who said, "Maybe Kanye was right."

At the Costume Institute Gala, Swift hesitated for a second, and then, realizing that there was no time to wait for advice, continued walking up the stairs toward West. As she neared the door, he held a hand out, and the two exchanged a studiedly casual, "down low" high five. When it was over, Swift stopped just inside the museum, looking giddy. Erickson let out a breath and exclaimed, "That wasn't bad!"

Feeling my eyes on her, Swift didn't comment on what had just happened. Instead, she said, "I'm so glad I didn't bring a purse this year!" Erickson handed her a ticket for the ball, and she ran upstairs to the party.

Swift wandered through the museum's Alexander McQueen exhibit, passing mannequins in bondage-inspired ensembles, ominous quotations painted on the walls: "There is no way back for me now." During the cocktail hour, in the Petrie Sculpture Court, waiters in kilts held trays of champagne, but Swift sipped soda

water and chatted with Gwyneth Paltrow. "I met her at Faith's house," she told me, referring to Faith Hill. "She is the best. You just end up telling her everything!"

Wendi Murdoch eyed Swift with approval. "I have a seven- and a nine-year-old daughter, and they love her music," she said. "She makes me want to listen to country music more. Also, she's such a professional and an artist. You don't hear about any of the bad kind of behavior all the other famous young stars have. I love her music."

Early adulthood is an awkward time for teen stars, but Swift's has been free of embarrassing incidents. She doesn't drink or go to clubs, and she has avoided the trip to rehab that marked the coming-of-age of the former Disney star Demi Lovato. She also hasn't made the jarring transition to the darker, sexier material embraced by former teenyboppers Miley Cyrus and Britney Spears. Swift describes this decision as an artistic rather than a moral one. "I don't feel completely overcome by the relentless desire to put out a dark and sexy 'I'm grown-up now' album," she told me. Still, her most recent record makes subtle references to more adult relationships, including lines such as "There's a drawer of my things at your place."

According to reports in the press, Swift recently bought a Colonial-style house in Beverly Hills that would be right at home on Nantucket. ("I just love New England-y things," she told me.) But her primary residence is in Nashville, a city that she said "is just *everything*. It's just my favorite place ever." A little over a year ago, she moved out of her parents' house, in the suburbs, into a four-thousand-square-foot duplex penthouse in a Trump-like glass building called the Adelicia, in midtown Nashville. The building has concierge service and a pool scene, where a crew of Vanderbilt grads like to socialize around a fire pit. Swift bought the apartment when she was nineteen, when her friends all went off to college, and spent two years decorating it with antiques. "I was obsessive about turning my apartment into an art project," she told me. "Everything's mismatched, everything's quirky." The condo has an indoor moat, a night-sky motif on the ceiling, and a birdcage-shaped observatory.

At home, Swift spends most of her off time with band members, friends, and

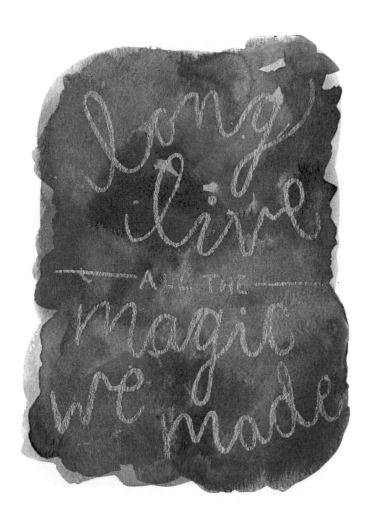

I WAS ENCHANTED TO MEET you

family—going out for coffee, cooking group dinners. When she's on tour, she watches TV on her computer: *Teen Mom*, *CSI* (on which she has guest-starred), and, recently, History Channel documentaries. "I'm just so obsessed with the whole history of JFK and RFK," she said. She recently announced that she had completed a nine-hundred-page book called *The Kennedy Women*.

When I visited Swift, she was rehearsing inside the Bridgestone Arena, home to the Nashville Predators. Twenty-two eighteen-wheelers were parked outside, bearing gauzy portraits of her face, along with the logo of CoverGirl, which is sponsoring her tour. In addition to her perfume, she has sold greeting cards, a line of $14 Walmart sundresses, Jakks fashion dolls—they wear Swift's outfits and carry mini versions of her Swarovski crystal–encrusted guitar—and, on her website, calendars, iPad skins, Peter Max posters, robes, headbands, journals, and gift bags. Swift professes a kind of auteur approach to marketing. "I don't believe in endorsing a product that you don't want to endorse," she said, with feeling. "I've *always* wanted to be a CoverGirl. I've *always* wanted to have a fragrance, and so when it comes time to go on *Good Morning America* and wake up really early in the morning to promote that fragrance I'm going to do it with a smile on my face."

Swift approaches her career with the seriousness of a CEO. Every two years, she puts out an album, for which she writes about forty songs. She composes by singing melodies onto her iPhone as voice memos, and writing down lyrics in the Notes section. "When I'm eighty," she told me, "I imagine that I'll wish that when I was twenty-one I'd gotten up early and gone out and walked to Hills-boro Village"—a shopping area near her condo—"and gone out and hiked and taken pictures of everything. And written in my diary more."

Swift clacked around the arena's empty concrete halls in gladiator sandals, a flowered skirt, a tank top, and a long, droopy orange sweater. (She gets cold easily.) Her hair was in a loose ponytail, with curly tendrils falling down around her face, and she had on her bright-red lipstick.

One of the dancers in the show ran by in a hillbilly outfit. "That's cuuuute!" Swift said, pointing. The dancer did a little curtsy and said, "Do you want some grits?"

"That's Charity, who's one of my best friends," Swift said. She is especially close with Liz Huett, a backup singer, and Caitlin Evanson, her violinist. The three share a dressing room, and, when I was there, they were all lying on a couch with their legs draped over one another.

Despite this coziness, the atmosphere of a Taylor Swift tour is professional, if not downright corporate—less *Almost Famous* than Apple board meeting. The tour is run by Robert Allen, a pudgy, gray-haired Englishman whose brother is the drummer for Def Leppard. Allen is given to rah-rah statements about the size of the production. He told me, "On the scale of all the tours that I've done,

personally, it's as big as it gets. The fact that we're in seventy-one arenas and eight stadiums and two of those stadiums are back-to-back—that's a 'wow.' That's rarefied air there." The other major player is Swift's mother, Andrea, a large, imposing woman with a blond bob and Swift's narrow eyes. When I arrived, she was holding a list of statistics to recite when giving backstage tours—"all my facts," she called them. She handed the list to Swift, who read them out: "We travel an average of three hundred and fifty miles per night. Eighty-two set carts. Ninety instruments—violins, percussions, banjo, a harp. Approximately

eight miles of electric cable get put up per day."

"Eight miles," Andrea Swift repeated, proudly.

Taylor Swift contributes to every detail of the show. "You have to," she told me, "or else you'll have these surprises pop up. And you don't ever want to be caught by surprise when you're touring." As a manager, she cuts a figure not unlike that of the teenage monarch in the 2009 film *The Young Victoria*, gracious and vulnerable but also, given her position of power, a bit terrifying. People bring her things: bottles of water, a Styrofoam bowl of Cinnamon Toast Crunch.

At one point, Swift and her mother were backstage, preparing for a meeting about onstage video content. Swift said, "Do we have the DVD? Because the ones that they gave me yesterday I left in my condo."

It turned out that an assistant had forgotten them. Andrea Swift groaned. "How many ways did we express to Britney that we needed those DVDs?"

Swift took the fall. "It's my fault, 'cause I was watching them last night," she said, sounding dejected.

Her mother adopted a gentle tone: "Honey, if we had to count on you to remember every little detail it certainly wouldn't work."

Swift's businesslike approach could be considered a natural result of her background. She was born not in the small-town South but in Reading, Pennsylvania. She was brought up in the nearby suburb of Wyomissing, where, she told me, "it mattered what kind of designer handbag you brought to school." The older of two siblings—her brother is a student at Vanderbilt—she grew up on a Christmas-tree farm, but her parents were not exactly farmers. Her mother worked

in finance, and her father, a descendant of three generations of bank presidents, is a stockbroker for Merrill Lynch. (He bought the tree farm from a client.)

Early on, Swift assumed that she would follow her parents into business. "I didn't know what a stockbroker was when I was eight, but I would just tell everybody that's what I was going to be," she recalled, during an online Q&A with fans. "We'd be at, like, the first day of school and they're, like, 'So what do you guys want to be when you grow up?' And everybody's, like, 'I want to be an astronaut!' Or, like, 'I want to be a ballerina!' And I'm, like, 'I'm gonna be a financial adviser!'" But she eventually had a country music epiphany, inspired by listening to '90s crossover hits—Faith Hill, Shania Twain, the Dixie Chicks. The melodies were good, but she especially liked the storytelling. "It was just such a given—I want to do that!" she said.

Swift's adolescence was dominated by a yearlong period of exile, when a group of friends ditched her, pronouncing her "annoying." "That's quoted," she said. "We had these catty little IM conversations when we were in sixth grade." The ditching probably had something to do with the fact that Swift was becoming recognized for her singing: she had performed at a 76ers game. (There is a YouTube clip of a chubbier Swift, in a headband and cardigan, belting out the national anthem.) But it might also have been related to her natural primness. She recalled an incident from seventh grade: "At the beginning of the year, we were all sleeping over at somebody's house and"—she broke into a mock whisper—"they were all talking about how they wanted to sneak over to this guy's house because this guy had beer. And I was just, like"—she affected a pan-

after the label decided to keep her in development for too long—but by then she had also secured a songwriter's publishing deal with Sony/ATV Nashville: she was the youngest songwriter the company had ever signed. Arthur Buenahora, the Sony executive who signed Swift after she played a few songs for him on her guitar, said, "The songs were great, but it was her, really. She was a star. She lit up the room." He added, "I liked her attitude. She was very easy to root for."

Swift, as a teenage singer-songwriter, was an anomaly in the country music industry. The predominant model is the songwriter workshop: writers churn out material in groups of two or three, and the results are hawked by a song-plugger, so that superstars like Tim McGraw can pick their favorites. There had, of course, been other teenage singers—from Tanya Tucker to LeAnn Rimes—but they often performed material written by and for middle-aged listeners. Swift recalled, "I remember auditioning for record labels and having them tell me"—she adopted a snobby voice—"'Well, the country-radio demographic is the thirty-five-year-old female housewife. Give us a song that relates to the thirty-five-year-old female, and we'll talk.'" It's since become a Nashville truism that Swift tapped into an audience that hadn't previously been recognized: teenage girls who listen to country music.

Swift's songs were different both in their personal dimension and in their subject matter. Peter Cooper, of the Nashville *Tennessean*, suggested that the best precedent might be Janis Ian, whose song "At Seventeen" swept the charts in the '70s with its raw portrayal of adolescent angst. "At its best, country music is a reality format," he said. "What Taylor did was to write her own experiences, nearly in real time, and speak directly to

icked voice—"I want to call my mom! I want to call my mom! I want to call my mom!'" She told me, "My whole life I've never felt comfortable just being . . . *edgy* like that."

Swift had already decided to become a songwriter. When she was ten, her mother began driving her around on weekends to sing at karaoke competitions. Then she persuaded her mother to take her to Nashville during spring break to drop off her karaoke demo tapes around Music Row, in search of a record deal; they didn't succeed, but the experience convinced Swift that she needed a way to stand out. Songwriting became a sanctuary from the horrors of middle school. "I couldn't wait to get home every day and write," she said.

The Swifts continued to return to Nashville, where Taylor played in industry showcases; at thirteen, she was offered a development deal by RCA, a Sony Music subsidiary. The following year, the Swifts moved. Her father transferred to the Nashville office of Merrill Lynch, and the family bought a large house on a lake in Hendersonville, Tennessee, a borderline rural area where Johnny Cash used to live. (It provided the small-town imagery for Swift's lyrics.) Swift enrolled at a public school and experienced a social revelation: "Everybody was so nice to me! They're all, like, 'We heard you're a singer. We have a talent show next week—do you want to enter?'" The RCA deal eventually fell apart—Swift walked away,

her audience about what she was going through—which was what they were going through, too."

She didn't do it completely alone. As part of her publishing deal, she was matched with professional songwriters. Her mother would set up the writing sessions and drive her there. She eventually began writing regularly with Liz Rose, a middle-aged Texan who cowrote many of the songs on her first two albums. Rose perhaps has a career incentive to play up Swift's role in their collaboration, but they both describe it as an equal one, with Swift providing a line, a scenario, or a hook—often about something that was going on at school—and the two of them improvising the rest. For the hit "You Belong with Me," a song about having a crush on a boy who is with someone else, Swift said, "I just came in and played the pre-chorus and the first half of the chorus for Liz"—she started singing—"'She wears short skirts / I wear T-shirts,' and she goes, 'Something about bleachers!'" The finished line: "She's cheer captain / and I'm on the bleachers."

Some have objected that Swift promotes a noxious, '50s-style ideal of virginal, submissive femininity. Critics take issue with "Fifteen," a song that Swift wrote, at seventeen, about the joys and pains of first relationships. The song sketches out the experiences of Swift and her best friend from high school, Abigail, a University of Kansas student who has become a demi-celebrity among Swifties. It moves from Swift's positive memory ("And then you're on your very first date and he's got a car and you feel like flyyyyin'!") to Abigail's disappointing one ("Abigail gave everything she had to a boy who changed

his mind") and concludes with a coy hint about Swift's future: "In your life you'll do things greater than dating the boy on the football team." Sady Doyle, the author of the blog *Tiger Beatdown*, interpreted "Fifteen" as an implicit morality tale. "The narrative here goes as follows," she wrote. "There's a girl who gets semi-sexual and regrets it (because BOYS want SEX, and GIRLS DON'T), and a girl who doesn't get up to much of anything sexual and ends up wise and happy." One mother recently wrote on the *Huffington Post*, "*Speak Now* tour? More like Speak softly and smile a lot."

But Swift's lyrics, though they are not subversive, have a certain sophistication. There's often a tension between the words

---

"If I was ever a headliner I would want to pick out people in the audience that were just so crazy and fanatical—*they'd* be the ones that got to come back."

---

and the music: angry songs sound upbeat, and sentimental songs are laced with intimations of future disillusionment. In person, Swift has a quietly ironic sense of humor. When I first met her, discussing the Costume Institute Gala, I asked, "So how do you feel about balls in general?" Swift seemed confused. Then she let out a cackle and said, "A-*ma*-zing! That was incredible. It's going to be my new moment of the century."

In her sophomore year, Swift bought a car with the money she'd earned from songwriting—a silver Lexus SC430 convertible. "It was the car that Regina George drives in *Mean Girls*," she said.

"Because all the girls back in Pennsylvania idolized her, and I think I just thought it would be fun to have that car."

Swift's story is often framed as an underdog saga, the triumph of a nice girl over mean ones, and of teenage pluckiness over industry gatekeepers. It's a legend that de-emphasizes the role of adults, although Swift's parents have been a constant presence in her life—she has even written songs about them. I spoke to Andrea Swift one afternoon in Nashville, in what is called the T-Party Room. At every stop on the tour, six workers take five hours to transform a cinder-block holding room into an exotic tented emporium to greet fans. It feels like the refuge of a prosperous Bedouin teenager: a central column is decorated with snapshots (Swift making a heart symbol with Steven Tyler), and swaths of purple, yellow, green, and red silk are draped from the top, maypole style, forming a billowy ceiling. "Virtually everything in this room she's picked out, either herself or through text," Andrea Swift told me.

During each show, Andrea Swift or an assistant scouts the arena and selects the most enthusiastic fans. She gives each lucky girl (they are usually girls) a wristband and invites her backstage later. The idea behind the T-Party dates to Swift's early years, when she was opening for other country stars—Rascal Flatts, Brad Paisley, George Strait. "She would wait until the headliner got back to his bus, was having his nightcap, and was going to bed," Andrea Swift told me. "And that's when we would hit the concourse level for her to sign autographs." She said that her daughter was unimpressed with the way meet and greets usually worked. "She was, like, 'You know, if I was ever a headliner I would want to pick out people in the audience that were just so crazy and fanatical—*they'd* be the ones that got to come back.' She didn't want you to VIP your way in or bribe someone or sob-story your way in. It's just basically the fans who it would really mean the world to just sit down and have fun and talk to her."

Andrea Swift affected a note of non-chalance when I asked her about her involvement in her daughter's career. "Well, you know, she's just been doing this for so long that, to me, this is just like soccer practice," she said. Swift's father, Scott, whose look includes tasselled loafers, was more direct. He said, "I'm not taking her money, if that's what you're saying."

While I was in Nashville, I went to see Scott Borchetta, the head of Swift's record label, Big Machine. Borchetta, a former Universal executive, left to start his own operation, and Swift was his first client. At the time that he signed her, he already had a reputation for being, in the words of the songwriter and producer Robert Ellis Orrall, "one of the best radio-promotion guys in the business." His office is on Music Row, in an unmarked frame house whose exterior state of dilapidation, an assistant explained, is a disguise: "So we don't have eight-year-old girls knocking on doors giving us their CDs." Behind the peeling paint, the building resembles an outpost of Soho House—diamond-plate-steel-covered doors and scores of gold and platinum records on the walls. In the basement is a map of the world stuck with multi-colored pins. "Those are our territories," Borchetta, a paunchy man with a goatee, told me. Swift has sold more than three

million albums internationally—an extraordinary number for a country act—and Borchetta outlined the plan of attack: Australia is next. "We were able to really infiltrate Japan over the last year," he said. "I think she's at the point now where it's probably time for her to do a movie and soundtrack. Because she's gotten to this kind of embeddedness, if you will, with where we are in American culture."

Since 2007, the Swifts have been in litigation with Dan Dymtrow, a former manager of Britney Spears, who claimed that they had violated a 2004 contract with him before Taylor signed with Borchetta. In papers filed in a New York court, Dymtrow challenged Swift's origin story: "How does an eighteen-year-old singer from a small town in Pennsylvania make it to the cover of *Rolling Stone*'s 'Best of Rock 2008'? If you believe the version of the story being told to the world, Taylor Swift knocked on record-company doors when she was just thirteen years old." Dymtrow argued that, instead, he had launched her career by bringing in branding consultants, setting up performances (one, he noted, was a venue known as Rudy Giuliani's Camp), and securing marketing deals with companies like Abercrombie & Fitch. The case is being settled out of court; a judge threw out all of Dymtrow's claims except one, for unjust enrichment. While the litigation didn't derail Swift's career, it did provide glimpses into the adult negotiations inevitably at work behind a teenage success story. At one point, Dymtrow's lawyers released an e-mail written by Swift's father to Borchetta that was quoted in the press: "Enough with the Dymtrow. You asked me to break both his legs, wrap him in chains, and throw him in the lake. I did."

"Hey, check, one, two. Hello? Hello, hey. Stadium. Hello?" Swift's phone was not getting a signal. It was late afternoon, and she was now in Detroit, preparing to play the first stadium of her tour: Ford Field, which seats fifty thousand people, and, five years ago, hosted the Super Bowl. Like all her tour dates, it had sold out in less than five minutes. "The only time when I'm alone is when I come into the venue earlier than everybody else," she said. She sat on the floor of her dressing room, a bare stadium space accessorized with scented candles, puffy purple couches, and lamps with the tags still on them. She was barefoot, wearing jeans and a red plaid shirt, with her hair in a ponytail. Except for a certain high-sheen

Swift's penchant for thank-you notes and thoughtful gestures may be a talisman against the fickleness of public opinion—or fate. She is an incessant worrier. "I've been watching *Behind the Music* since I was five, and I became fascinated by career trajectories," she told me. "Like"—she adopted a TV-announcer voice—"'This artist peaked on their second album. This artist peaked on their third album. This artist peaked with every album. These are singles artists. These are album artists.'" She went on, "And I sometimes stress myself out wondering what my trajectory is—like, if I sleep in and wake up at 2 p.m., because I'm so tired from the night before, sometimes I'll beat myself up, because what if I was supposed to wake up earlier that day and write a song?"

Swift's career role models are not the Madonnas and Beyoncés of the world but the singer-songwriters—Bruce Springsteen, Kris Kristofferson, and Emmylou Harris. "They're so known for their thoughts, and the things that they've written, and the things they've created," she told me. "They've evolved, but they've never abandoned their fans." (Robert Christgau thought that Harris made sense, but he said that the Springsteen aspirations were a stretch: "She has a much more contained and crafty relationship with words.")

Swift told me that she is taking control of her career, now that she's no longer a teenager. Her parents, she said, "have

exquisiteness—thinness, the lipstick—she looked like a regular college student.

"Yeah, check, one, two," Swift said. She was talking to her management office about an album of pictures from the tour, which would be sold at merchandise stands. Beside her on the floor was a stack of dummy pages, which she'd covered with Post-it notes. She flipped through the pages and read off critiques: "I'd really like to take out the 3-D element"; "Does it bother you that I have a hair scrunchy on my wrist for some of the pictures?"; "Okay, 'Love Story'? The one where I'm coming down the stairs? I look like a big, giant cat."

When I arrived, she had been bent over a glass coffee table, writing thank-you notes to local radio-station managers. The cards, which she had helped write and design, were from the American Greetings line. Some of the styles are glitter-encrusted, with Swift's handwriting on them, and messages that echo her song lyrics: "You know how sometimes—right in the middle of a moment—you already know it's one you won't ever forget?" Swift had contacted American Greetings with the idea for the cards. "Part of the reason I wanted to do it was because I go through so many cards on a weekly basis," she said. "I like writing 'em. And I like stamps." As she wrote her thank-yous, Swift referred to notes about each radio-station worker that she had made on her iPhone. She signed a card:

been staying home more" (although one of them was at all the shows I attended). And, although she has acted in the movie *Valentine's Day*, and hosted *Saturday Night Live*, and plans to do more acting, she flinched when I mentioned the plan for global domination that Borchetta had mapped out for her.

In Detroit, Swift seemed somewhat melancholy. Once in a while, I had the feeling that she was on the verge of bursting into tears. She said that she had recently decided that life is "about achieving contentment. . . . You're not always going to be ridiculously happy." She had written about ten songs so far for her next album. Asked to characterize them, she said, "They're sad? If I'm being honest." The most recent one, she said, "is about moving on."

At one point, her security guard, Greg, came in, carrying a pair of portable iPod speakers. "Yes!" Swift said. "Where did they find them?" (Swift's life sometimes resembles an extended iPhone commercial.) She plugged her phone into the speakers, and played a mournful country song: "Well, they ain't gonna make a movie about a couple of fools like us." "This is my time to hang out with Lori McKenna, who I want to be when I grow up," Swift said, of the singer. "She's a mom, and she lives in New England with her five kids. And she wrote 'Stealing Kisses,' by Faith Hill. She wrote that!" She fixed me with an intense look before cuing up another song, and asked, "Have you ever had your heart broken?"

Listeners to Swift's most recent album will get the impression that she has. The songs, which she wrote without collaborators, are extra long, and cover a multitude of relationships, in moods that range from regret to a surprising, and somewhat satisfying, cattiness. Besides "Dear John," about John Mayer, the upbeat, guitar-driven

"Better Than Revenge" is, according to fan speculation, a takedown of the actress Camilla Belle, who dated a former boyfriend of Swift's. The chorus rhymes "she's an actress" with "she's better known for the things that she does on the mattress."

A perusal of the songbooks begs a logistical question: where does she find the time to date so many people? The answer seems to be that a little goes a long way. Many of the songs are based on a memory or on a flirtation. In "Enchanted," Swift murmurs in a pleading voice, "Please don't be in love with someone else." It was inspired, apparently, by a brief conversation that she had, in New York, with the musician Adam Young, who performs under the name Owl City. The interaction was "just small talk and stuff," Young told me. "She talked about how she grew up in Pennsylvania, I talked about how I grew up in Minnesota. She's very genuine." Swift's hint in the liner notes spelled A-D-A-M. Her fans decoded it by tracking a word, *wonderstruck*, which Young had used on his blog. The word is now the name of Swift's perfume—a seamless mixture of reality, romance, and marketing.

When I asked why so few of her songs are about work, she said, "I don't want to write songs like"—she switched into a monotone voice—"'Today, I woke up in a hotel and went to a venue and wrote cards.' Nobody wants to hear a song about that."

One song from her current album is, however, about a professional dustup. "Mean," an upbeat, unusually twangy number, calls out a bully ("You, with your switching sides and your wildfire lies and your humiliation"), and alludes to her success ("Someday I'll be big enough so you can't hit me"). At one point, Swift taunts, in a singsong way, "All you are is mean, and a liar, and pathetic, and alone in life."

The consensus is that the song is aimed at Bob Lefsetz, a former L.A. entertainment lawyer who blogs about the music business. Lefsetz, who had at first praised Swift, reversed himself after her live performance at the 2010 Grammys, announcing, "Now, everyone knows that Taylor Swift can't sing." I talked to Lefsetz, who said that the song "Mean" had brought him daily hate e-mail. "I wrote that she couldn't sing. People are saying, 'Little kids like her, so who the fuck are you to speak the truth?'" But he stood by his argument: "Let's say that you're ugly, and you're on the cover of *Vogue*, does that work for you? And the defense is 'I'm a good person!' Let's say that you're a really nice guy and play baseball for the Yankees and bat .100. 'Oh, but he's a nice guy!'"

Swift refuses to defend her singing voice. She told me, "I write songs, and my voice is just a way to get those lyrics across."

A Taylor Swift concert begins with the massing, hours before showtime, of little girls outside the concert venue—the Hajj at Mecca, if it were sponsored by My Little Pony. There is a uniform: sundresses, cowboy boots. (Swift's look during her early years.) Fans curl their hair into loose ringlets and write the number 13 on their hands. Many also carry signs, in the hope of being selected by Swift's mother for the T-Party. For example: I WOULD BE ENCHANTED TO SEE YOU. Inside, video screens above the stage project text messages from the audience:

Taylor you're my idol <3
We love you more than we can say!!!

At one concert I attended, Tom Petty's "American Girl" was playing on the sound system as fans filed in, a nod to the middle-aged chaperones in the arena.

There are lots of mother-daughter pairs at Swift's shows. In New Jersey, a mother accompanying her thirteen-year-old said, "There's nothing like Taylor. I'm not worried about the words coming out of her mouth. Growing up, I remember my mom making me return a Rod Stewart album because of the song 'Hot Legs.'" (For a contemporary example, one can attend a concert by Katy Perry and listen to a stadium full of thirteen-year-olds chant along with the song "Peacock," which goes, "I want to see your peacock-cock-cock! Your peacock-cock!")

Swift's entrance is all pomp and circumstance. First, her mother appears on the floor, and a wave of screaming breaks out. Andrea Swift walks the aisles of the arena, smiling and waving like a political wife, giving the occasional hug, and takes her place near the soundstage. Then Swift's entrance is announced by sonic rumbling and by her recorded voice: "There's a time for silence and a time for waiting your turn. But if you know how you feel and you so clearly know what you need to say, you'll know it. I don't think you should wait, I think you should Speak Now!" As the music starts, she sprints onstage in a glittery dress, and launches into the first song. Then she does her standing-still ritual, her eyes misting over while the audience screams.

Swift's songs may be wistful expressions of a teenager's inner life, but her shows are huge externalizations of them—featuring a two-story stage, "pyro" displays, dancers, aerialists, and nine costume changes. Although the stories in her songs are somewhat oblique, her dance troupe acts them all out literally: "Speak Now," a fantasy of a woman interrupting her crush's wedding, is performed on a church set, complete with pews and bridesmaids. Swift, her hair in a ponytail, bobs and sings, "Don't say

yes / run away now / I'll meet you when you're out of the church at the back door," and runs offstage with the dancer dressed as the groom. Cheesy, yes, but once, during this song, I noticed a grizzled rock critic in the row in front of me, cotton stuffed in his ears, tapping his feet.

Eventually, Swift moves to the B stage, a little island with a glittery tree. She plays the ukulele and banters about love, saying, "We're all hopeless romantics," and "I think there's really something special about a first kiss." The subject of the songs, it becomes clear, is not really men—it's more about the love affair between Swift and her audience. In Detroit, she said, "You know when you know someone really well and they can finish your sentences? I'm curious to know what it would be like to have fifty thousand people finish my sentences."

She began to sing a soft, acoustic version of "Fearless"—"In a storm in my best dress, fearless"—and the entire stadium sang along. Standing on the floor in front of the stage were six sixteen-year-old girls holding hands and swaying, and a girl in a hijab sobbing as she sang the words. It was hard not to be a little moved, and not to feel relieved that the words being sung were, more or less, safe. At the show's high point, the crowd-pleasing song "Love Story," silver and gold confetti rains down, and Swift, wearing a princess gown, is launched above the crowd in a flying balcony.

Toward the end of the show, I followed a production assistant, Gabby, up to a row near the nosebleed seats, where two girls were holding a sign that read SPEAK NOW, illuminated by clip-on book lights. They were Lidia Hencic and Anna McWebb, fourteen, of Waterloo, Ontario. They wore braces and Birkenstocks, and were jumping up and down like pogo sticks.

"Have you ever met Taylor?" Gabby asked.

"No!!!!!"

"Want to meet her?"

"Yes!!!!!"

She handed them wristbands and said, "Taylor's mom handpicked you." The girls began convulsing with screams.

In the T-Party Room, the lights were low, and the anointed fans stood around in stunned clumps. An assistant had briefed each person on the protocol: "They have one group photo and absolutely no video. Taylor signs one thing per person. When she's coming, that's when to start the 'Tay-lor!' chant."

Hencic and McWebb stood in a corner. They said they had sleepovers oriented around watching Swift's videos. "We're not really the boy-crazy type," McWebb said. "We just want to be her friend."

Hencic said, "I can relate to what she's saying, even though I've never had a boyfriend."

As the fans chanted "Tay-lor! Tay-lor!," Swift appeared, in a baggy pink striped sweater, her hair in loose braids and her skin showing a faint layer of sweat. She started giving out hugs, her eyes crinkling as she smiled.

Swift approached Hencic and McWebb, and said, calmly, "Hey, dudes!," and gave them each a hug. She stood back to admire their sign, with its book lights. "This is so good," she said, matter-of-factly. "I've never seen anyone do this before. It's so crafty."

"You're our idol," McWebb said. "We watch all of your blogs."

Swift put a hand to her heart and said, "Thank you. That's awesome."

They stood there while she worked the rest of the room, very close, but very far away. ◆

EMMA DUGAN

STUDENT, 14, ILLINOIS

My first memory of Taylor is when my aunt went to the *Fearless* concert and brought me and my sister some of the confetti that fell at the end of the show. She also brought us back a super-long poster. I remember wishing that I'd been there.

My favorite place to listen to Taylor is in the car. I love to look out the window and either watch the music video in my head or make one up if there isn't one.

I was in a car the first time that I heard "Shake It Off." We were driving to one of my former teachers' houses to have lunch. I was like, "This sounds like Taylor." I got so excited when I realized it was.

If I ever meet Taylor, I'll probably go into shock. I don't think the fact that I'm talking to Taylor Swift will really register until it's over. Then I'd probably cry a lot and keep looking at the pictures and wishing that I could go back in time.

It's impossible to pick a favorite song, but if I had to, I would probably say "Mine." It's the story of a girl who's seen love fail before but still has the courage to find and be happy with the love of her life.

Her funniest lyric has to be "This morning I said we should talk about it / 'Cause I read you should never leave a fight unresolved / That's when you came in wearing a football helmet / And said 'Okay, let's talk.'"

I'm obsessed with Taylor's style. She can pull off anything. I'm also super obsessed with her red lipstick.

My favorite moment at a concert is right before Taylor comes onstage. When you know that in about thirty seconds you'll see the most amazing person in the world. It's so exciting and nerve-racking and emotional all at the same time.

I was terrified when it started raining right before the concert I went to. I was worried that it might be canceled because it was storming really badly. There was thunder and lightning and everything.

Something that cracks me up about Taylor is when she just fools around. I love it when she's just her usual goofy self.

It makes me sad when people say that Taylor isn't talented or has dated too many people. Taylor is just like any girl, going through a string of boyfriends until she finds the love of her life. If Taylor wasn't a celebrity or hadn't written most of her songs about love, people wouldn't even notice. Also, when people say that Taylor isn't talented it's so irritating. If Taylor wasn't talented then she wouldn't be this successful and have so many amazing fans.

Nobody gets "Blank Space"! When I tell them that it's about the media I always have to give a long explanation and even then some people don't get it.

It makes me incredibly happy to imagine Taylor happy and married with kids. Although it makes me sad that she might not go on tour or anything. But she is going to be such an amazing mom. I just want Taylor to be happy.

> "It makes me incredibly happy to imagine Taylor happy and married with kids. . . . I just want Taylor to be **happy.**"

DeC. 2015

HA PY BIRTHDAY TAYLOR!! I YOU'LL WAIT FOREVER AND EVER T MEET YOU! -EMMAD

#WhatLiftsYou
#NashvilleGulch
@KelseyMontagueArt

WE ♥ TAYLOR SWIFT FOREVER AND ALWAYS

Love Taylor Swift

STAY EXTRAORDINARY
Diet Coke
THE RED TOUR

A REVIEW OF *RED*
2012 ROBERT CHRISTGAU

So if Stephin Merritt can make a big deal out of sixty-nine love songs, why can't Taylor Swift make a fairly big deal out of sixteen? His being formally savvy in his pop-polymath way and hers being formally voracious in her pop-bestseller way? Need either deal be autobiographical? One hopes not in both cases, although verisimilitude has its formal aspects for best-sellers. Swift hits the mark less often than Merritt—65 or 70 percent, I'd say. But one could argue that the verisimilitude requirement forces her to aim higher. I like the feisty ones, as I generally do. But "Begin Again" and especially "Stay Stay Stay" stay happy and hit just as hard. That's hard.   **A–**

ACROSS

1 Spanish for "daddy"
5 Broadcasted again
10 "What's all the ___?"
14 Supply and demand subj.
15 "Let It Go" crooner Menzel
16 Slanted font type: Abbr.
17 Angry tirade
18 Heredity transmitters
19 Singer Bareilles
20 Start of a Taylor Swift lyric
23 Muslim holiday that marks the end of Ramadan
24 Cambridge univ. home to an annual Mystery Hunt
25 Car that's been crashed
28 Owned
31 Civil rights org. founded in 1909
35 Part 2 of the lyric
38 Caesar's question to Brutus
39 [nail polish] or [face with tears of joy]
40 Steve of sports or Miranda of modeling
41 Some four-year degrees: Abbr.
43 1.609 ___ = 1 mi.
45 Hospital scan: Abbr.
48 *The Canterbury Tales* writer Geoffrey
52 Medicine-approving org.
55 Part 3 of the lyric
58 Pitcher ___ Ryan
59 Part 4 of the lyric
60 Quaggy bogs
61 ___ out (distributed)
63 Perspectives
64 ___ Newton (fruit-filled snack)
65 2013 memoir ___ Malala
67 Tater ___
68 Snug ___ bug in a rug
70 Part 5 of the lyric
74 Madonna's "La ___ Bonita"
75 Cow mascot married to Elmer the Bull
76 Combines numbers
77 Root in root beer
80 Taxi alternative
82 ___-Alt-Delete
85 End of the lyric
91 Fine spray

92 Sierra ___ (Freetown's country)
93 Grand Ole ___ (weekly Nashville concert)
95 Civil rights activist Parks
96 "___ you clever!"
97 Ye ___ Shoppe
98 Unforeseen problem
99 Medicine amounts
100 Goes from brunette to blonde, say

DOWN

1 Flawless, for short
2 Trendy smoothie berry
3 Ping ___ table
4 Out dancing, getting bottle service, etc.
5 Inflexible
6 Biblical garden
7 Boxing enclosure
8 Over again
9 *SNL* alum Pedrad
10 Bowls for aquatic pets
11 Salt Lake City's state
12 South Asian garment
13 Poetry competition
21 ___ torch (Polynesian-inspired decoration)
22 Apple- suffix, in a bar
25 "Raw" sports org.
26 Lab rodent
27 Numerical guess: Abbr.
28 Stitched edge
29 From ___ Z (all-encompassing)
30 B-ball legend with a medical nickname
32 Get older
33 Midpoint: Abbr.
34 "___ favor" (Spanish for "please")
36 One-named "TiK ToK" singer
37 "That's scary!"
42 "Act III, ___: JULIET enters alone"
44 He went to Washington in a 1939 film
45 AOL alternative
46 People you share a bathroom with
47 Like running a red light
49 Inits. of the official name for Obamacare
50 Large coffee server
51 Atlantic food fish
52 "Spring ___, fall back"

53 Wearing clothes
54 Commercials
56 Winery container
57 Golfer Michelle
62 Confused states
63 Person in a booth on election day
64 Part of 67-Down: Abbr.
66 "Cool" sums of money
67 "So glad this week is over!"
69 Real jerk

71 Game involving infrared guns
72 U.S. government org. known for its domestic surveillance
73 Clint who played Dirty Harry
78 Ms. Grande, for short
79 Room coolers: Abbr.
80 Labor group
81 "Blame It on the ___ Nova"

83 Respond to an email
84 One-named "Royals" singer
86 Storage bag brand
87 Villain's foe
88 "Little piggies"
89 Hathaway of *The Devil Wears Prada*
90 They hang from basketball rims
91 ___ Fields (cookie brand)
94 "You betcha!"

For the solution, see page 280

If You Listen Closely, *TAYLOR SWIFT*
Is Kind of Like Leonard Cohen

THE ATLANTIC, **NOVEMBER 2012** | BRAD NELSON

Taylor Swift's new album opens with heaving drums and vague lyrics. The percussion—near-ponderous, seemingly pulled from a mammoth rock record—lopes along; the guitars ease in and flutter U2-like. Swift, though sounding more confident and focused than ever, lingers in abstraction and cliché for a verse: "We fall in love 'til it hurts or bleeds / or fades in time."

But then something happens: She gets writerly. "We are alone, just you and me / up in your room and our slates are clean / just twin fire signs / four blue eyes." Those are the kinds of details that detach from a narrative and stretch over it like clouds, casting shadows that introduce nuance. They have a similar effect on the music itself for "State of Grace," intensifying and unlocking it: Swift's delivery enters a kind of double time, the drums become varied and alive, and the guitars spin bright webs.

Swift, an underrated and overselling pop-country songwriter, has been getting better and better at telling stories through song. On her new, fourth album, *Red*—which moved a decade-record-setting million copies last week—the twenty-two-year-old seems to have picked up a few

techniques from classic, acclaimed masters of narrative rock and roll. There's a critical and cultural bias against artists like Swift, whose bright, booming production and songs about ex-boyfriends can seem juvenile and unserious. But Swift brings intricate craft to seemingly simple pop about the teenage experience.

In an interview with YouTube from 2011, Swift talked of how, when she was a kid, her mother would speak extensively in figurative language. "I grew up just understanding metaphor and just kind of loving that," she said. "How you could take something you're going through and speak about it in a different way that applies how you're feeling to something completely different but connects it."

The mingling of concrete and abstract detail in "State of Grace" reminds me most immediately, of all things, of Steely Dan: how Donald Fagen and Walter Becker would introduce an image to their songs that could change the entire character of a story. "Glamour Profession," from 1980's *Gaucho*, begins with their characteristically vague and ominous scene setting: "6:05 / outside the stadium / Special delivery / for Hoops McCann." It's all transparent allusions to drugs until

the next lyric lends the scene color, recasting it in a kind of shrapnel gray: "Brut and charisma / poured from the shadow where he stood." The narrative, before a deranged and incomplete puzzle, experiences poetry, which deepens the song and gives it three dimensions. "Glamour Profession" eventually becomes a cascade of disturbed people and events—it's sort of Steely Dan's ultimate dead zone of cynicism. The cascade in "State of Grace," meanwhile, is mostly of worn phrases: "hands of fate," "Achilles' heel," etc. But small, unexpected lyrical flourishes transform their surroundings, like milk pluming in a cup of coffee.

"Holy Ground" recalls another tradition, this time without doing much to disguise itself. The percussion, the cadence, and the electrified air all point directly to Bruce Springsteen. On her earlier records, Swift would often employ the Springsteen trope of escaping a small town and entering the blurry resolution of a city, but the only hints of his city darkness were in "Never Grow Up" ("It's so much colder than I thought it would be / so I tuck myself in and turn my night light on"). "Holy Ground," though, isn't Springsteen in subject. It's Springsteen in style. The

song's tempo feels his. There's no real trace of producer Jeff Bhasker, who's worked with Kanye West and fun., except in the drums, which, as in fun.'s "We Are Young," are pure bombast. They're faster here, though, and are insistent enough to act as punctuation for the lyrics, which practically tumble out of Swift and fit into one another strangely, like how early Springsteen rhymed as if by accident of memory. The drums add syllables to the words—"I was / remin / iscing / just / the / oth / er / day"—just as every snare roll divides "Candy's Room" into kinetic fractions.

Most of all, Springsteen and Swift share a sensibility: that a story can be reduced purely to its rising action. There's a central relationship to "Holy Ground," and Swift refers tidily to its end with the

lyric "Well I guess we fell apart in the usual way / And the story's got dust on every page." But the song is focused inflexibly on a single, revelatory moment that happened during the course of the relationship. The second verse begins "Took off faster than a green light—go," and the song builds itself in the shape of this line. The shape resembles ghostly restraint of "I'm on Fire" or "Brilliant Disguise," with intense, variable emotions flickering beyond a fire door. There's no climax; it's a tense framework of expectations and barely contained ecstasy. It's like the seconds right before you run into the middle of traffic. It lasts three and a half minutes.

"Holy Ground" also shows off a relatively recent development in Swift's storytelling: ambiguity. Her songs about

destroyed relationships mostly come from the perspective of someone distinctly wronged. In 2010's "Dear John," her triumph over a bad boyfriend is stratospheric: she ends the bridge "shining like fireworks / over [his] sad empty town." In a 2011 interview with MTV, Swift described this attitude as a product of age and experience, and she refers to a particularly embittered song from her first record, "Picture to Burn." "Now the way that I would say that and the way that I would feel that kind of pain is a lot different," she said. "It's a lot different as you grow up and you kind of understand that there are different ways of saying things." In "Holy Ground," her way of processing a breakup has become charmingly complicated. In the chorus ("Right there where we stood / was holy ground") she enshrines a moment of mutual discovery, but the moment has passed. Later in the song, a ghostly chorus of "hooray"s drifts into the mix. They make for a frail celebration, commemorating a small, happy instant in a longer, murkier story.

Ambiguity runs throughout *Red*, most explicitly in the title and expressive waltz-ing of "Sad Beautiful Tragic." But it works best on "All Too Well," perhaps Swift's finest narrative. There's even a Chekhov's gun in the first act—a scarf left at a boyfriend's sister's house—but its reappearance, during a relationship's messy unravel, is thoughtful and brutal: "But you keep my old scarf from that very first week / 'cause it reminds you of innocence / and it smells like me / You can't get rid of it / 'cause you remember it all too well." It's an exhilarating piece of writing. A detail snaps into place, and the thrill experienced is half from the detail itself and half from how it refers to a haunted object, like a road sign remembered drowsily and a little too late.

The rest of the track renders the rela-

tionship and its dissolution so delicately that I'm both surprised and unfazed to discover myself contemplating it as intensely as I might a Leonard Cohen song. In the center of "All Too Well" is a lyric that's at once intricate, tender, and lucid: "And I forget about you long enough / to forget why I needed to." While not as precisely formed as the lines in "Chelsea Hotel No. 2" or "Famous Blue Raincoat," it feels of a piece with "That's all / I don't even think of you that often," or "I guess that I miss you / I guess I forgive you / I'm glad you stood in my way."

This isn't to suggest Swift is operating on the level of Cohen, Springsteen, or Steely Dan. She's a pop musician; her words function less as demonstrations of artistry than they do as practical, inclusive stories. Her nearest lyrical analogue is still Ashlee Simpson's totally under-respected and still-great *Autobiography*, a collection of observations so specifically teenage that they come out sophisticated and strangely applicable to adulthood. But there are also songs on *Red* that lack immediate reference. "Begin Again," like "All Too Well," lingers in a cloudy, uncertain space, between the end of one relationship and the start of another. Swift addresses the previous boy by listing contrasts: "He didn't like it when I wore high heels / but I do." But when someone new enters a scene, she preserves the "I do" structure, and it flourishes newly in this setting, like a flower returned from darkness to a sunlit windowsill: "We tell stories and you don't know why / I'm coming off a little shy / but I do." These small, rich differences are derived from the traditions of great songwriters, but they're delivered with such ease that they sound entirely Swift's own. ◆

ALYSSA WALTERS

STUDENT, 19, MINNESOTA AND FLORIDA

I listen to Taylor at least once a day, so it's crazy to think of how often I've heard her music in the past ten years. Her lyrics are the advice I listen to because I never had an older sister to give me any.

I once screamed the lyrics to "Blank Space" in a hospital at 1 a.m., but I don't remember it. I broke my ankle and was on anesthetics. My mom says that when I was coming off the meds I started screaming Taylor's lyrics and had the nurses quiz me on her music. Apparently I got every question right! I guess I am a major Swiftie no matter what the circumstance.

My two favorite songs are "Enchanted" and "Wildest Dreams," so when I found out there was a mash-up of those songs on the *1989* tour, I almost cried from being so excited. That was my favorite performance by her, ever.

I've been to every one of her shows in Minnesota. The *Fearless* tour was my very first concert ever and I've been back to every show since. I even flew two thousand miles home from college in Florida just to go to the *1989* tour with my best friend. Best. Night. Ever.

"All Too Well" helped me get over an abusive relationship. That song made me realize that it's okay to not be okay. I hope someday I can thank Taylor for writing it.

I listen to "Blank Space" or "Style" when I want to walk confidently. They are my secret to looking like I know what I'm doing (when most of the time I don't).

I've always wished that Taylor would have put the song "I'd Lie" on an album. That's my favorite song from her earlier music.

Taylor made me realize that you can celebrate other people's accomplishments without devaluing your own.

One time I had a dream that Taylor had a dog and our dogs were siblings. Because they were related, I got to meet her. It was weird but hey, I got to meet Taylor!

My favorite quote from Taylor is "Hang on. It gets easier, and then it gets okay, and then it feels like freedom." I'm not sure where I saw it but it stuck with me.

If someone insults Taylor in front of me they'd better be prepared to get a long lesson. I try to stay calm and use facts to prove how impressive she is.

Taylor's song "Jump Then Fall" was playing when I had my first kiss. I love that Taylor's music was a part of that memory.

To me, Taylor's albums represent different eras in life. *Speak Now,* an era that makes me think of magic and love, was released when I fell in love for the first time. *Red,* which makes me think of heartbreak and betrayal, was released when I lost that love. *1989,* which was about Taylor finding herself again, was released when I had found my happiness again. I have grown up with Taylor's music as the soundtrack to my life, and I'm so grateful for it.

> "Taylor made me realize that you can **celebrate** other people's accomplishments without devaluing your own."

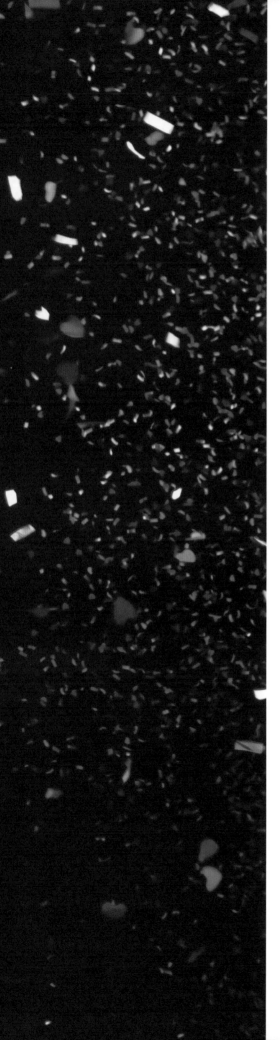

TAYLOR SWIFT
in Wonderland

ROLLING STONE, OCTOBER 2012 | BRIAN HIATT

This is what it sounds like when Taylor Swift totally loses it: "Oh, my God. OH, MY GOD. OH, MY GOD. OH, MY GOD. OH, MY GOD. OH, MY GOD. OH, MY GOD. OH, MY GOD. OH, MY GOD. OH, MY GOD. OH, MY GOD. OH, MY GOD."

Her summer tan is turning ashen; her very blue eyes are practically pinwheeling with panic. But she didn't do anything *that* bad just now, didn't start a nuclear war or curse on country radio or upload her new album to BitTorrent: We're on a bleak industrial road outside a Nashville rehearsal studio one stiflingly hot late-August evening, with Swift behind the wheel of her black Toyota SUV—which she just backed directly into a parked car.

She's never learned how to use her SUV's built-in GPS, was messing with Yelp and Google Maps on her iPhone instead, realized she was going the wrong way, started to turn around, still clutching the phone, and . . . *crunch*.

"Oh, my God," she repeats, pausing for air. She takes another look at the car she hit. "Oh, is that my bass player?"

It totally is. "It's fine, it's my bass player!" She couldn't look more relieved if she had received a death-row pardon. Popping out of the SUV, she apologizes to her bemused employee, a Ben Stiller look-alike named Amos Heller, who had been walking toward his now slightly dented car. "I'm gonna pay for it, I promise! I'm good for it! Oh, my God, Amos, I'm so sorry. I freaked out 'cause I went the wrong way and he was gonna think I'm a bad driver and then I backed into another car. This is the worst interview he's ever had, already!"

One of her security guys, who was supposed to be discreetly trailing us, gets out of his own SUV, looking shaken: "You okay?" Soon enough, we resume our journey to a local restaurant, this time with Swift following her bodyguard, who's serving as a human GPS at her behest. Problem solved.

Swift is still recovering for the whole ten-minute drive. "I cannot believe there was a car behind me. I thought that— because I could only see the security car, and Amos's car was so low and I didn't look in the back camera and I was so sure no one was behind me and . . ."

The moment she crashed, she pictured herself being taken away in handcuffs, sitting in jail in her blue polka-dot shirtdress. "I have a lot of anxieties that end in me

being put into a police car," she says, ponytail bopping as she shakes her head. "I am so, like, rules, and not getting into accidents. So this is perfect."

At twenty-two, Swift is always waiting for her luck to run out. This week, her new single, the irresistible, distinctly un-country "We Are Never Ever Getting Back Together," became her first No. 1 Hot 100 hit—and for all she knows, it could all be downhill from here. "I'm always terrified that, like, something's going to happen," she says, "and I'm not going to be able to do this anymore and it's gonna all end in one day. Part of the fear comes from loving this so much and not wanting to lose it."

Watch her segment of MTV's *Punk'd*, where Justin Bieber goads Swift into setting off fireworks from a waterfront balcony—then makes her think that they started a huge fire on a nearby boat: her face betrays the same *ohmygodohmygod* terror. "You know I had serious nightmares where I'd wake up in the middle of the night for, like, three weeks after that? I really thought that was it for me. I was thinking, 'Justin is seventeen, so he's going to juvie, but I'm going to big-girl prison.'"

She nearly made it all into a self-fulfilling prophecy during her performance at the 2010 Grammys, when stage fright knocked her voice flat during an awkward duet with Stevie Nicks on "Rhiannon." Nonfans were instantly, and unfairly, convinced that she was an Auto-Tune baby who can't sing live. "I had a bad night," says Swift, who's since refocused on vocal lessons. "It's one of those things where you've rehearsed over and over and when the camera turns on, the nerves kick in and you just can't think straight."

Mostly, though, it's been a smooth ride, with so few speed bumps she could practically tick them off on crimson-tipped

fingers: She was terrible at fourth-grade soccer, couldn't parlay her height into basketball glory, never managed to do a split, had a hard time with math. There were some mean middle school girls, and more recently, as you may have heard, a few totally exhausting boyfriends. She has that slight overbite; at five feet eleven, her posture isn't great. And yeah, there was that time Kanye West snatched her microphone and started yelling stuff about Beyoncé—still *so* not funny, as far she's concerned.

But she's come to understand that life—even hers—is unpredictable, uncontrollable. Messy. The Kanye episode helped her to "realize nothing is gonna go exactly the way that you plan it to," she

says. "Just because you make a good plan, doesn't mean that's what's gonna happen."

Case in point: later that evening, Swift is driving back from dinner, singing along to Third Eye Blind's "Never Let You Go" (which came out when she was nine)—when, unbelievably, we get into another car accident.

This one is random, terrifying, and utterly not her fault. As Swift cruises down a four-lane street, what looks like an old Corvette blazes out of an intersection and veers into our lane—smacking the driver's side of Swift's SUV, then speeding off. They were driving, as Swift later puts it, like they had just robbed a bank.

"Okay, that was my life flashing before my eyes," she says, voice trembling. "What

is this day? This is some strange alternate reality where things just go wrong a lot. That was the second time today! I'm going to have a nervous breakdown!" Her phone rings—it's her poor security bro, who sounds like he's already had one.

There is a pond, complete with koi fish, in the middle of Swift's astonishing, many-colored Nashville condo. It sits beneath a wrought-metal spiral staircase leading to a human-size birdcage that faces floor-to-ceiling windows, with a view stretching to the green mountains beyond downtown. ("It's the most comfortable place in the world," she says of the wooden cage, built from a sketch she made. "It's just, like, pillows and comfiness.")

Under the previous owner, this was an ultramodern bachelor pad. Over eighteen months of remodeling, Swift gave the condo a sex change and a heavy dose of well-funded OCD whimsy. The ceiling is arranged in multiple motifs—billowing curtains here, a painted indigo night sky there. In one corner, under hanging crystalline stars, sits a giant bunny made of moss. He's wearing a hat. "It's a whole *Peter Pan, Alice in Wonderland* structure here," she says, welcoming me the next morning. "It's what the inside of my brain looks like, essentially."

On the custom-built walls—some brick, some purple-wallpapered—are an endless array of photographs in ornate gold frames, some with matching gold-cursive captions:

Swift with her high school friend Abigail (complete with lyrics from "Fifteen," in which said friend gave a boy "everything she had"); Swift with James Taylor; Swift making that heart-hand-symbol thing with buddy and Bieber-*fräulein* Selena Gomez. Above the fireplace, which is emblazoned with a small heart, there's even a photo of the moment Kanye stormed her VMA stage (captioned, "Life is full of little interruptions," a phrase that's also in the liner notes of her last album), right next to what is presumably the actual award in question under glass.

The place is immaculate, and there's no sign that any other living thing—besides her unusually friendly Scottish fold cat, Meredith (named after a favor-

ite *Grey's Anatomy* character)—has been here recently. But a gossip item circulating that morning suggests otherwise: as the story goes, she missed her boyfriend, eighteen-year-old Conor Kennedy—an incoming prep-school senior—so she "kidnapped" him, via private jet, flying him to Nashville.

Swift stopped reading her own press after the Grammy incident, and instituted a self-Googling ban. "What did I do? Don't tell me! Is it bad?" she says, clutching a pale-blue knitted pillow and curling her mile-long legs beneath her on a swiveling love seat. She's barefoot, wearing a V-neck white blouse and high-waisted, vintage-y floral shorts. Her knees have some fresh white scars on them ("I fell

on rocks on the beach, and I fell during volleyball. Kind of eight-year-old-child injuries"). When she hears the day's gossip, her eyes widen under feline makeup. She looks faintly nauseated: "How did I kidnap him? You can't kidnap a grown man! These are serious accusations, now!"

She laughs, but she's swiveling furiously in the chair, like it might move her away from this topic. "It's an interesting way to spin something into a story," she says. "See, this is why I don't read stuff."

So is Conor chained to something upstairs, then? "*What?* God!"

She is aware of another recent rumor: that she and Kennedy crashed his cousin's wedding, then flatly refused to leave. "I have no idea what happened there," she says, spinning again, fidgeting with some chipped nail polish on her index finger. "I think that story was based on the biggest misunderstanding, 'cause I would never knowingly show up somewhere that I

thought I wasn't invited to. And I would never want to upstage anybody."

She's come to grips, sort of, with the fact that her days of exclusively good press are over. "I just gotta take it day by day," she says. "I don't think anyone is ever truly viewed as only one thing, as only good, as only well-behaved, as only respectful. In the beginning, when there would be a tiny news story about something that wasn't true, I thought that meant my fans weren't gonna show up to my next concert. But now, knock on wood—where's wood? I need to knock on wood—I feel like my fans have my back and I have theirs."

And she knows that she can't always be the good guy. "It's just part of the dynamics of a good story," she says. "Everybody is a complicated character."

It's somehow not surprising to learn that Swift had her first drink ever on her twenty-first birthday. "I knew I couldn't get

away with it until then," she says the night before, sipping a Diet Coke through a little red straw that matches her lipstick. We made it into the restaurant without fuss, except for a pigtailed little girl who gaped with I-just-saw-the-Easter-Bunny joy. "I didn't really care to know what I was missing, and I knew it was illegal, and that my luck would be that I'd get caught. And then you think about all the moms and little girls who would have thought less of me. I'm still not much of a drinker, but I'll have a glass of wine every once in a while." And has she gotten drunk? "I'm not gonna talk about that! No one wants to picture that!"

It can't be easy, living like this. Gomez recalls going out to dinner with Swift when she noticed another patron eavesdropping. "She got startled that they were listening," Gomez says, "and she got nervous, and then the person left and she felt awful. She was like, 'I hope he didn't leave because of me. I hope he doesn't think

I'm mean. Do you think he's going to tell everyone I'm mean?' She cares so much."

Swift has recurring anxiety dreams, and, predictably enough, one of them involves being arrested for something she didn't do. "I keep trying to tell them that I didn't do anything," she says, "and they won't listen, or my voice doesn't work."

Another one is quite vivid. "I'll be in a room with piles of clothes all over the floor, and I can't clean it. And no matter what, they keep piling up and I can't move. It freaks me out! It makes me wish I could clean it, 'cause I love cleaning. But the piles get bigger, or there's piles on the ceiling, and I don't even know how that's possible."

She knows what that one's about. "I think I have a big fear of things spiraling out of control," she says. "Out of control and dangerous and reckless and thoughtless scares me, because people get hurt. When you say 'control freak' and 'OCD' and 'organized,' that suggests someone who's cold in nature, and I'm just not. Like, I'm really open when it comes to letting people in. But I just like my house to be neat, and I don't like to make big messes that would hurt people. . . . I don't want to let people down, or let myself down, or have a lot of people that I know I wronged."

Swift has never seen a therapist. "I just feel very sane," she says.

It takes only a cursory listen to Swift's songs—or a visit to TMZ—to figure out the one part of her life where she allows messiness to reign. "The way I look at love is you have to follow it," she says, "and fall hard, if you fall hard. You have to forget about what everyone else thinks. It has to be an us-against-the-world mentality. You have to make it work by prioritizing it, and

by falling in love really fast, without thinking too hard. If I think too hard about a relationship I'll talk myself out of it."

And why would she go from dating men in their thirties—John Mayer, Jake Gyllenhaal—to her current, SAT-prepping guy? "I have rules for a lot of areas of my life," she says. "Love is not going to be one of them."

Before she got together with Conor, she was publicly touting her interest in the Kennedy family's history, and had mentioned reading a 960-page book called *The Kennedy Women.* "Weird," she says. "Oh, my God, I know. It's like—things happen in my life in coincidental ways that are weird."

> "Nothing is gonna go **exactly the way that you plan it to.** Just because you make a good plan, doesn't mean that's what's gonna happen."

But it does look funny. . . . "You're telling me," she says. She looks comically aghast at the idea of Elvis superfan Nicolas Cage marrying Lisa Marie Presley—he got the ultimate collectible. "That's not what's happening," she practically yells, sending her eyes skyward.

It may also help that a friend did it first. Ask fellow minicougar Gomez if Swift got the idea from her relationship with Bieber (who's almost two years younger), and her answer is quick and cheerful: "Probably!"

Swift has written some of her generation's most seductively romantic songs—she may be the world's leading proponent of kissing in the rain. "I love the ending of a movie where two people end up together," says Swift, who further explores this theme on a new collaboration with

Snow Patrol. "Preferably if there's rain and an airport or running or a confession of love."

She's also written breakup tunes that, in their own way, rival "Idiot Wind" for mercilessness. "Dear John," 2010's presumed John Mayer evisceration, may be the most brutal: "Don't you think nineteen's too young to be played by your dark, twisted games?" But the new album's "I Knew You Were Trouble" comes close: "You never loved me or her or anyone," she sings.

"In every one of my relationships," she says, "I've been good and fair. What happens after they take that for granted is not my problem. Chances are if they're being written about in a way they don't like, it's because they hurt me really badly. Telling a story only works if you have characters in it. I don't think it's mean. I think it's mean to hurt someone in a relationship."

Mayer told *Rolling Stone* that "Dear John" "really humiliated" him, and accused Swift of "cheap songwriting." When I first try to ask her about that over dinner, she literally presses her hands against her ears, saying, "Be kind, and don't tell me."

The next day, I'm unkind enough to relay Mayer's quotes, and she turns steely. "I didn't write his first and last name in the song! So that's him taking it on—when he had an album to promote."

But didn't she use his first name? "I didn't say anything about the person's identity. 'Dear John' is a well-known concept."

And why not just pick up the phone and tell these guys off directly? She looks at me like I'm insane. "What's the fun in that?" ("She's so tough," says Gomez. "Sometimes she'll tell me, like, 'You should be a little mean sometimes.'")

In addition to heavy rom-com viewing (*Love Actually* is her favorite), Swift's daunting ideal of love comes from her maternal grandparents, who were married for fifty-one years, and died a week apart. "They were still madly in love with each other in their eighties," she says. There are no mere hookups in Swift-land. "No," she says, nose wrinkling. "Where's the romance? Where's the magic in that? I'm just not that girl." And by the way, hackers shouldn't bother with her cell phone: "There's interesting things on there, like text messages," she says. "But you wouldn't find any naked pictures."

She's uncomfortable discussing a line from her new album—"I'll do anything you say if you say it with your hands"—that seems to break new ground. "I don't know if I'm interested in writing about, um, blatantly sexual things out of the context of how it affects a relationship," she says, then pauses. "Oh, I should just totally say that Dan thought of it," she adds, meaning cowriter Dan Wilson. "I could get myself off the hook so quick!"

Swift loves the idea of long relationships, though she's never really had one. "It usually lasts four and a half months, and then it all just disintegrates. Then I spend, like, a year and a half mourning the loss of it."

Eventually, she would like to have a lot of kids: "Like, minimum, four," she says. "My fantasy has always been having a bunch of kids running around. I would love to become as dedicated a mom as my mom was." Which brings her to another recurring nightmare. "I have a kid and the paparazzi is taking pictures, and it's scaring my baby. And I know that I caused it, and I can't figure out how to stop it."

A few days later, Swift is sitting in a dressing room in MTV's New York studio, wearing a fluffy blue bathrobe and borrowed hotel slippers, talking business on her phone. Her two beauty coordinators are ministering to her wavy hair with a flatiron as she speaks. She waves me in, mid-conversation.

"I resent the idea that you can just start a sentence with 'respectfully' and then you can just say whatever you want," she says, sounding like someone with whom you wouldn't want to negotiate. "I don't understand how we resolve this— is it him giving points? Ah, okay, good call. Absolutely, if he calls me I'll tell

> "It was a surreal moment. I knew we were doing what her grandmother wanted us to do. There was a kind of passing of the torch."
> **—Andrea Swift**

him that. Okay, cool. Mm-hmm. Yeah, respectfully." Instead of a manager, Swift has a management team, which she leads herself.

Her parents, Scott and Andrea, both have business backgrounds and have been involved in her career from the start. "I think my earliest memory is my mom would set up an easel in the kitchen when I was three," says Swift. "And she'd give me finger paints and I'd paint whatever I wanted, and it was always good enough.

"My mom would have conversations with me before I could talk," she says. "So I started talking really early." Her first word was *yellow*, which had something to do with fellow tall creature Big Bird.

The rest is already a familiar story: She grew up on a Christmas-tree farm in rural Pennsylvania, became unaccountably obsessed with Shania Twain and the Dixie Chicks, started singing and writing songs, and by age fourteen, persuaded her parents to move near Nashville. They signed to a fledgling label called Big Machine Records, founded by a former Universal executive named Scott Borchetta. Swift's dad, a Merrill Lynch stockbroker, was a minor investor in the label, which was more of an idea than a company when they signed: "Scott Swift owns 3 percent of Big Machine," Borchetta says. "But I hear people go, 'Oh, well, he funded the whole deal, and that's why Taylor's No. 1.' It's like, 'Please, people.' Everybody wants to say, 'Well, there's a reason.' Yeah, there is a reason. 'Cause she's great. That's the reason."

As she prepares to release her fourth album, *Red*, Swift is at the very center of pop—more than any other putatively country artist before her. That's why MTV is sacrificing valuable *Teen Mom* airtime to debut her new video in a live segment tonight. But first, she has to endure nine or so taped interviews with various network offshoots. Now in a tight red top and blue pants, she displays such ease with a parade of interrogators—and the random little kids who come by for autographs—that it's not hard to imagine her running for office someday. "Really? I might have to be a college graduate, though," she says. "I guess I better start figuring out my platform."

This ease with glad-handing comes from her father, who, as Borchetta says, "never meets a stranger. You send him into a room, and he'll walk out and go, 'Hey, I just met a guy on the board at Papa John's.' True to form, when I eventually meet Scott Swift—an affable silver-haired guy in a Brooks Brothers–y suit and rimless glasses—he immediately goes for common ground, sharing tales of a brief stint in journalism.

Taylor's maternal grandmother, Marjorie Finlay, was a professional opera singer who sang around the world. "I feel like my karma in life is being in a backstage area or being in front of the house," says Andrea Swift, whose mother died around the time Taylor was signing her record deal. "We were in Nashville when she passed away, and it was a surreal moment, because I knew we were doing what she wanted us to do. There was a kind of passing of the torch."

Swift is convinced she's an exact mix of her parents' personalities—she thinks like her mom but acts like her dad. "My mom is, like, all about the worst-case scenario," she says. "My brother and I call her Central Intelligence Andrea. If you have a headache, she could tell you fifteen different things it could be, all of which end in emergency room or death. But she also knows how to throw the best party. She's also really compassionate and kind and disciplined and has a really good head on her shoulders for advice."

Her father is the designated dreamer, though she won't say if her lyric about "a careless man's careful daughter" is autobiographical: "My mom thinks of things in terms of reality and my dad always thinks in terms of daydreams—and, 'How far can we go with this?'" He was the one who envisioned her success: "I never really went there in my mind that all of this was possible. It's just that my dad always did."

As Swift waits for her video debut, racing around the room on a wheeled ottoman, network executives Van Toffler and Amy Doyle show up. Many smiles and hugs ensue. "How huge is that single?"

says Toffler, who's wearing jeans and a blazer, his hair slicked back. "It's like the most ginormous thing in history."

"It's the highest female debut in iTunes history," Swift says. "I'm, like, what?"

"And you know," says Toffler, "or I don't know if you do know, but you're going to be closing the VMAs."

"Oh, my God," says Swift. "I'm gonna pass out. What? When were you guys gonna tell me that? Thank you, that's amazing. Now I really do feel like I might pass out." She's happy, but there's a familiar hint of terror in her eyes. *Ohmygod.*

A viral video called "Taylor Swift Can't Believe It" shows Swift winning award after award, acting lottery-winner astonished every time, continually mouthing, "What?" (See Kristen Wiig's brutal Swift impression.) Needless to say, Swift has never seen it. "I really get my feelings hurt when people make fun of me," she says. "I never won anything in school or in sports, and then all of a sudden, I started winning things. People always say, 'Live in the moment'—if you really live in the moment at a big awards show and you win, you freak out!"

"Those are just her mannerisms," says one of Swift's best friends, stylist Ashley Avignone. "She does the same thing if I tell her something on the couch at home."

The morning after the VMAs, we meet for breakfast in Beverly Hills—her security sneaks her through the back of the restaurant. *Us Weekly*'s headline for the performance was "Taylor Swift Gets Sexy"—because she wore shorts. "It's a really interesting idea that you wear shorts and all of a sudden it's very edgy," she says. "Which, you know, on the bright side gives you room to grow—I don't have to do too much to shock people."

It's 11 a.m. and she's totally bright-eyed

and un-hungover in her cream-colored blouse and polka-dot pants ("not shorts," she says, "that would be too sexy"). She skipped the afterparties and had sushi with her band instead. When she hears that Lady Gaga tweeted "Swifty is so cute" after her performance, she offers a taste of jaw-drop-awards face: "No way! Are you serious? I need to see that! Thank you for telling me that." She spends three minutes trying again and again to load the tweet on her phone, without success.

It would be easy to watch Swift at those awards shows and conclude that she's a phony—in her terms, a cheerleading captain pretending she still belongs on the bleachers. But if she lacks self-consciousness, that's the idea. "I just don't want to live that way," she says. "I never want to get jaded, because then you get really protective and hard to be around. That's what can happen if you're too aware of people second-guessing every move you make. So I try to be as blissfully unaware of that as possible." She laughs. "Please don't ruin it. I'm living in such a happy little world!"

Swift may just experience life a little more intensely than the rest of us, which is one reason her songs can hit so hard—along with the ache in her voice, and her instinct for the minor fall and the major lift. Her songs sneak past our emotional defenses because she has so few of them.

Swift has one more thing to do before she leaves L.A.—a performance at a Stand Up to Cancer telethon, broadcast live on more than twenty channels. She has a bunker-buster of a song for the occasion, called "Ronan." Swift's eyes grow wet telling me about it: it's the true story of a not-quite-four-year-old boy who died of cancer, told from the perspective of his mother. (Swift incorporated ideas from the mom's blog, giving co-songwriting

credit.) Nearly every line is unbearably upsetting—it makes "Streets of Philadelphia" sound like "Party Rock Anthem." (The lyric that keeps getting me: "It's about to be Halloween / You could be anything you wanted if you were still here.") Andrea—blond, warm-eyed—passes out tissues as Swift rehearses the song at the Shrine Auditorium. I take one.

As showtime approaches, Swift keeps her mind off the song, doing her extensive vocal warm-ups (which, at one point, involve actual meows) and discussing food options for tonight's plane back to Nashville. She's sprawled sideways in a director's chair; her flats have cartoon-cat heads by the toes. "Buffalo tenders? Okay! And rigatoni with truffle meat sauce—can I get it with spaghetti, though? Rigatoni

makes me feel weird. It's like a wheel, and what's it trying to do? It's like an unfinished ravioli."

Soon, trailed by a small entourage that includes her mom and her stylist, Swift enters the theater's darkness. She stands just offstage, biting her lip, head down, as Alicia Keys sings. In a similar moment before this year's Grammy performance—which earned her a redemptive standing ovation—Swift told herself, "This is either where you prove the people who like you right, or prove the people who hate you right. It's up to you. Put on your banjo and go play."

She un-hunches her shoulders, breathes deep, and walks toward the stage. "Come on baby with me," she sings with exquisite tenderness, over a hushed guitar. "We're

gonna fly away from here / You were my best four years."

Swift makes it through the song. But afterward she breaks into a jog toward her trailer, weeping uncontrollably the whole way, smudging her eye makeup into wild streaks. Ten minutes later, when I say goodbye, she hasn't stopped. "I was trying not to cry the whole song," she says, shrugging helplessly.

Some of the event's stagehands were watching Swift from the sidelines, beefy arms folded. Goateed, ankle-tattooed, wallet-chained, they would've looked at home wielding pool cues at Altamont. But they're soon frozen in place, transfixed by Taylor Swift, and by the time she's halfway through "Ronan," I catch one of them silently brushing away a tear. ♦

Tavi

+

Taylor

JUST KIDDING, LOVE SUCKS

Notes on Taylor Swift

THE BELIEVER, JULY/AUGUST 2013 | TAVI GEVINSON

The general public has managed to make Taylor Swift's greatest strength seem like her greatest weakness, and it makes me feel sad and angry and like people are really missing out on something great. By "general public" I mean email-hosting sites and sometimes Fancier Publications, and by her "greatest strength" I mean Taylor's unique ability to focus in on one detail or exchange and magnify it completely in this way that makes it feel at once universal and deeply personal. I don't want to devote too much of this holy ink and paper to haterz, but I do want to free your mind from any reservations about the Swift Power in order to fully prepare you for a MAGIC-CARPET ROLLER-COASTER RIDE across this CANDY LAND BOARD of a DECLARATION OF INDEPENDENCE from BRITAIN (= NOT LIKING TAYLOR SWIFT).

Swifties see the characteristic at hand for what it is: writing. Her songs are her point of view, making it her job to blow up the most minor event into something that more accurately represents the way *she experienced it*. As Tay quoted Neruda in her *Red* liner notes, "Love is so short, forgetting is so long." This is basic Nabokov shit, right? Everything hits harder in memory. Everything changes color. Her first album will tell you she is a natural crusher, daydreamer, hopeless romantic. Obsessing over the briefest of encounters is *what we do*. She was just born to translate it for millions of people. And I don't think her commercial responsibilities detract from her genuine passion for her craft. Have you ever watched her in interviews when she gets asked about her actual songwriting? She becomes that kid who's really into the science fair. Her hands go crazy and she explains all the different categories she breaks emotions into and how they all have their own individual sounds. Then the interviewer totally doesn't get it because it's *60 Minutes* and they were hoping for a pleasant little soundbite instead of, like, an Andrew Kuo–style verbalization of the human psyche. And Taylor smiles, perfectly aware she just weirded them out, perfectly aware it's the same weirdness from which she pulls all these beautiful songs.

So the fact that people think they're, like, Nancy Drew for claiming that none of her relationships have lasted long enough for her to be able to write a song about them really proves only that she has this uncanny talent for dressing up an experience until what *happened* matches how it *felt*. I don't care that her relationships aren't long-term—she's a little busy running a goddamn empire! I don't care if she only dates guys to write songs about them, like people say—she dates people, she writes songs about her life, naturally many of these songs are about people she's dated, and many of them *aren't*, as well. Mostly, basically: I DON'T CARE, I LOVE IT.

These are some of my favorites, severely edited down for word count. I almost didn't want to publish it, because her music is so close to my heart, but I also really wanted to publish it because her music is so close to my heart. Please handle with care.

ALBUM:
TAYLOR SWIFT

"Our Song"

Somewhere in the dark depths of deleted YouTube videos is a circa-sixth-grade recording of my childhood best friend and me singing this while I play guitar. Taylor's one of the reasons I learned guitar (along with some vague image I had of ROCK STARS and PEOPLE IN COOL HATS), and I was very serious about imitating her country twang. While Taylor is not technically an exceptional vocalist on this first album, she knows exactly how to make each word sound on an emotional level. Her instincts are just *right*, her cadence is so *her*. Like, it's not just that her lyrics perfectly match up with the music and together they accurately capture a certain emotion—you can also just *hear* it when she's smiling, or looking up, or thinking. This, I would argue, is more important than technically good vocals, and it's also very rare.

"Picture to Burn"

So much sass! Pickup trucks! Dads who are gonna beat up ex-boyfriends! I'LL TAKE IT.

"Stay Beautiful"

This song KILLS me because I only ever listened to it a few times way back when, which means rediscovering it was like seeing someone you didn't even know you missed but you're suddenly so grateful they're in your life. The lyrics totally apply to young Taylor: "Don't you know, you're really gonna be someone. / Ask anyone." UGHHH. I think I get so emotional listening to her first album because it's just so heartening to think about where she was when she wrote these songs (lonely, bullied, awkward phase, bad at boys, country-music nerd) and where she is now (BFF to PLANET EARTH). She's a prime example of how you can turn a middle-school-rooted inferiority complex into beautiful, relatable art. She's like Chris Ware, except not, except *totally*.

"Should've Said No"

PERFECT for singalongs. There's a great live performance where she starts out seated, wearing a black hoodie, angstily banging it out on a guitar and looking at the ground, and by the end she's become this beautiful butterfly, like a really emotional deodorant commercial.

"Tied Together with a Smile"

Whenever people are like, "Ugh, ew, Taylor Swift, stop acting like you know pain when you are beautiful/famous/etc.," I want to play them this song. It reminds me of really bad school hallway art of girls looking in mirrors and feeling sad but in a way that makes me love everyone and want everyone to love themselves.

ALBUM: FEARLESS

"Fearless"

This song is *made* for daydreaming; when I listen to it, it's OK that I'm alone in my room and not with some boy, because I'm exactly where I'm supposed to be. There's a great liner note in this album where she says fearlessness isn't being totally fearless, it's owning up to having fears and being flawed and being OK with life anyway, which is sort of just like very basic Fiona Apple theory for twelve-year-olds.

"Fifteen"

I'm not going to touch on the feminist argument as it applies here (in short: girls who have sex "early" with people who don't love them will feel broken afterward), because this album came out five years ago and since then she's put out two albums that give a total seal of approval to sexy-times. Plus, I mean, these lines: "In your life you'll do things greater than dating the boy on the football team." "Back then I swore I was gonna marry him someday but I've realized some bigger dreams of mine." That blew my mind when I first heard it!

But I will touch on the feminism debate in *general*, because I am both a feminist and a seventeen-year-old girl who feels empowered by Taylor. I think the "fairy-tale-obsessed" and "slut-shaming" criticisms just aren't relevant anymore, since there's no hint of either on the latest album. As for her writing so much about boys, that's just a lazy summary of her body of work. And, frankly, I would *love* for every girl to aspire to be Patti Smith, but for the ones who don't relate to that, let them still have a role model who displays her own version of strength and does dole out some sage advice. As for her supposedly acting all weak and self-victimizing, I don't think she acts that way at all. She's just a gracious interviewee, a paranoid hard-worker, and a cautious prodigy. If you watched any of her tour movies (*Journey to Fearless*; *Speak Now World Tour Live*), you would see that she makes it pretty clear that she thinks she's awesome and wants you to think *you* are also awesome. If you looked at any Swiftie tumblrs, you would see that her young female fans admire her not because she seems weak and submissive, but because they admire her wit, her sense of humor, how much control she still has over what she does, and her passion for her fans and for making good music. From the Kathleen Hanna school of thought:

Some of the themes she writes about are stuff I wish was there for me when I was in high school, and I'm so happy she really cares about her female fans. She's not catering to a male audience and is writing music for other girls. I don't care if she calls herself a feminist or not. There is something that she's doing that feels feminist to me in that she really seems to have a lot of control over what her career is doing.

"Love Story"

Taylor's parents wouldn't let her date some guy, so she stomped into her room and wrote this in twenty minutes. The intro sounds like footsteps and whispers and secrets in the woods.

"White Horse"

Seriously important to this album as her moment of being like, "Maybe the fairy-tale Romeo and Juliet shit doesn't always happen and maybe other things will make me happy?" (Paraphrasing.) The whole song swings between her blaming herself and her wild heart to her being like, "Wait, maybe I can go have my own life now." Essential counter to the songs of hers that are just total fairy-tale lovefests.

"Forever & Always"

This was introduced on her *Fearless* tour with a video of her giving an interview, and the interviewer asking her, "Why do

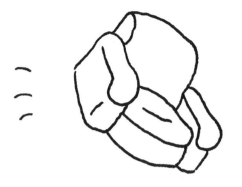

the interviewer rise from below the stage on a platform, and Taylor says, "No more questions!" and THROWS A FUCKING GIANT RED CENTRAL PERK ARMCHAIR OFF THE PLATFORM. Then the phrase "They shouldn't do bad things" shows up, like, eighty times on each Jumbotron.

secretly so into despite fully committing to the vignette of an angry teen wearing headphones in the backseat of a minivan.

you think any guy is going to date you?" and Taylor saying, "If guys don't want me to write bad songs about them, then they shouldn't do bad things." Then she and

"You Belong with Me"

I once listened to this song on repeat while driving to Michigan with my family and it was the kind of melancholy that you're

---

ALBUM:
SPEAK NOW

"Sparks Fly"

If Britney or anyone who we think of as damaged by pop-star sexytimes-repression had just been allowed one song with the hormonal power of "Sparks Fly," they might have turned out OK. "Drop everything now. / Meet me in the pouring rain." "Give me something that'll haunt me when you're not around." Staaahhhhhp! (Sidenote: Recently I've been writing out, color-coding, and diagramming Stevie Nicks lyrics, and there are a LOT of similar motifs between hers and Taylor's.)

"Back to December"

I used to listen to this song ALL THE TIMEEEE. Sad and powerful and guh-hhhh. Also a good example of her taking the blame for a relationship ending even though the common misconception is that she always blames the guy.

"Speak Now"

Next time you are stressed out just listen to this stoned and you will be OK because there have been times when listening to Taylor Swift stoned was the only thing keeping me from becoming a combination of Vincent Gallo and both Edie Beales. P.S.: Don't do drugs. P.P.S.: You are proba-

bly older than me and can do whatever you want and thank you for reading this article.

"Dear John"

Has there ever been a revenge love song that cuts this deeply? It has the equal parts classy and witchy SECRET BITE I love so much about her. I mean, come ON: "All of the girls that you've run dry / have tired, lifeless eyes / 'cause you've burned them out. / But I stole your matches before fire could catch me, so don't look now, / I'm shining like fireworks over your sad, empty town." The imagery! The metaphor she draws out as long as possible before it just explodes in a moment of triumph! This song is one of her absolute best, lyrically. Another ingenious layer to this one: John Mayer–esque guitar farts in the background. (It is about John Mayer.)

Oh, and she said this is the one where, when she looks out during her tour, girls are crying the most. How did she write a song that's both such a GIANT BURN to her ex AND a victory bonding moment for girls who have been in toxic relationships?

"MEAN"

Famously wrote this after a critic turned his back on her and people get mad that she seems to victimize herself in it but HER ART IS HER TRUTH, MAN, JUST LAY OFF.

"THE STORY OF US"

Listening to this song is the only time I can ever see myself fist-pumping.

"ENCHANTED"

The very beginning shows how aware she is about the bullshit parts of her job, though she never sounds like she's whining about how hard it is to be famuzz. "There I was again tonight, / forcing laughter, faking smiles. / Same old tired, lonely place." Then, what's this? A fixation on a flirtation as a creative way to distract from the mundanity of the Kids' Choice Awards or whatever toilet flush of stupidity was going down at the time? "Your eyes whispered, 'Have we met?' / Across the room, your silhouette / starts to make its way to me." At last, the chorus just SLAYS ME: "This night is sparkling, / don't you let it go. / I'm wonderstruck, / blushing all the way home. / I'll spend forever / wondering if you knew / I was enchanted to meet you." God, just typing it out makes me remember hearing it for the first time and feeling like absolutely nothing else in the world existed or mattered. SO jealous if it's new for you.

"LONG LIVE"

This was my number one before *Red*. The way you can hear her smiling when she says, "You traded your baseball cap for a crown." The simultaneous football homecoming victory/fairy-tale king-and-queen imagery. The joy that must exist in the world when she plays this live, as she wrote it for her band and fans.

"IF THIS WAS A MOVIE"

Another cathartic moment of her sort of questioning her own daydreams.

ALBUM: RED

"STATE OF GRACE"

"We are alone, just you and me, / up in your room and our slates are clean. / Just twin fire signs, / four blue eyes." By the end of this album you will have a complete visualization of her world.

"TREACHEROUS"

The hopeful and in-love energy is at "Sparks Fly" levels of intensity. Almost too much for me to handle. "Put your lips close to mine / as long as they don't touch. / Out of focus, eye-to-eye, / till the gravity's too much." Every time I hear this line I just shake my head repeatedly until I feel I know what it's like to be a GIF.

"I KNEW YOU WERE TROUBLE."

Like "Forever & Always," begins with the lyric "Once upon a time" and goes on to be like "JUST KIDDING, LOVE SUCKS," only this one is in 4-D and with dubstep.

"ALL TOO WELL"

"You call me up again just to break me like a promise. / So casually cruel in the name of being honest." Aiiiieeee! The song's structure, the visuals, EVERYTHING IS PERFECT. She revives a Stevie-esque

"Did I scare you with my FEELINGS and my HONESTY?" kind of haunting (daunting? taunting? all of them?) challenge that makes me feel less bad about my bad feelings. From her recent *Vanity Fair* interview:

> For a female to write about her feelings, and then be portrayed as some clingy, insane, desperate girlfriend in need of making you marry her and have kids with her, I think that's taking something that potentially should be celebrated—a woman writing about her feelings in a confessional way—that's taking it and turning it and twisting it into something that is frankly a little sexist.

"22"

OMG OMG OMG. Perfect "Girls Just Wanna Have Fun"–type jam about going out with your friends and dancing and flirting haaaaay. I wanna jump around to it all the time. Also: "It feels like a perfect night to dress up like hipsters." WHAT DOES THAT EVEN MEAN? Whatever, I totally get it on a cosmic level.

"I Almost Do"

Classic cinematic walk-in-the-rain Taylor goodness.

"We Are Never Ever Getting Back Together"

ALREADY EASILY ONE OF THE BEST POP SONGS OF ALL TIME OF ALL TIME. Here's where she's like, "I know I'm not some fucking hip, tortured indie artist and also I don't care, OK, cool": "I'm really gonna miss you picking fights, and me / falling for it, screaming that I'm right, and you / would hide away and find your peace of mind, with some / indie record that's *much* cooler than mine." I reeeeally didn't want to bring any exes' names into this—her music is more enjoyable when all that gossip is ignored—but apparently this song is about Jake Gyllenhaal and I can just *so* see Donnie Darko being like, "Can't you see how FUCKED UP the world is, man? I don't have time for your bullshit teen tiger beats!" Wait—OMG—is this why there are furries in the music video? TAYLOR, YOU CARD. I hated *Donnie Darko* so much that I looked it up on Facebook to see which of my friends liked it and then silently judged them and then probably got food and went to sleep.

"Stay Stay Stay"

"I just like hanging out with you / all the time." Taylor is a big fan of *Girls* and I wouldn't be surprised if this song was inspired somehow by the speech Hannah delivers at Adam's door in the fourth episode of season one. I also think this song shows her sense of humor about herself and her own lovesickness/crazy-girlfriend-ness: "I threw my phone across the room at you" is sung so cheerfully! Over, what, a ukulele?! All-around delightful. The very beginning sounds like some happy commercial with cartoons bouncing around because it's spring and you need new laundry detergent or something.

"Holy Ground"

This feels like drinking every energy drink at every gas station from every Lana Del Rey song ever. By the end it has a "Long Live"–esque kind of HUZZAH feel that I'm sure will make it amazing in concert.

"Sad Beautiful Tragic"

HER VOICE. All of it. So delicate and fragile and then the bridge is absolutely heartbreaking. "Could you just try to listen?" *kills me.*

"The Lucky One"

Taylor is a smartypants about fame some more.

"Everything Has Changed"

The little bit about the butterflies is just perfect. The whole thing is perfect. This is a perfect song.

"Begin Again"

"He didn't like it when I wore high heels. / But I do." This is the last track

on the album, like her parting words with us are just an FYI that she's growing up and she does things for herself now and she's BEGINNING AGAIN and changing. In "You Belong with Me," from ye olde *Fearless* phase, she goes, "She wears high heels, / I wear sneakers." I feel like now she's established herself as both a sneaker-wearer and a high-heels-wearer and I am totally cool with that. Beautiful and famous and good at performing, but capable of feeling lonely and small, and unafraid to talk about it.

One of my most passionate waves of TS love hit when I had been working for thirty hours straight without sleep and just wanted something that was so HIGH SCHOOL and NORMSIES and made me feel part of that demented girl culture that I was left out of in middle school because I looked like a boy/grandma and that I eventually stopped wanting because It Gets Better™ but that I still desire in a corner of my soul when I'm doing my adult job. This is not supposed to read like one of those weird side comments people make for pity, because #WritingAnArticleAbout-TaylorSwiftForTheBeliever #Summer2013 #NoRegrets. But for a long time, I did use her music to feel part of a teen experience that I just wasn't meant for, and to feel connected to something so many people like in this way I had become rather opposed to due to my own middle-school inferiority complex. Those first three albums helped me believe I was still someone who could relate to something that had no irony to it, who could genuinely enjoy a completely earnest expression of desire and love. Letting myself geek out over Taylor's music was legit good for my mental health.

In the time since then, however, two things have happened and fucked me over completely. For one, I embarked on a relationship with a person I love, meeting my once-harmless wistfulness with a scary, real thing that I care about. For another, *Red* was released—an album free of any fairy-tale bedazzlement, set outside the high-school vacuum of the other three, sung in screams and whispers and nothing in between. It's not daydream material; it hits too hard. It's not just catchy chemical power satisfying my perpetually slight yearning for an adolescence I just wasn't cut out for; it's a musical manifestation of my very own brain and soul and blood and tears.

It almost makes me angry, having to deal with these dumb, real feelings now. I feel like a Kevin James character, middle-aged and moderately depressed because I thought I was just picking up a lady at a sports bar but we ended up getting married instead. I feel like TAY-LOR SWIFT HERSELF dated me and "tricked" me into staying in it long enough for a relationship and then wrote a song about me that GETS ME COMPLETELY, whether I like it or not.

But one thing you become shockingly OK with when you do reach this scarier understanding of the music of Taylor Swift is these dumb, real feelings. You start to see each one, no matter how painful, as just another layer of your emotional spectrum, another experience, another inexplicable circumstance valuable in itself because it's another thing you get to feel. It is suggested, perhaps, that her music is less about being in love or mourning the loss thereof, but how incredible it is that we can know what it's like to have these emotions at all.

This facet of Taylor Swift's strength I spoke of four thousand words ago, the most heartstopping one of all, can be best summarized with this sentence from a letter Frida Kahlo wrote Diego Rivera: "It's not love, or tenderness, or affection, it's life itself."

Long live. ♦

ANNA PERILLO

22, NEW YORK

Whenever I was bored in high school I would write lyrics to Taylor Swift songs in my notebook to make it look like I was taking notes.

Her most romantic song is easily "You Are in Love." I want to find that kind of true love. It will certainly be my wedding song.

One thing that makes me different from a lot of fans is that I rock a light-up foam finger at every Taylor Swift concert I attend. It says *#1 swifty* and I am very proud of it.

The song that made me realize she's a genius was "All Too Well." In college our final assignment for my Literary Perspectives course was to write an analytical paper about a meaningful poem or song. I chose "All Too Well." The verse "You call me up again just to break me like a promise / So casually cruel in the name of being honest" gives me chills. It's about the fragility of love and how difficult is to forget once it goes away.

I met Taylor on August 18, 2014, aka the most magical day of my life. She handpicked eighty-nine of us to attend a top-secret event in New York City where she announced *1989,* released "Shake It Off," and debuted the music video on a livestream. After that we all got the surprise of a lifetime when we were put on a coach bus and driven to Taylor's apartment building. I stepped into the lobby of the building in a state of shock and disbelief. I remember hugging the girl standing next to me because we were so excited. A few minutes later we ran up like ten flights of stairs to Taylor's apartment. She was standing at the door and gave every single person a hug. When it was my turn and Taylor made eye contact with me all I managed to say was, "Taylor, I love you. Thank you so much for this!"

I'm obsessed with Taylor's cats. I shared a moment with "Dibbles," which is Taylor's nickname for Olivia, when I was petting her and she was playing with the dangling tails of my Taylor Swift leather bracelet that I've worn to all of Taylor's concerts. She is the cutest fluffball in all the land. Taylor's dad also showed me Meredith's "trick" where she drinks from the kitchen faucet. They're truly adorable kitties with very different personalities.

At one point that night "Shake It Off" started playing on Z100 and we had an impromptu dance party in her kitchen. I have a Polaroid of me standing next to Taylor holding one of her Grammy Awards. What more could you ask out of life?

My favorite car song is "22" because I am currently twenty-two-ooh-ooh. (Sorry, couldn't help myself.)

My friend Sarah thinks I'm insane because I'll wait months before listening to bonus tracks on an album because I always want to have "new" Taylor music to look forward to. It takes a ton of self-control.

Taylor started following me on Tumblr on August 27, 2015. I was at work when I saw it. My follow-up post was, "Taylor Swift is following me. I can't breathe."

I find it impossible to listen to "You Belong with Me" without thinking about the guy I had a crush on in high school. He sat next to me in orchestra. His girlfriend was the captain of the kickline team, so I could relate to the lyrics. Picture the music video with Taylor dancing in her bedroom like a dork using a hairbrush as a microphone. That was me.

I can see her writing a cookbook someday.

It makes me incredibly happy to imagine Taylor finding true love and living happily ever after in her own love story.

Keds
ON TOUR

#KEDSONTOUR #OHSOFAMOUS

THE 1989 WORLD TO

Best. Night. Ever.

Keds
#KEDSONTOUR

PLATINUM UNDERDOG

Why Taylor Swift Is the Biggest Pop Star in the World

NEW YORK, **NOVEMBER 2013** | JODY ROSEN

Taylor Swift worries a lot about security. It's an understandable concern. This spring, a man was arrested in the wee hours of the morning near her estate in Watch Hill, Rhode Island. Police reportedly spotted him walking out of the ocean; he told the arresting officers he had swum two miles to meet Taylor Swift. The singer has two other homes—a modest house, which she calls a "cottage," in Beverly Hills, and her main residence, a penthouse apartment near downtown Nashville—and her team makes every effort to keep the addresses hush-hush. But fans have a way of sniffing these things out. On a Sunday morning in late September, a twelve-year-old girl and her mother, who had flown to Nashville from Connecticut to see Swift's concert at the Bridgestone Arena the night before, walked into the lobby of her building. This was celebrity stalking at its most benign: the mom and daughter had a gift for Swift, a big container of homemade chicken soup, which they left with her doorman.

Swift needed the soup. When I arrived at her apartment later that day—my visit was scheduled—she was audibly under the weather. She looked the picture of health: she greeted me in her big, open-plan kitchen, wearing a loose-fitting white-lace frock and friendly grin. But when she spoke, what came out was a croak, a husky voice pitched about two octaves lower than Bea Arthur's. "I made these, and I'm super-proud of them," she said, pushing a plate of cookies across the counter. "They're pumpkin-chocolate-chip. I didn't cough on them, just so you know. You're safe."

Swift had been sick all week, fighting the kind of head cold best treated by curling up in bed with a magnum of NyQuil. She didn't have that luxury. She'd come home to Nashville to wrap up a seven-month-long North American tour in support of her fourth album, *Red*, which was released in October 2012. The concert the previous evening was the final one of the tour, and the toughest. "It was a struggle," she said. "I found it a little bit easier to sing than to talk, which was, like, a miracle."

In fact, Swift's cold had provided one of the show's Kodak moments. About halfway through, she settled in front of a microphone to perform her 2010 hit "Sparks Fly." Suddenly, she thought better of it. "I'm sorry, guys, but I just really have to blow my nose," she said. "I swear I'm gonna do this really fast, can you please scream to fill the awkward silence, please?" She scurried down a flight of steps offstage, where, presumably, a roadie was waiting with Kleenex.

For another star, the move would be inconceivable: a mystique-shattering breach of the fourth wall. Can you imagine imperial Beyoncé or imperious Lady Gaga telling a sold-out arena: *Hang on a sec, I've gotta go snort into a napkin*? But for Swift it was a *coup de théâtre*. The crowd—fourteen thousand plus, mostly female—erupted in a deafening, inhuman roar. Twenty seconds later, Swift was back onstage, strumming her twelve-string acoustic guitar and singing "Sparks Fly."

Swift's *Red* tour is her biggest yet, and it has all the trappings of a stadium-pop blockbuster. There are Jumbotrons and LED lights, multilevel stages and hydraulics and confetti drops, a seven-piece band, four backup singers, fifteen dancers,

nearly as many costume changes. Yet the heart of a Taylor Swift show is intimacy: moments like the tissue break, when the razzle-dazzle recedes, the band and dancers step into the shadows, and Swift bathes cavernous arenas in a homey campfire glow. Introducing "Mean," a song about bullying, Swift stood at the lip of the stage, picking at a banjo. "I always wanted to know and I always used to daydream about what it would be like to stand on a really big stage and sing songs for a lot of people, songs that I had written . . . Daydreaming was kind of my No. 1 thing when I was little, because I didn't have much of a social life going on. I didn't always have fourteen thousand people wanting to hang out with me on a Saturday night."

This is the signature Swift humble-brag, modesty that has at times seemed so false that it earned its own meme, the Taylor Swift Surprised Face—a reference to the *What? Me?!* gasps of astonishment she unleashed once too often when her name was called at awards ceremonies. Still, can you blame her for being shocked? The scale and scope of Swift's success is startling. In an age of catastrophic music-industry contraction, Swift stands apart; sometimes she has seemed like a one-woman bulwark against the collapse of the traditional record business. In the seven years since the release of her self-titled debut, Swift has sold twenty-six million albums. Sales of Taylor Swift song downloads have

topped seventy-five million; according to the Recording Industry Association of America, she is the No. 1 digital singles artist of all time. Since 2006, she has placed forty-three songs in the Top 40 of *Billboard*'s Hot 100 pop chart as the lead performer, more than any other artist in that period. She's had thirty-one Top 40 country singles, including thirteen No. 1's.

These numbers are especially improbable when you consider the music, and the musician, behind them. Swift is an oddball. There is no real historical precedent for her. Her path to stardom has defied the established patterns; she falls between genres, eras, demographics, paradigms, trends. She is a Pennsylvania Yankee turned teen-pop country singer, a Nashville star who crossed over to Top 40, a confessional singer-songwriter who masquerades as a global pop diva. Her music mashes up the quirkily homespun and the gleaming pop-industrial, Etsy and Amazon, in a way we've never quite heard before.

Swift herself is a figure of contradictions. She's a rock critic's darling who hasn't the faintest whiff of countercultural cool about her. Raunchiness is the norm in today's pop, but Swift is prim, rated G. She is a model of can-do twenty-first-century girl power whose vision of romance is positively medieval—fairy-princess, shining-knight, prancing-unicorn medieval. She can write the sickly sweetest love song you've ever heard and churn out the most bilious, vindictive, name-naming, slut-shaming breakup ballad; often, they're the same song. Swift's influence has reverberated through popular music, yet she remains sui generis, a genre of one. By rights, she should be a fringe figure, a cult artist. But as 2013 rounds the corner toward 2014, as Swift puts a bow on her fourth album and begins work on her fifth, there's no mistaking it: Beyoncé, Rihanna, Gaga, Katy, Miley, Justin, Justin, Usher, Jay Z, Kanye—they're all vying for second place. How, why, is Taylor Swift the world's biggest pop star?

The best place to seek answers may be Nashville, the city that shapes Swift's approach to art, business, and the intersection of the two. Her apartment, a three-bedroom corner duplex with soaring ceilings, sits more or less in the center of town, about two miles southwest of the Cumberland River, near the campus of Vanderbilt University. Swift did the interior design herself, a project she says took years to complete. It's easy to see why. The apartment is a very pleasant, very visually busy place. There is a lot of decor for the eye to absorb.

There's rustic hardwood furniture, Oriental rugs, a giant hearth where an electric fire flickers even when the temperature outside is in the high seventies. There are cabinets cluttered with books and tchotchkes; there's a kitchen backsplash in the shape of a giant heart. In a corner near a window, there's a topiary rabbit, as tall as an NBA shooting guard, wearing a marching-band hat. On the wall of her living room, I noticed a photograph in a gilded frame: the famous image of Kanye West, stage-crashing Swift's acceptance speech at the 2009 MTV Video

---

Swift is an oddball. **There is no real historical precedent for her.** Her path to stardom has defied the established patterns.

Music Awards. Underneath the picture is a caption, handwritten by Swift: *Life is full of little interruptions*.

Swift's ceilings are hung with all kinds of things: gathered silk, wooden birdcages, chandeliers, lanterns. Ornate railings line the apartment's second-floor balconies; it looks like a stage set for a production of *Romeo and Juliet*—or for the scene in the final verse of Swift's 2008 hit "Love Story." In short, it's exactly the kind of apartment you'd expect Taylor Swift to inhabit: whimsically girly, dreamy, appointed in a style you might call Shabby-Chic Alice in Wonderland. Swift showed me one of the guest bedrooms, which holds an eye-popping cacophony of patterned wallpaper and fabrics. "I wanted, like, every color," she said.

Swift is a homebody. Even when she's

touring, she tries to sleep in her own bed, picking the shortest distance to one of her three residences and flying home in her private jet after shows. "It's not a bad gig," she deadpanned. You might not know it from her public persona, but Swift is funny; she has a dry, ready wit. I told her about the strange man who was seated next to me at the concert the night before. He looked to be in his early forties and was wearing a Taylor Swift T-shirt covered with Taylor Swift pin-back buttons. He announced that he was alone and had driven to Nashville from Oklahoma for the show; he filmed the whole concert on his phone, mouthing every word to every song with unnerving intensity. "He's probably in a file somewhere," Swift said.

The most impressive features of Swift's apartment are the twenty-foot-high windows, which wrap around a corner of the building, offering panoramic views of Nashville. If you look out those windows to the west, you can see the famous epicenter of the country-music industrial complex, the strip of song-publishing firms, recording studios, and record labels known as Music Row.

Swift first saw Music Row in 2001. At the time, the Swifts were living in Wyomissing, Pennsylvania, near Reading, on an eleven-acre Christmas-tree farm that the family owned as a secondary business. (Her father, a successful stockbroker, worked for Merrill Lynch.) Taylor had discovered country music a few years earlier, when her parents bought her a LeAnn Rimes album. At age eleven, Taylor persuaded her mother to take her to Nashville during spring break, so she could go door-to-door on Music Row, armed with a demo CD of karaoke performances.

She came up empty on that first trip, but three years later the family relocated to Hendersonville, Tennessee, an affluent suburb about twenty miles northeast of Nashville, so Taylor could pursue her musical dream. For once, it is not glib to say that the rest is history. In 2004, when she was fourteen, Swift signed a songwriting contract with Sony/ATV Nashville; she may have been the youngest professional songwriter in Music Row history. A year later, she inked a deal with Big Machine, a fledgling label run by former Dream-Works Nashville Records executive Scott Borchetta, and released her first album, *Taylor Swift*, in October 2006.

Revisiting Swift's debut, you're reminded just how much of a country record it was. The lead single, "Tim McGraw," tipped a Stetson to the country superstar; on the album cover, Swift looked like a mini-me version of McGraw's wife, Faith Hill, whom she thanked in the liner notes "for being the most graceful woman in the world." The songs were genre fare: lyrics about Chevy trucks and bedtime prayers and slammin' screen doors, sung by Swift in a Dixie drawl, an accent she couldn't possibly have picked up in the Keystone State.

There is a long tradition of country carpetbaggers: musicians from points north who squeeze into cowboy boots, start dropping their g's, and make a beeline for Nashville to launch, or revitalize, their careers. The country star Alan Jackson lampooned the phenomenon in a 1994 hit, "Gone Country," and the trend has been pronounced in recent years, with rockers like Sheryl Crow and Darius Rucker migrating to Nashville, one of the last places hospitable to guitar-based pop-rock in an era dominated by hip-hop.

You could make the case that Swift traveled that well-worn path herself. In fact, she did a bait-and-switch maneuver, planting roots in loamy country soil, then pivoting to pop. With each album, her drawled vowels have become more clipped; she's pushed the fiddles and mandolins down in the mix, or jettisoned them altogether. The tale is told by two of her biggest hits, "You Belong with Me" (2008) and "We Are Never Ever Getting Back Together" (2012). The former is a

power-pop song with a country twang; banjos are prominent amid the surging guitars, and Swift still sounds like she's a Southerner. (Listen to her sing the phrase "typical Tuesday night.") "We Are Never Ever Getting Back Together," on the other hand, is a pure bubblegum-pop ditty, which Swift sings—and in funny asides, speaks—in a Valley Girl accent purged of all down-home traces. Goodbye, twang; hello, vocal fry.

Yet Swift's ties to Nashville are still strong, crucial to her music and to what can only be called the Taylor Swift Brand. Radio is a major force in country, and Swift has remained a country-radio favorite the old-fashioned grassroots way: by schmoozing and glad-handing station executives, program directors, and disc jockeys.

"Country radio is much more like a family than any other group of people that I've met," Swift said. "They just say, 'Look, we've known each other for years. You've stood by us, and we've stood by you. That's how this works.'"

Swift has made splashier gestures toward the country Establishment. In October, the singer attended a gala ribbon-cutting ceremony for the Taylor Swift Education Center at the Country Music Hall of Fame and Museum, which she personally endowed with a $4 million donation. "I love being a part of the country-music community," she told me.

Those feelings are, to say the least, reciprocated. Swift is Nashville's sweetheart; it can't stop lavishing her with accolades and honors. This fall, the Nashville Songwriters Association International named her Songwriter/Artist of the Year for a record sixth time. She has been nominated for twenty-one Country Music Association Awards, and she's won nine. Midway through this year's CMAs ceremony, a phalanx of eight of the biggest stars in country—McGraw and Hill, George Strait, Brad Paisley, Keith Urban, and the three gaudily moussed simps in the trio Rascal Flatts—appeared onstage to present Swift with the Pinnacle Award, a special prize that had only been given out once before, to Garth Brooks. Brooks won his when he was forty-three; Swift turns twenty-four next month.

The Swift-Nashville love affair works for both sides. She is country's first truly global star, its ambassador not just to the nation's mall-rat hordes but to Ireland and Brazil and Taiwan. She confers modernity, cosmopolitanism, youth on a genre that traditionally has stood for the opposite values. The country Establishment may not be crazy about pop music, but it loves having a pop star in its midst, and is willing to follow Swift anywhere she goes, sending songs like "We Are Never Ever Getting Back Together" to No. 1 on the Hot Country Songs charts. Nashville barely even flinched when confronted with "I Knew You Were Trouble," surely the only record with a dubstep bass-drop ever to get spins on country radio.

For Swift, Nashville offers plenty in return. The country audience is music's most loyal and reliable; in a decade of record-industry decline, country sales figures have been notably more buoyant than other genres. Nashville turned out to be the perfect staging ground, the ideal base of operations, for Swift's broader conquest of pop culture. If you ask Swift to reconcile her musical impulses, she gives an answer that has the virtue of being both true and politically savvy boilerplate. "I love country and I love pop," she told me. "I love them both."

But Swift's relationship to country is not merely a matter of careerist calculation. Nashville is a song town, and Swift is first and foremost a songwriter, steeped in Music Row's values of craftsmanship and storytelling. This was evident from the beginning, on Swift's debut record, when listeners were amazed to hear a scrawny teenager—who in early publicity photos looked like she'd been awkwardly airdropped into a debutante's ball gown—singing self-written songs that showed such sure-footed command of form. Her songs had catchy verses that erupted into catchier singalong choruses, and the kinds of clever lyrical twists and switchbacks for which country songwriters are renowned. Her first country No. 1, "Our Song," which she wrote for a talent contest as a high-school freshman, bounded out of the speakers, grabbing your ears from the first bar. The lyric was a little Mobius strip: a teenage romance tale, which looped around, in a nifty final verse, to Swift, the songwriter: "I grabbed a pen / And an old napkin / And I wrote down our song." With each album, she's refined her craft. Consider a refrain from another big hit, "Mine" (2010): "You made a rebel of a careless man's careful daughter." That's awfully deft writing: a little miracle of narrative concision, vacuum-packing a novel's worth of backstory into ten words and two bars of music.

Swift told me she could imagine a time when she'd stop performing and just be a writer. "When I'm forty and nobody wants to see me in a sparkly dress anymore, I'll be, like: 'Cool, I'll just go in the studio and write songs for kids.' It's looking like a good pension plan."

Perhaps. But Swift's songwriting may be too quirky, too personal, to fit all comers. Swift's parents named her after James Taylor, and she has a '70s-folkie's soul; she is a confessor, a memoirist. On *Red*, Swift made the big leap into high-gloss pop, cowriting three songs with the wizardly Swedish hit-makers Max Martin and Johan "Shellback" Schuster, who are responsible for dozens of pop smashes over the last decade and a half. You could hear Martin and Shellback's touch in the bright, punchy sound of those songs, "We Are Never Ever Getting Back Together,"

"I Knew You Were Trouble," and "22." Yet the songs are unmistakably Swiftian; unlike other Martin songs, you can't imagine them being recorded, interchangeably, by Katy Perry, or Pink, or any of the other usual suspects. Listen to a key line in "22": "We're happy, free, confused, and lonely at the same time / It's miserable and magical." It's a classic Swift lyric: purple but precise, self-involved yet self-aware—all in all, about as spot-on a description of a young woman's turbulent inner life as you're likely to hear on hit radio.

"I think that allowing yourself to feel raw, real emotions in public is something I am never going to be afraid to do," she said. "Hopefully that's the case, if I can remain a real human. I'm fine with being honest with my fans about the fact that it's okay that everything *isn't* okay all the time. I love my life, I love my career, I love my

friends—but things are not okay all the time. So I don't sing about things being okay all the time."

She never has. The second song Swift ever wrote, when she was twelve, was a lament about junior-high-school ostracism called "The Outside." (The song appeared on *Taylor Swift*.) Swift quit Hendersonville High for good when she was sixteen, but her songs have never quite left the schoolyard: she still obsesses over castes and cliques and social hierarchies. In "22," Swift sings about fleeing a party packed with "cool kids"; in "We Are Never Ever Getting Back Together," she scoffs at the ex-boyfriend who plays "some indie record that's much cooler than mine." One explanation for Swift's immense popularity may be her insistence on playing the unpopular girl— 36.7 million Twitter followers be damned. Other divas project invulnerability, striding through videos like jackbooted superheroines. Swift offers a different image. To put it in the teen-movie terms of "You Belong With Me": in life Swift is, unmistakably, a "cheer captain"—blond, leggy, confident, talented, and, oh, yeah, world famous. But in her songs she's staked out a different persona: she's a bleacher warmer, a wallflower, an underdog.

Swift is best known, of course, for writing love songs, and lost-love songs—and, especially, vengeful, scorched-earth lost-love songs. The liner notes to her debut album included this dedication: "To all the boys who thought they would be cool and break my heart, guess what? Here are fourteen songs written about you. HA." Back then, the boys in question were Swift's high-school classmates, but she's since moved on to dating musicians and movie stars. These days, spotting-the-celeb in Taylor Swift's lyrics is a favorite media parlor game.

Like many famous people, Swift complains about the prying of tabloid gossips. In fact, she does a lot to encourage the attention. Accepting the Best Female Video award for "I Knew You Were Trouble" at the VMAs this August, Swift said: "I also want to thank the person who inspired this song, who knows exactly who he is"—a statement that unleashed a torrent of tweets about One Direction singer Harry Styles, the song's reputed target.

At such moments, you can't help but conclude that you are watching a shrewd businesswoman at work: It doesn't hurt Swift's bottom line to keep gossip mills whirring. But Swift's vengeful streak has also brought censure—lots of it. She's been maligned as a serial kisser-and-teller, as an entitled rich kid, as a mean girl with a victim complex. Swift can be shrill. When singer Joe Jonas dumped her and began dating actress Camilla Belle, Swift's (alleged) response was "Better Than Revenge" (2010), a song that spent as much time shaming the girl as the rake ("She's an actress / She's better known / For things that she does / On the mattress"). "Dear John," allegedly about Swift's reported fling with John Mayer, had a delectable melody, but Swift's self-righteousness, her immature insis-

tence on her own immaturity—"Don't you think I was too young / To be messed with?"—curdled the drink.

Swift has heard the criticism, but she waves it off. "There's a spin on every single celebrity out there," she said. "I know that one of my spins is: 'Oh, Taylor's heartbroken. Oh, Taylor fell in love and the guy broke her heart. She's sad all the time, and lonely.'

"I mean, they can say that all they want. Those are real feelings that every single person goes through. I think that it's okay to be mad at someone who hurt you. This isn't about, like, the pageantry of trying to seem like nothing affects you. I'm a songwriter. Everything affects me."

"I'm a songwriter," surely, is the apt response. The tradition of musical score-settling stretches all the way back to medieval troubadours and lyre-plucking ancients; it's been a mainstay of American song at least since the first bluesman aimed an acidic twelve-bars at the woman who'd done him wrong. Bob Dylan is an incorrigible, at times malicious, kisser-and-teller; for decades, rock critics have been quoting with admiration Elvis Costello's famous dictum: "The only motivation points for me writing all these songs are revenge and guilt." Drake's new album *Nothing Was the Same* is, as usual, a vérité catalogue of his "bitches" and booty calls, in which he goes so far as to name one of his civilian exes, "Courtney from Hooters on Peachtree"—a creepier move by far

than Swift's sly swipes at her famous former beaux. It's hard not to detect a sexist double standard in the policing of Swift's confessions, especially when you consider the routine misogyny in the songs of rockers, rappers, and woebegone beardy indie balladeers. Taylor Swift is a young woman who dates guys, falls in love, falls out of love, and writes some songs about it. Must we begrudge Swift her muse?

You could call Swift a generational bard: she merges the pleasures of old-fashioned songcraft with millennial social-media oversharing. There's no doubting the artfulness of Swift's best status updates. *Red*'s centerpiece is "All Too Well," cowritten with songwriter Liz Rose, a frequent collaborator. If the internet is

to be believed, "All Too Well" is about Jake Gyllenhaal, whose romance with Swift convulsed the tabloids in late 2010. It's a ballad that rises, like a slow-cresting wave, over a bass line similar to the one in U2's "With or Without You." There are the usual recriminations, which arrive in tight, crackling couplets: "You call me up again just to break me like a promise / So casually cruel in the name of being honest." But "All Too Well" is also a montage of fond memories, vividly drawn: The song catches a couple "singing in the car, getting lost upstate" and dancing around the kitchen "in the refrigerator light." Here is Swift, watching her boyfriend react as she pages through childhood photographs at his mother's house: "Photo album on the counter, your cheeks were turning red / You used to be a little kid with glasses in a twin-size bed." It takes a special songwriter to craft a sneering kiss-off that's also tender valediction.

"I heard from the guy that most of *Red* is about," Swift said. "He was like, 'I just listened to the album, and that was a really bittersweet experience for me. It was like going through a photo album.' That was nice. Nicer than, like, the ranting, crazy e-mails I got from this one dude. It's a lot more mature way of looking at a love that was wonderful until it was terrible, and both people got hurt from it—but one of those people happened to be a songwriter."

She rolled her eyes. "So what are you going to do? Did you not Wikipedia me before you called me up?"

These days, Swift is thinking a lot about her next record. While on the *Red* tour, she'd been writing songs and stockpiling ideas: reams of lyrics, thousands of voice memos in her iPhone. Swift will end the year by performing in Australia and New Zealand and will play a few dates in London and Berlin in February. But she plans to spend much of 2014 writing and recording the new album, a prospect she finds exhilarating and terrifying.

"I worry about everything," Swift said. She was sitting in her dining room, at the head of a large antique wooden table. "Some days I wake up in a mind-set of,

like, 'Okay, it's been a good run.' By afternoon, I could have a change of mood and feel like anything is possible and I can't wait to make this kind of music I've never made before. And then by evening, I could be terrified of the whole thing again. And then at night, I'll write a song before bed."

Swift hopes to collaborate with new songwriters and producers. But she planned to begin, she said, by heading back into the studio with Max Martin and Shellback. "I want to go in with Max and Johan first, just to figure out what the bone structure of this record is going to be.

"I have a lot of things to draw from emotionally at the moment. But I have to draw from them with a different perspective than on *Red*. I can't say the same

things over and over, you know? I mean, I think it's just all the more important that I don't ever allow myself to coast.

"At the same time, there's a mistake that I see artists make when they're on their fourth or fifth record, and they think innovation is more important than solid songwriting. The most terrible letdown as a listener for me is when I'm listening to a song and I see what they were trying to do. Like, where there's a dance break that doesn't make any sense, there's a rap that shouldn't be there, there's like a beat change that's, like, the coolest, hippest thing this six months—but it has nothing to do with the feeling, it has nothing to do with the emotion, it has nothing to do with the lyrics. I never want to put things in songs just because that might

make them popular, like, on the more rhythmic stations or in dance clubs. I really don't want a compilation of sounds. I just need them to be songs."

As for the theme of those songs: That's a foregone conclusion. "I only write songs about crazy love," Swift said. "If I go on two dates with a guy and we don't click, I'm not writing a song about that. It didn't matter in the emotional grand scheme of things. There's a lot that goes on in daily life that isn't really worth turning into a verse and a chorus."

Swift is definitely in the right line of work: popular song is, to a large degree, the art of setting crazy love to a tune. But Swift's romanticism has brought disdain from certain quarters. In a post on the website *Jezebel* titled "Taylor Swift Is a Feminist's Nightmare," Dodai Stewart scorned the singer as retrograde, a prude infatuated with white-knight romance. "For Taylor, fifteen means falling for a boy and dreaming of marrying him. My fifteen was more like: flirt with this one, make out with that one, try a cigarette, get drunk, lie to your parents, read some Anaïs Nin . . . [Swift's] image of being good and pure plays right into how much the patriarchy fetishizes virginity, loves purity, and celebrates women who know their place as delicate flowers."

Swift is practically Victorian compared with stars like Beyoncé, Gaga, and Rihanna, to say nothing of another daughter of Nashville who's been in the news lately, Miley Cyrus. Those women represent an aggressively sexualized feminist pop, harnessing big beats and skimpy outfits to work through questions of power and self-determination. Swift's songs aren't totally chaste: sex is there in the rush and flush of the music, and it peeks through, discreetly, in the lyrics. But she is demure. Among other things, this is an excellent marketing strategy. Swift has moved from teen-pop stardom to adulthood, bringing her old fans along while staying wholesome enough for the next generation of tweens and their parents.

Still, is Taylor Swift really a "feminist's nightmare"? You could argue the opposite. Her straightlaced fashion sense and dance moves—the fact that she's never writhed across a concert stage wearing a negligee, or less—may make her more square than some other singers. But she's also less beholden to that old feminist bugbear, the Male Gaze.

In fact, seeing Swift live is revelatory: it's in a setting like Bridgestone that her uniqueness, the weirdness of her conventionality—and, yes, her feminism—snaps into focus. I've been going to arena shows for three decades; I've never experienced a louder, more rabid crowd than at Swift's concert. Nor, for that matter, a more female crowd, music critics from New York and creepy dudes from Oklahoma to the contrary. Even at a Justin Bieber show—even at a women's-studies seminar—you won't find as pronounced a female-to-male ratio, nor such a wide age range: toddlers and teens and tweens and their moms, for sure, but also college co-eds, and grandmothers, and rowdy thirtysomething office workers, like the gals who sat in the row behind me, passing a flask of

> The message of her concerts is a different one: that **great power is unleashed** when a female takes a guitar and pen in hand and makes some art.

booze. To push through the turnstiles of a Taylor Swift concert is to enter, as the saying goes, a women's space. Swift has the power to turn a hockey arena into a room of one's own.

She puts on a good show. In the past, Swift's singing has been shaky—who can forget the wounded-water-buffalo harmonies in her duet with Stevie Nicks at the 2010 Grammys—but these days her pitch is sure; she sings confidently, prettily, if not quite muscularly. The concert is elaborately choreographed, and she hits her marks like a pro. But the most fascinating bits come between songs, when Swift speaks to the crowd. Her banter consists almost entirely of talk about songwriting. It is a rather eccentric brand of stage patter: more hippie arts-camp counselor than rock star.

I think for me, a question that I get asked sort of a lot is: How do you write a song? Like, where do you start? I just imagine that I am putting a message in a bottle and sending it out into the ocean.

I remember being really young, and the thing I would write songs about, mostly, was the fact that I really didn't really fit in in school. Songwriting became a coping mechanism for me early on.

I think it was Joni Mitchell who said that 'songs are what you think of on the drive home.' You know, the Great Afterthought.

At Bridgestone the loudest cheer of an earsplittingly loud night came when Swift was sitting at the piano, in the middle of a rambling introduction to "All Too Well." "I'm sure," she said, shooting a sidelong glance at the audience, "we have a lot of people here tonight who write songs." Call Swift a stooge for the patriarchy if you like, but the message of her concerts is a different one: that great power is unleashed when a female takes a guitar and pen in hand and makes some art.

At her apartment, I ask Swift to explain her rapport with her fans.

"There's more of a friendship element to it than anything else," she said. "Maybe it's a big-sister relationship. Or it's a *Hey, we're the same age*—and we were both sixteen when my first album came out, and we've both grown up together.

"Audiences respond differently to different effects that artists have on them. I've noticed this, from bringing lots of special guests onstage. Crowds scream for lots of different reasons. There's a certain cuteboy scream. And there's, like, a certain 'I identify with this lyric, this lyric is my life' scream. I guess that's the scream that I hear in my concerts." ♦

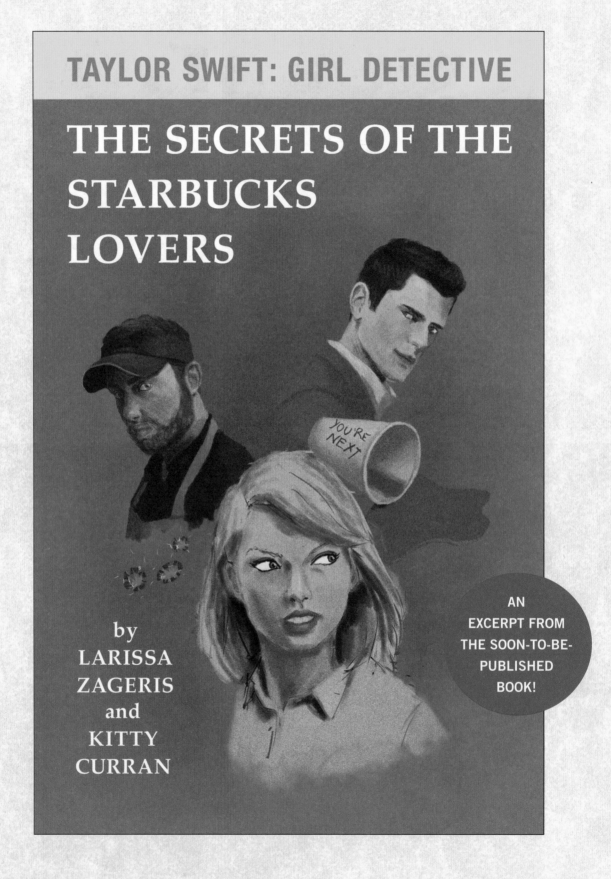

TAYLOR SWIFT: GIRL DETECTIVE

THE SECRETS OF THE STARBUCKS LOVERS

YOU'RE NEXT

by

LARISSA ZAGERIS

and

KITTY CURRAN

AN EXCERPT FROM THE SOON-TO-BE-PUBLISHED BOOK!

A Note *from the* Chron\.CHRONICLERS

To the undiscerning eye, it may seem that Taylor Swift is "just" an internationally beloved musical living legend as much known for her good humor, impeccable style, and all-around acumen as she is for her enduring pop anthems.

But to the perceptive peepers of Kitty and Larissa, her secret life as an internationally beloved musical living legend as much known for her good humor, impeccable style, and all-around acumen as she is for her enduring pop anthems who *also* moonlights as a girl detective is revealed.

Lifelong students of intrigue, art, and run-on sentences with a nose for extended metaphor, Kitty and Larissa hope you enjoy this kind and gentle parody of everyone's favorite pop star, girl detective, and also the world's most popular maker of fine caffeinated beverages.

Stay Mysterious!
Kitty & Larissa

P.S. This book is in no way affiliated with Starbucks, and we do not actually think that they are the front to an international jewel smuggling ring. Though it would be quite exciting if they were, and we are extremely charmed by the prospect of a line of diamond-dusted Frappuccinos. Ethically and organically sourced, of course.

This book is also not affiliated with Taylor Swift, Lorde, or any other member of Taylor's squad. We do hope they like it, though, and if they were to embark on new careers as detectives, we would be thrilled to translate their adventures for the large and small screen.

Taylor and Lorde were writing their first duet, but couldn't figure out a good rhyme for "feminism."

CHAPTER I

A Latte Danger

TAYLOR SWIFT, an attractive music legend and girl detective, was sitting in a Tribeca Starbucks with her musician friend Lorde. The two were writing their first duet, but couldn't figure out a good rhyme for "feminism."

"Darwinism? Ecosystem?" Taylor suggested.

"How 'bout *prism*, mate?" Lorde smirked. She was attractive, like Taylor, and a Kiwi who loved to show off her tomboyish edge.

Taylor furrowed her delicate brow. "Oh, Lorde. There's one direction for this pop-dance hit about the power of female friendship to take . . . and it looks like it's going to take us another round of skinny caramel lattes to find it."

The girls got up to order. They had scarcely passed the display of Colombia Medium Roast coffee beans when a scream shattered the midday calm. Taylor rushed to the source of the sound: a pretty young woman staring in horror at a grande skinny mocha she had spilled on the floor.

"Why's she packing a sad? Skinny mochas are shite," said Lorde.

"Look closer," Taylor countered, and ran her eyes over the scene. "Where her name should be written. It says—"

Both girls fell silent as they read the two words scrawled in angry Sharpie on the side of the screaming girl's cup.

"You're Next."

CHAPTER II

THE MISSING SISTER

"LET'S GET ahold of ourselves, Bianca." Taylor calmed the girl with a heavy dose of her intelligent blue eyes. "I've gotten you a new skinny mocha and autographed your phone. Now will you please tell me what's going on?"

"I wish I knew!" Bianca exclaimed, before falling back into her overstuffed chair. "You see, I'm an actress." Lorde rolled her eyes, but unrolled them almost instantly at the sight of Taylor's expertly arched eyebrow.

"Continue, Bianca." Taylor gave the girl a smile as warm as one of her fan-appreciation blog posts. A barista, who looked not unlike a young Paul Bunyan, angrily mopped up the remnants of the spilled beverage as Bianca told Taylor her tale.

"And my sister is—was—too. We used to look for auditions in this very Starbucks, every day, until a month ago. That was the day I got my first big part. I was cast as Struggling Murder Victim #2 in an upcoming episode of *Law & Order: SVU.*"

Bianca let this news hang in the air. Lorde did her best to stifle a snicker. Taylor eyed Lorde, and urged the girl on. "That must have been exciting for you."

"It was!" Bianca wailed. "But it was also the last day I saw my sister. We were both up for the same part. At first I thought she was jealous that I got my big break and she didn't and she just wanted

Taylor gave the girl a smile as warm as one of her fan appreciation blog posts.

some space. But then I started looking for her at all our favorite Starbuckses. Now every time I order a drink, someone writes something scary on my cup."

"Scary like . . . your definition of a big break?" joked Lorde. The bearded barista could not help but suppress a gruff giggle in the near distance.

"Scary like, *'You're next.'* Or *'Keep away.'* At first I thought they were having a hard time spelling 'Bianca,' but honestly, it isn't that hard to spell!" Bianca worked herself into a fresh fit of tears.

Taylor and Lorde shared the look they always shared before playing concerts and solving mysteries.

"So, mate. Is Taylor Swift, Girl Detective on the case?" Lorde asked.

"When am I not?" Taylor responded, sweeping up her coat and Dolce & Gabbana Agata bag.

"Where are we going?" asked Lorde.

"To Starbucks." Taylor put on her trademark really cool sunglasses.

"Which one?" Lorde did the same.

Taylor applied a fresh coat of her signature red lipstick and smiled.

"All of them."

CHAPTER III

A Helpful Stranger

LORDE AND TAYLOR accompanied Bianca to several different Starbuckses throughout the city, concluding their journey in a frighteningly long Frappuccino line at the Astor Place store. Promptly upon receiving her Java Chip Light Frappuccino blended coffee beverage, Bianca screamed. She even more promptly spilled her drink all over Taylor.

"What's it say this time, then?" Lorde asked.

"*Shake the pop star off*," Taylor read, while shaking bits of blended coffee beverage from her wrist.

Lorde and Taylor shared a look. "Someone wants me off the case more than I never ever want to get back together," Taylor said.

"And someone right ruined your Katherine Hooker Cape Coat," Lorde intoned sadly.

"Never say 'ruin' when a bashfully charming British man is about," said a charming British man who approached Taylor, bashfully. "It's bound to force us to say something horrifying, like 'keep calm and carry on.'"

He handed a packet of stain-removing wipes to Taylor. She accepted them with a winning smile and took a deep drink of his tweedy handsomeness.

"Erm. Uh, keep calm and carry on, Ms. Swift," the handsome stranger stammered.

"I always do, Mister—" Taylor attempted, but before she could catch the helpfully handsome British man's name, he was lost in a crowd of Frappuccino-rabid NYU students.

CHAPTER IV

TIP YOUR LUMBARISTA

LATER that evening, Lorde had a concert and Taylor had a hunch.

"I bet whoever is writing these messages is doing so under the instruction of some other authority," Taylor confided to her Scottish Fold, Detective Olivia Benson. "It seems to be the only way to explain the consistency of the threats across so many different Starbucks stores. The real question is: who? And the second real question is: why?"

Detective Olivia Benson purred.

"You're right, Detective Olivia Benson. I'm not going to get anywhere asking a cat."

*

The Paul Bunyan–esque barista from earlier was wiping the counter to within an inch of its life when Taylor entered the Tribeca Starbucks for the second time that day. He was completely absorbed in his work, and, Taylor decided, handsome in a grumpy lumberjack sort of way. She would call him The Lumbarista.

"If you're coming in here ten minutes before close to order a Frappuccino, you'd better be the President or—"

"Taylor Swift?" Taylor asked with a smile.

The Lumbarista sighed deeply. "Can I tell you we're closed without you writing a song about it?"

"You can tell me you're ten minutes from closing, which you are, and no promises." Taylor smiled winningly.

The Lumbarista didn't. "Eight minutes. And counting."

"I can get a lot done with three minutes and thirty-five seconds."

"And I can get a lot done without living legends loitering in my store. What do you want, Swift? Take it to the bridge."

Taylor was not dissuaded by The Lumbarista's sass. It had been a while since she'd enjoyed some decent banter, and this was tastier than

6

A charming British man approached Taylor, bashfully.

the skinny vanilla latte she'd planned on ordering. "The girl I was in here with earlier—"

"Ole Butterfingers Bianca, the scream-spiller from hell?" asked The Lumbarista, in a deadpan growl.

"Yes. Do you have any idea of who could be behind all of these threats she's been receiving?"

"Gee. She's pretty annoying, so my guess is . . . literally anyone." With that, The Lumbarista attacked a patch of dried mocha sauce with renewed vigor. "Ouch!" he cried, and grabbed his left elbow in pain.

"You're wincing!" Taylor rushed to his aid.

"You're observant!" The Lumbarista snapped, but softened at the sight of her pulling an elbow support wrap from her bag. He snatched the wrap from her outstretched hand, but his eyes spoke volumes of gratitude. "It's probably why your lyrics are so relatable," he added.

"I've a touch of the occupational arthritis myself." Taylor gestured to the guitar slung across her back. "You know, we're not all that unlike each other, you and I."

"I can see some subtle differences." The Lumbarista applied the wrap to his aching elbow.

Taylor noticed an angry set of scratches running along his underarm. "We're both people this entire city—world, even—counts on to get through their day," she probed.

"Yeah . . ." The Lumbarista said dubiously, eyes narrowed.

"And," Taylor continued, the concern in her voice going from grande to venti, "even though I'm compensated well for running the world, yours can't be a terribly high-paying position."

"The benefits are good," The Lumbarista responded, but hesitation shot through his voice like the espresso in a caramel macchiato. Taylor took this as her cue.

"It would be perfectly understandable for someone in your position to, say, accept a bribe from an unknown third party to write threatening messages on a certain customer's cup." She adjusted the fit of the support wrap on his elbow ever slightly. "It would also be perfectly acceptable for someone in your position to tell someone in my position who that other someone is."

"I knew you were trouble when you walked in," The Lumbarista snapped. "Time's up. I've got enough dishes to do tonight without cleaning up your mess."

Taylor's eyes flashed, but she kept her voice calm. "There's no need to be—"

"*Mean?* C'mon, Swift." The Lumbarista smirked unkindly. "I could see that one coming a mile off."

*

A few paces away from the Starbucks, Taylor's beloved Scottish Fold poked her head out of Taylor's handbag.

"I know, I know, Detective Olivia Benson," Taylor said, and sighed. "All that effort, just to come up as dry as a cappuccino."

"I knew you were trouble when you walked in,"
The Lumbarista snapped.

CHAPTER V

COVER GIRL

THE next day, Lorde and Taylor found themselves comforting an inconsolable Bianca at a Gramercy Park Starbucks. A puddle of *"Stay Away!"* latte lay at their feet. Bianca sobbed into her infinity scarf.

Lorde rolled her eyes. "Jaysis. Save something for *SVU*."

Taylor arched an eyebrow in Lorde's direction before placing her well-manicured hand on Bianca's knee. "There's no need to despair, Bianca. I'm as good at getting to the bottom of things as I am writing indelible pop hits with massive crossover appeal."

"So what are you going to do now?" Bianca asked, her voice quavering.

"I'm going to do what Taylor Swift: Music Legend can't—but what Taylor Swift: Girl Detective always does," Taylor said, reassuringly. "Go undercover."

"I'm as good at getting to the bottom of things as I am writing indelible pop hits with massive crossover appeal."

CHAPTER VI

TRAINING TAY

TAYLOR adjusted her newly minted Starbucks employee visor over her impeccable blond shag. She had been embedded in a West Village Starbucks for several hours, but so far her work had turned up more chores than clues.

"Meredith! What's the holdup?" Tam, her new coworker, called to her over the roar of the industrial dishwasher. "I need those Trenta lids, pronto!"

"In a tic, Tam!" Taylor called out, suppressing a small smile at the use of her preferred undercover name. She made a show of looking for the lids, while actually scanning the stockroom shelves for evidence of any kind. An out-of-place box, an old clock, a locket . . . evidence could take any form. More than likely, it was in the overstuffed bag of coffee beans marked COLOMBIA MEDIUM ROAST ESPECIAL squeezed between some bags of Pike Place Roast and Veranda Blend.

"Come on," Tam snapped, and snatched up a sleeve of lids. "I still have to teach you seasonal lattes."

"I'll be out front in a minute." Taylor smiled brightly. Tam shot her a suspicious look. "I need to clean up some beans I spilled."

She made a show of looking for the lids, while actually scanning the stockroom shelves for evidence of any kind.

CHAPTER VII

THE COLD HARD GROUND

TAM rolled her eyes and left Taylor to her own devices. One of those devices was her knife from the "Blank Space" video, which she promptly used to slice open the bag of Colombia Medium Roast Especial.

Instead of beans pouring out of the bag, countless glittering emeralds tumbled out and onto the stockroom floor.

"Emeralds," Taylor whispered out loud. "How will the pumpkin spice latte compete?"

"You'll never learn how to make a pumpkin spice latte, Meredith Grey." A livid Tam had appeared in the doorway. "Because you'll never make it out of here alive!"

With that, plumes of thick, black smoke erupted from the industrial dishwasher, filling the room with a disorienting haze. Coughing, Taylor tried to feel her way toward the door, collapsing just short of it.

"The plot thickens," she whispered aloud.

"As does the smoke," a tweedy voice responded. Taylor's last memory was a pair of strong, but delicate, hands wrapping themselves around her waist. Then the world went black.

Plumes of thick black smoke erupted from the industrial dishwasher.

CHAPTER VIII

TRENTA-SIZED TROUBLE

BACK at the Tribeca Starbucks, the refreshing scent of Jade Citrus Mint Green Tea brought Taylor back to her senses. She awoke to see the concernedly handsome face of the helpful British stranger, and Lorde yelling dead into it.

"*Allen Lagh-Jeaky?* What kind of posh prat's name is that?" Lorde demanded, roughing up the perturbed-looking gentleman with her eyes.

"It's . . . uh . . . Welsh," Allen stammered, an undignified blush reddening his ears.

"Yeah right, ya bloody royal!" Lorde shouted, forcefully.

"Lorde!" Taylor could not arch her eyebrows high enough at her well-meaning friend. Lorde slumped back in her seat. "Allen is a friend. He saved me from whatever happened back in Gramercy Park."

"Still don't trust him." Lorde snorted.

"Pardon me, ladies," Allen Lagh-Jeaky said, and smiled charmingly. "But could one or the other of you please inform me of what is going on? I had the pleasure of running into the lovely Miss Swift at another Starbucks I frequent, only to save her from some sort of smoke monster. The devil's guess as to why. Perhaps we should flag a constable to apprehend that knavish woman for her near murder of you, Miss Swift?"

"You playing twenty bloody questions then, mate?" Lorde snarled. This time, Taylor did nothing to stay her friend's belligerence. This

Allen Lagh-Jeaky fellow was handsome, but, if Taylor were being as honest as her poignant, bittersweet lyrics about young love, he was gratingly slow on the uptake.

"Tam is long gone by now. Besides, involving the authorities is sometimes more a hindrance than a help, if the Case of the Jellybean Ruby has taught us anything." Taylor shook the last remaining trace of Starbucks hat hair from her honey-blonde locks. Lorde nodded knowingly. Allen Lagh-Jeaky fluttered his eyelids in a way that called to mind peak-career Hugh Grant.

"I'm, er, eh, erm, I—" Allen stammered, Hugh Grantishly.

Taylor took a deep breath and collected herself. "Allen, you know I am an international music legend and style icon. What you may not know is that I am also a detective."

Allen Lagh-Jeaky's aristocratically blue eyes widened. "A Girl Detective?"

Taylor disguised a slightly disappointed sigh. "For lack of a catchier-yet-still-feminist term, yes. And you have met me in the middle of quite a mystery. I'm trying to discover the connection a certain actress's sister has to Colombia. You see, Starbucks is famous for their Colombia Medium Roast, and Colombia is famous for its blood emeralds."

"Why, yes!" Allen said, excitedly. "Colombian emeralds! The Green Cocaine!"

"Exactly," Taylor said, in a voice as lyrical as her hit songs. "Someone has been using at least one Starbucks as a front for an international gem-smuggling trade. They're likely moving the jewels in with the coffee, but why or what this has to do with Bianca, I don't know."

"One thing is for certain, Miss Swift. You'll use your wits to figure this out . . . and likely turn it into one of your American Top 40 hits." In his excitement, Allen Lagh-Jeaky had gathered Taylor's elegant hands into his. At the precise moment they both noticed how long their hands had enjoyed this union, a piercing scream startled them apart. . . .

In his excitement, Allen Lagh-Jeaky had gathered Taylor's elegant hands into his.

Will Taylor Swift: Girl Detective *crack the case?*

Will she find true love . . . or maybe a kitten?

Will she at least incorporate that mysterious scream into her next chart-topping hit?

Find out the answers to these questions and more by obtaining your own copy of Taylor Swift: Girl Detective in The Secrets of the Starbucks Lovers, *available online.*

Snoop for clues on how to get your copy at http://taylorswiftgirldetective.tumblr.com.

Stay Mysterious,

Kitty & Larissa

About the Authors

LARISSA ZAGERIS

(AKA The Scribe With No Name Except Larissa Zageris)

Skilled in six different types of martial arts and a master of all weaponry, Larissa fought the law and the law . . . conceded defeat in the face of her badassery. These days she has calmed down somewhat, hung up her katanas, and spends her time writing tales of glory in her adopted home of Chicago. Still, on warm summer nights she will gaze upon the darkening sky and wonder what would happen were she to return to tread the path of the warrior.

KITTY CURRAN

(AKA The Artist Formerly Known as Miffy Von Tuffington III)

Originally from London, Kitty has been on the run from nefarious ne'er-do-wells ever since *The Incident*. She doesn't like to talk about what happened, but her body bears the scars of what was clearly an epic battle. At present she lives in Chicago, draws pretty pictures, and acts almost normal provided you don't sneak up behind her too quietly.

Own the original thrilling
TAYLOR SWIFT: GIRL DETECTIVE STORIES

- ☐ The Secret of the Old Blog Post
- ☐ The Clue in the Liner Notes
- ☐ The Haunted Locket
- ☐ The Haunted Mansion Mystery
- ☐ The Haunted Beach Mansion Mystery
- ☐ The Mystery at Last Chance Ranch
- ☐ The Mystery of the Double Standard
- ☐ The Curse of the Jelly Bean Ruby
- ☐ The Secret of the French Kiss
- ☐ The Hidden Recording Studio
- ☐ The Haunted Recording Studio

- ☐ The Hidden Haunted Recording Studio
- ☐ The Mystery at Last Chance Ranch
- ☐ The Secret of the #Squadgoals
- ☐ The Haunted Sunglasses
- ☐ The Sinister Lipstick
- ☐ The Met Gala Mystery
- ☐ The Secret of the Baked Goods
- ☐ The Haunted Topiary Garden
- ☐ The Great Social Media Caper
- ☐ The Clue in the Tour Bus
- ☐ The Clue in the Pop Culture Think Piece

Own the action-packed
ED SHEERAN ADVENTURES

- ☐ High Tea at Intrigue Estates
- ☐ The Cursed Cross-Stitch
- ☐ The Ginger League
- ☐ The Clue at the Brit Awards
- ☐ The Guitar on Mystery Moor

- ☐ Ed Goes Mad in Dorset
- ☐ X Marks the Spot
- ☐ Ed Goes Down to the Tenerife Sea
- ☐ Mystery at Sheeran Farm
- ☐ Shenanigans at the Royal Albert Hall

Coming Soon—
Taylor Swift is still a Girl Detective, but Edgier in...
THE TAYLOR SWIFT CASE FILES

- ☐ Out of Style
- ☐ Trouble Walks In

- ☐ Blank Target Space
- ☐ Bloodstains On My Guitar

To order: Simply find someone you are great friends with. Fall deeply and irrevocably in love with their truest soul. Take this love to a dance, but do not dance with said Love. Instead, watch them longingly from across the room, making occasional (and meaningful) eye contact. Return home. Practice guitar and songwriting basics until you are able to craft songs that will make the whole world sing. Write a song that will make the whole world sing, and casually mention to said Love that it is about them once they have started singing it too. Make an intelligent and hasty escape when said Love reveals they work for The Wrong Hands, a nefarious crime syndicate. Nurse your wounds. Reconnect with friends you are not in love with. Make friends with people you may or may not one day fall in love with. Write songs all the while. You can't afford to lose this skill. Achieve self-actualization. Write the most mysterious song you possibly can about this process. Make it catchy. Then, and only then, release it on social media, along with a list of titles in the Taylor Swift: Girl Detective library you wish to possess. Await further instructions.

And always, always, always: Stay Mysterious.

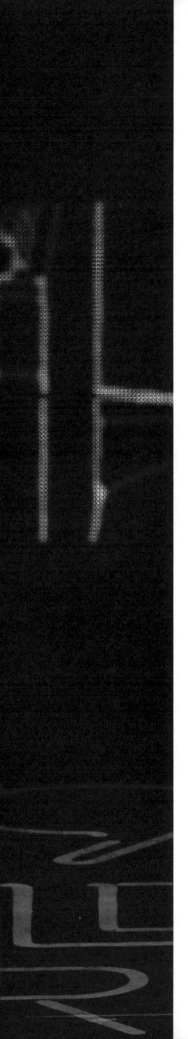

PART THREE

1989 AND BEYOND

Even calling this record 1989 was a risk. I had so many intense conversations where my label really tried to step in. I could tell they'd all gotten together and decided, "We gotta talk some sense into her. She's had an established, astronomically successful career in country music. To shake that up would be the biggest mistake she ever makes." But to me, the safest thing I could do was take the biggest risk. I know how to write a song. I'm not confident about a lot of other aspects of my life, but I know how to write a song. I'd read a review of Red that said it wasn't sonically cohesive. So that was what I wanted on 1989: an umbrella that would go over all of these songs, so that they all belonged on the same album. But then I'd go into the label office, and they were like, "Can we talk about putting a fiddle and a steel-guitar solo on 'Shake It Off' to service country radio?" I was trying to make the most honest record I could possibly make, and they were kind of asking me to be a little disingenuous about it: "Let's capitalize on both markets." No, let's not. Let's choose a lane.

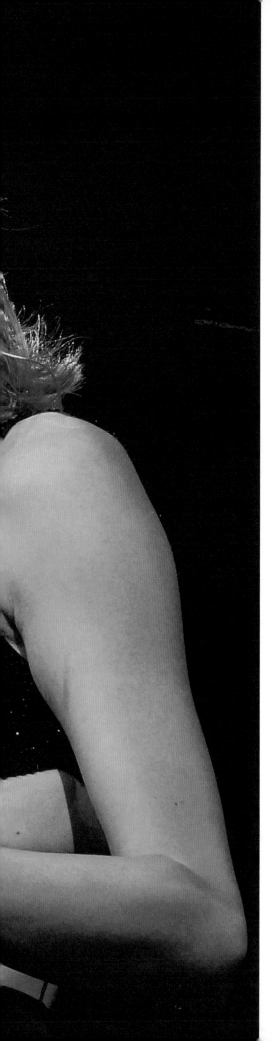

TO APPLE, LOVE TAYLOR

JUNE 2015 | TAYLOR SWIFT

I write this to explain why I'll be holding back my album, *1989*, from the new streaming service, Apple Music. I feel this deserves an explanation because Apple has been and will continue to be one of my best partners in selling music and creating ways for me to connect with my fans. I respect the company and the truly ingenious minds that have created a legacy based on innovation and pushing the right boundaries.

I'm sure you are aware that Apple Music will be offering a free 3 month trial to anyone who signs up for the service. I'm not sure you know that Apple Music will not be paying writers, producers, or artists for those three months. I find it to be shocking, disappointing, and completely unlike this historically progressive and generous company.

This is not about me. Thankfully I am on my fifth album and can support myself, my band, crew, and entire management team by playing live shows. This is about the new artist or band that has just released their first single and will not be paid for its success. This is about the young songwriter who just got his or her first cut and thought that the royalties from that would get them out of debt. This is about the producer who works tirelessly to innovate and create, just like the innovators and creators at Apple are pioneering in their field . . . but will not get paid for a quarter of a year's worth of plays on his or her songs.

These are not the complaints of a spoiled, petulant child. These are the echoed sentiments of every artist, writer and producer in my social circles who are afraid to speak up publicly because we admire and respect Apple so much. We simply do not respect this particular call.

I realize that Apple is working towards a goal of paid streaming. I think that is beautiful progress. We know how astronomically successful Apple has been and we know that this incredible company has the money to pay artists, writers and producers for the 3 month trial period . . . even if it is free for the fans trying it out.

Three months is a long time to go unpaid, and it is unfair to ask anyone to work for nothing. I say this with love, reverence, and admiration for everything else Apple has done. I hope that soon I can join them in the progression towards a streaming model that seems fair to those who create this music. I think this could be the platform that gets it right.

But I say to Apple with all due respect, it's not too late to change this policy and change the minds of those in the music industry who will be deeply and gravely affected by this. We don't ask you for free iPhones. Please don't ask us to provide you with our music for no compensation.

Taylor

A REVIEW OF *1989*

ROLLING STONE, OCTOBER 2014

★ ★ ★ ★ ☆

ROB SHEFFIELD

When Taylor Swift decides to do something, the girl really knows how to overdo it. So on her fifth album, when she indulges her crush on '80s synth-pop, she goes full blast, spending most of the album trying to turn herself into the Pet Shop Boys. *1989* is a drastic departure—only a couple of tracks feature her trademark tearstained guitar. But she's still Taylor Swift, which means she's dreaming bigger and oversharing louder than anyone else in the game. And she still has way too many feelings for the kind of dudes who probably can't even spell "feelings."

Swift has already written enough great songs for two or three careers. *Red*, from 2012, was her *Purple Rain*, a sprawling I-am-the-cosmos epic with disco banjos and piano ballads and dubstep drops. But as every '80s pop star knew, you don't follow one epic with another— instead, you surprise everybody with a quick-change experiment. So rather than trying to duplicate the wide reach of *Red*, she focuses on one aspect of her sound for a whole album—a very Prince thing to do.

Max Martin produced seven of these thirteen songs, and his beats provide the Saturday-night-whatever soundtrack as Swift sings about the single life in the big old city she always dreamed about. In "Welcome to New York," she finds herself in a place where "you can want who you want / Boys and boys, and girls and girls." She hits cruise mode on the floor in "Blank Space" ("I can make the bad guys good for the weekend") and the hilariously titled "Style," where she swoons, "You got that James Dean daydream look in your eye."

The best moments come toward the end, when Swift shakes up the concept. "How You Get the Girl" mixes up the best of her old and new tricks, as she strums an acoustic guitar aggressively over Martin's expert disco surge. "This Love" brings back her most simpatico producer, Nathan Chapman, for the kind of tune that they were just starting to call a "power ballad" in 1989. (The precise equivalent would be Bon Jovi's "I'll Be There for You.") On the killer finale, "Clean," English singer Imogen Heap adds ethereal backup sighs to Swift's electro melancholy ("You're still all over me like a wine-stained dress I can't wear anymore").

If there's nothing as grandiose as "All Too Well" or "Dear John" or "Enchanted," that's because there wasn't meant to be. *1989* sets the record for fewest adjectives (and lowest romantic body count) on a Swift album. Most of the songs hover above the three-minute mark, which is a challenge for Tay—she's always been a songwriter who can spend five minutes singing about a freaking scarf and still make every line hit like a haymaker. But if you're into math, note that the three best songs here— "How You Get the Girl," "This Love," "Clean"—are the three that crash past four minutes. This is still an artist who likes to let it rip. Deeply weird, feverishly emotional, wildly enthusiastic, *1989* sounds exactly like Taylor Swift, even when it sounds like nothing she's ever tried before. And yes, she takes it to extremes. Are you surprised? This is Taylor Swift, remember? Extremes are where she starts out.

darling
i'm a
nightmare
dressed like a
daydream

TAYLOR SWIFT:
"Sexy? Not on My Radar"

THE GUARDIAN, **AUGUST 2014** | HERMIONE HOBY

In Manhattan's chichi Sant Ambroeus restaurant, the pair of smartly dressed women at the next table are making not-so-surreptitious "eek" faces at each other, having clocked that their neighbor for lunch is Taylor Swift. And that's nothing compared to the commotion gathering outside: wherever Taylor Swift dines, a swarm of fans and paparazzi soon forms on the pavement.

This is normal life for the biggest force in pop right now, a global superstar whose songs soundtrack lives, whose tours sell out stadiums in seconds, and whose every facial expression generates a million tweets. Taylor Swift in 2014 is an extraordinary phenomenon. She began as a ringletted country singer, teenage sweetheart of the American heartland, but between 2006's eponymous first album and now she's become the kind of culturally titanic figure adored as much by gnarly rock critics as teenage girls, feminist intellectuals, and, well, pretty much all of emotionally sentient humankind. Unlike Beyoncé with her indomitable run-the-world warrior-queen stylings, or Nicki Minaj, with her cartoonified, amplified self and pantheon of alter egos, there is very little image-making going on with Taylor Swift, pop star. Instead, it's her "realness" that's made her; as well as, of course, some clever choices and heavy doses of charisma and songwriting talent. She is, as her friend the teenage media magnate Tavi Gevinson put it, nothing less than "BFF to planet Earth." Which, for one thing, entails talking to planet Earth at a moderate volume.

"When I'm doing a concert, it's not

"I've **wanted this life** since I was a kid."

---

like, 'WHAT'S UP LONDONNNNN!' I pretty much just speak at this level," she says. As a result, her stadium shows have the confessional good feeling of mass sleepovers and she communicates with her vast audiences "as if I'm talking to them across the dinner table."

Swift releases an album every two years without fail, which means it's time for a follow-up to 2012's *Red*. We meet in the week before she announces new album *1989* and its lead single, "Shake It Off," a breezy, uptempo number about ignoring the haters. She explains: "In the last couple of years I've had to come to terms with the fact that anyone can say anything about me and call *TMZ* or *Radar Online* or something, and it will be an international headline. You can either go crazy and let it make you bitter and make you not trust people, and become really secluded or rebellious against the whole system. Or you can just shake it off and figure that as long as you're having more fun than anyone else, what does it matter what anyone else thinks? Because I've wanted this life since I was a kid."

Her cheery, stoical take on celebrity and tabloid intrusion has served her well. "I am not gonna let them make me miserable when I could be enjoying my life," she says. "That's why you see these artists become a tabloid regular and then become artistically and musically irrelevant, because they let [gossipy websites] stifle them. It's not going to happen here."

For the "Shake It Off" video, she enlisted one hundred fans as well as a load of professional dancers: "Ballet dancers, break-dancers, modern dance, twerkers—and me, trying to keep up with them, sucking." She adds: "I feel like dancing is sort of a metaphor for the way you live your life. You know how you're at a house party and there's a group of people over there just talking and rolling their eyes at everyone dancing? And you know which group is having more fun."

Dancing enthusiastically amid hauteur has become a Swift trademark; specifically, letting loose at awards ceremonies while everyone else remains seated and stiff. She's been attending these shows since she was a teenager and, after "eight years of these very stressful and competitive scenarios, sitting in the front row trying to figure out how you're supposed to act," she eventually realized that "I can process this as a huge pressure cooker or I can just look at it like I have a front-row seat to the coolest concert right now."

Dancing to Justin Timberlake with Selena Gomez at last year's VMAs was a particularly fine example of the latter.

But her most famous awards-show moment remains Kanye West's interruption at the 2009 MTV Awards. Such is Swift's global standing that the president himself called West "a jackass" and, five years on, the moment still hasn't quite died in the collective imagination. Or indeed, Swift's own: last year, she gave her friend Ed Sheeran a jar of homemade jam with a handwritten label that said: "Yo Ed

Im really happy 4 u and I'm gonna let u finish but this is the best JAM OF ALL TIME–T."

In short, the interruption only magnified good feeling toward her. Less fortunate was her Grammys appearance the following year in which she wobbled her way through a duet with Stevie Nicks and subsequently suffered an online shellacking. At this year's ceremony, she seemed determined to eclipse that with a rendition of the bruised "All Too Well," a song allegedly inspired by her relationship with

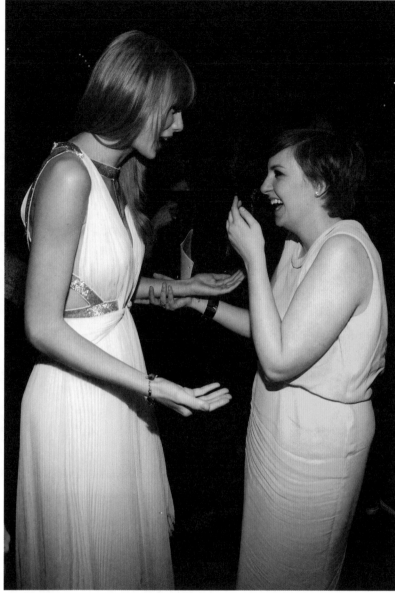

Jake Gyllenhaal. Her performance was fierce and focused. When she finished, she turned from the piano and faced the audience with an intent gaze of defiance and held it for several seconds. The message was clear: no more the victim. It's this song, incidentally, that contains one of the lyrics she's most proud of: " 'You call me up again just to break me like a promise / So casually cruel in the name of being honest.' " She pauses, pleased. "I was like, I'll stand by that one."

"All Too Well" was taken from 2012's *Red*, an album defined by wide-screen, wind-machined renderings of heartache, which confirmed that "country" could finally be dropped from her tag of "country-pop" singer. But *1989*, as she explains, is shorter on the "jilted, sad, pining." Instead, "it's the phase after that, when you go out into the world and make changes in your life on your own terms, make friends on your own terms, without [literally] saying 'C'mon girls, we can do it on our own!' "

Those words will kindle the hopes of those who've suspected Swift has expe-rienced some sort of feminist awakening over the last few months. Recently, she was spotted browsing the feminist section of a Manhattan bookshop. Even more heartening has been the array of BFFs filling her Instagram feed, Lorde and Lena Dunham among them. This seems to be one of the many fun things about being Taylor Swift: that pretty much any smart and interesting young woman in the public eye is yours for the friending. She loved Lorde's debut album *Pure Heroine*, so sent flowers to congratulate her on its

release. Lorde, in turn, got Swift's number from Gevinson (whom Swift recently counseled through her first heartache) and sent her a long message apologizing for once calling her "too flawless to be a role model." Unsurprisingly, Swift forgave her. The first time they hung out, she says, "We took a walk and sat in the park and ate Shake Shack burgers."

Her friendship with Dunham began even more simply. Swift had tweeted in praise of *Girls*, and the moment she followed Dunham on Twitter, Dunham responded with a direct message which said, "something like, 'Can we be friends please?' And then that was that."

Has female friendship become more important to her than romance? "Without a doubt. Because the other alternative"—as in having a boyfriend—"isn't really possible right now. It just doesn't seem like a possibility in the near future. It doesn't ever work. What works is having incredible girlfriends who I can trust and tell anything."

As for the endless "is Taylor Swift a feminist?" pieces—well, they can die now. "As a teenager, I didn't understand that saying you're a feminist is just saying that you hope women and men will have equal rights and equal opportunities. What it seemed to me, the way it was phrased in culture, society, was that you hate men. And now, I think a lot of girls have had a feminist awakening because they understand what the word means. For so long it's been made to seem like something where you'd picket against the opposite sex, whereas it's not about that at all. Becoming friends with Lena—without her preaching to me, but just seeing why she believes what she believes, why she says what she says, why she stands for what she stands for—has made me realize that I've been taking a feminist stance without actually saying so."

I ask if tabloid scrutiny over her lyrics

(and the string of famous exes they allude to) has dissuaded her from pursuing what rock critic Robert Christgau calls her "diaristic realism," or the clues she famously leaves in her liner notes. No, she says, because it's that sense of reading a journal that "has always connected me to my fans in this very intense way." Nonetheless, she concedes that "it's an interesting tightrope walk to write autobiographical songs in an age where mystery is completely out the window."

The way she sees it, there's a gender element to such scrutiny. "I really resent the idea that if a woman writes about her feelings, she has too many feelings," she says. "And I really resent the 'Be careful, buddy, she's going to write a song about you' angle,

---

"Are you ready for a photo shoot? **Take my hand.**"

---

because it trivializes what I do. It makes it seem like creating art is something you do as a cheap weapon rather than an artistic process. They can say whatever they want about my personal life because I know what my personal life is, and it involves a lot of TV and cats and girlfriends. But I don't like it when they start to make cheap shots at my songwriting. Because there's no joke to be made there."

True: Swift has always been a deft lyricist. "Our Song," for example—a perky early hit written when she was sixteen—indicates her precocious skill when it reveals itself as the "our song" of the title: in the last verse she sings, "I grabbed a pen / And an old napkin / And I wrote down our song."

The hysteria and scrutiny came later, with songs like 2010's "Better Than Re-

venge." Fired at the woman who took her man, rather than the man himself, it includes the snide "no amount of vintage dresses gives you dignity" and a chorus that's distinctly unsisterly: "She's an actress, whoa / But she's better known for the things that she does / On the mattress, whoa."

For a moment, Swift seemed in danger of typecasting herself as a victimized prude. "I was eighteen when I wrote that," she reminds me. "That's the age you are when you think someone can actually take your boyfriend. Then you grow up and realize no one take someone from you if they don't want to leave."

We're meant to assume that anyone making this much money (at *Forbes*'s estimate, she'll have raked in $64 million this year) or anyone this astronomically successful (seven Grammys, a Country Music Association lifetime achievement award when she was twenty-three, and so on) must be a cold-blooded and ruthless operator. But Swift's reputation for niceness is unrivaled—and, as I discover a few minutes later, completely deserved.

"It's always been important to me, that's always been a priority," she says. "Every artist has their set of priorities. Being looked at as sexy? Not really on my radar. But nice? I really hope that that is the impression." She agrees that "nice" is often used pejoratively. "Totally! But I don't care if that's not cool, to seem nice or not. I'm not that focused on being cool and I never have been."

Outside, a sea of big black cameras and upraised iPhones are aimed at the door that she's about to walk through. After a glance through the windows she wraps her arms around me in a very deliberate hug goodbye. Then she looks me in the eye and says, in a low voice: "Are you ready for a photo shoot? Take my hand." ♦

KELSEY EIHAUSEN

STUDENT, 16, NEBRASKA

I'm from a small town. It's the kind of place where you know you're welcome and where everybody knows your name. That's the way I feel Taylor is—welcoming to everyone who wants to know her. She makes an effort to get to know us, especially online.

At this point in my life the most relatable album is *Fearless*. I'm still trying to figure out my personality, and starting to experience love, like a regular adolescent, and "Forever and Always" and "Fifteen" are the songs that speak to me the most.

I've seen her in concert two times now—*Red* and *1989*.

The most incredible moments are when she first comes on stage, and when she plays the acoustic pieces and it's just her, the guitar, and the audience. I can't even describe the joy and excitement that rush through me. It's the best feeling in the world.

I met Taylor in Loft '89 with my friend Jocelyn. We were screaming in the crowd and Taylor's mom tapped us on the shoulder during "Style." We couldn't believe it. She told us that she'd been watching us and made us pinky promise that we hadn't been to a meet-and-greet before. I made a book for Taylor that re-created every photo from every album booklet, and I got the opportunity to give it to her. She was so grateful and loved that we'd handwritten it.

The thing that I admire the most about Taylor is her ability to be a great vocalist, songwriter, and performer at the same time. That's a combination that's hard to find these days.

The line I can never get out of my head is "And I know for me / it's always you" from "I Know Places." So simple, but unbelievably true. It's poetic, raw, and real.

I've always loved that she had a dream when she was young and achieved it as she grew up.

My favorite one of her friends is Ed Sheeran. I love their friendship, and I saw them perform together on the *Red* tour. They're both so charismatic and talented, and you can tell they really care about each other.

If Taylor could collaborate with any artist I'd want it to be 5 Seconds of Summer. They've interacted on social media and would sound so great together. Any songs that they would write would make me (and many others) ecstatic.

One time I had a dream that Taylor and I went shopping together and had lunch in a little café in NYC. I wish I could remember what specific stores we went to or where we ate, but I can't.

Taylor is a spectacular role model. She's taught me and other young girls like me that it's okay to be ourselves and that we can express ourselves through our hobbies and passions.

She's shown us not to be afraid of what other people think of us. And to dream big. Those are two things that have changed my life and will continue to change my life.

> "She's taught me and other young girls like me that **it's okay to be ourselves.**"

A REVIEW OF *1989*

2014   ROBERT CHRISTGAU

The NYC tourist jingle everybody hates on to prove they're not her shills is my favorite thing here. Having emigrated to Manhattan myself, albeit from Queens, I think it's silly to demand sociology from someone who can't stroll Central Park without bodyguards. I note that even from a limo you can tell that the "everyone" here who "was someone else before" includes many immigrants of color. And I credit its gay-curious moment even if she ends up with a banker like her dad. All that said, however, there's a big difference between Swift's Manhattan and the one I can afford only due to real estate laws as vestigial as the family grocery that just closed up across the street, and you can hear that difference in the music. In principle I'm down with the treated hooks and doctored vocals with which Swift makes herself at home. Freed of Nashville's myth of the natural, she echoes and double-tracks and backs herself up, confides with soft-edged subtlety and fuses the breathy with the guttural. But I have less use for the cyborg with feelings she's playing now than for the gawky fifteen-year-old she created on *Fearless*—the one who was a hundredth as talented and a tenth as self-possessed as the eighteen-year-old who imagined her, the one who gathered an audience of country fangirls Nashville didn't know existed. That fifteen-year-old obviously isn't much like me. But she's more like I was when I got here than the cyborg will ever be, or most bankers either.   **A–**

ACROSS

1 Pay for everyone
6 Lance of NSYNC
10 "Skedaddle!"
13 Humidifier's output
14 "And another thing . . ."
15 "I ___ feminist and she is a young and talented girl": Tina Fey, re Taylor Swift
16 Do some very inept twerking?
19 World Series org.
20 Happy as ___
21 With 50-Across, remark while sorting good apples from bad?
27 Oscar-winning actor Jared
28 Start a poker pot
29 *Amen & Goodbye* band
31 Singers Young, Diamond, and Tennant
33 Biopic about a boxer
34 Keep Jetson's boss from scoring at all in a game?
40 College, to a Brit
41 Massage, as a sore muscle
43 Reality show featuring a lot of icing
48 Major African river
49 "I wouldn't want to break up ___"
50 See 21-Across
53 Important exam
55 Body part that's frequently pierced
56 Theme of this puzzle
63 ___ Khan
64 NYC theater award
65 One of sixteen in a pound
66 Refusal in Rouen
67 Caring
68 One of the inert gases

DOWN

1 Things to watch videos for "Style" and "New Romantics" on, say
2 Cheer from the stands
3 Anti-pollution org.
4 All systems go
5 HBO series that was set in New Orleans
6 Musical about a *Weekly World News* cover subject
7 Words before mode or carte
8 Direction opposite NNE
9 Couch
10 Ship's kitchen
11 White Rabbit's cry

12 Julie who directed Broadway's *The Lion King*
17 ". . . and ___ write your name" (Taylor Swift lyric)
18 The Bruins' sch.
21 ___ *Can Cook* (PBS show)
22 Number and letter used to indicate a first baseman
23 Electricity or gas: Abbr.
24 Lugosi of horror movies
25 Kind of tide
26 Fancy event
30 Under the weather
32 Completely ignore
35 "I ___ Places" (*1989* song)
36 Enthusiastic agreement in Acapulco
37 Feminine suffix
38 General in *The Force Awakens*

39 Plural pronoun, for some
42 Susan of *L.A. Law*
43 Robe-like dress
44 Cheese used in some bagels
45 Nationality some conspiracy theorists believed Obama to be
46 Abbr. at the end of some lists
47 Tipsy
51 "Bali ___"
52 "Fantastic" title animal in a Wes Anderson film
54 "You got that James Dean daydream ___ in your eye" (Taylor Swift lyric)
57 19-Across stat
58 One of a deadly set
59 Day between Mon. and Wed.
60 Ramada ___
61 Novelist Umberto
62 Rep. counterpart in Congress

This puzzle is courtesy of avxword.com. For the solution, see page 280.

Taylor Swift:
A SOCRATIC DIALOGUE

McSWEENEY'S, 2014 | JARED SMITH

TAYLOR SWIFT: Tell me, Socrates, must the player always play, play, play?

SOCRATES: Well, that depends on what it is to be a player and what it means to play. Could you be more specific?

SWIFT: I'm thinking of the dirty, dirty cheats of the world. Those about whom so many get down and out while they could be getting down to sick beats. Alcibiades, for example, abandoned Athens and sought refuge in Sparta, then left Sparta for Persia before finally returning to Athens, leaving an inter-imperial trail of broken hearts.

SOCRATES: Yes, I see. Alcibiades is, in fact, a player who will play, play, play.

SWIFT: Yes, very much so.

SOCRATES: But must he? That is the question at hand.

SWIFT: I believe he must for, consider that the hater must hate, hate, hate, and the faker must fake, fake, fake. Why should the player be different?

SOCRATES: But might people change? Couldn't something convince the player to stay, stay, stay rather than play, play, play?

SWIFT: Ah, but you see Socrates, it is not the player that decides to stay, stay, stay. Rather, the player becomes a stayer when he ceases to play, play, play.

SOCRATES: So then one must eliminate the other. A player can never stay, stay, stay because, according to you, he would then be a stayer and not a player.

SWIFT: That is correct.

SOCRATES: Could a stayer, having previously been one to go on too many dates, fall into old habits?

SWIFT: Perhaps I've got nothing in my brain, at least that's what people say, but I'm afraid I don't follow.

SOCRATES: Pay no attention to what people say. The depth of this issue you bring up shows the substantial content of your brain. But, let me make myself clear. Might it be a matter of degree? Could a stayer who was previously a player, still have an urge to play, play, play but resist temptation and stay, stay, stay?

SWIFT: No, a player that appears to stay, stay, stay is nothing more than a faker. And as I said before, fakers gonna fake, fake, fake.

SOCRATES: Well then let's consider the avowed stayer. Having been one to always stay, stay, stay, perhaps he stays out too late, and giving in to temptation he's gonna play, play, play. What say you?

SWIFT: The case you describe, the stayer that's gonna play, play, play, is that of the heartbreaker. Not unlike the faker, the heartbreaker is gonna break, break, break.

SOCRATES: Let me see if I follow. The player that's gonna stay, stay, stay is a faker. And fakers gonna fake, fake, fake. Correct?

SWIFT: Yes.

SOCRATES: And is it the case that the stayer that will play, play, play is a heartbreaker who will break, break, break.

SWIFT: That's my position.

SOCRATES: It sounds like you speak from experience.

SWIFT: In some sense. But these experiences, if not completely universal, are at least easily relatable.

SOCRATES: Like a popular song that can't stop, or won't stop groovin'.

SWIFT: That's just the type of music that gets in your mind.

SOCRATES: Saying it's gonna be all right.

SWIFT: Indeed.

SOCRATES: Let us return to the beginning. Your hypothesis is that players gonna play, play, play. Is that right?

SWIFT: That is right.

SOCRATES: And so they cannot stay, stay, stay.

SWIFT: You're right again.

SOCRATES: But didn't you say also that the player that appears to stay, stay, stay, is really a faker. And as a faker, therefore, is gonna fake, fake, fake.

SWIFT: Yes, I did say as much.

SOCRATES: It seems we've reached an impasse—you say players will always play, play, play, but it's possible for them to appear to stay, stay, stay and yet this makes them a faker who will fake, fake, fake. But if they fake, fake, fake then they do not always play, play, play for there must be at least some stay, stay, stay for otherwise, they only play, play, play and hence, are a player and not a faker.

SWIFT: The human creature is a ponderous thing, full of complexities and contradictions. But what can one do? If only there was some sort of movement that would throw off the psychic troubles that follow from simply being.

SOCRATES: Maybe like a dog that has gone for a swim, you can shake, shake, shake.

SWIFT: Shake it off?

SOCRATES: Shake it off. ♦

CARLEE LANGHAM

SECOND GRADER, 7, MARYLAND

The first time I heard Taylor's songs (that I can remember) was when I was three years old. It was the song "We Are Never Ever Getting Back Together."

My mom and I like to listen to "22." I wish I was twenty-two—my mom also wishes she was twenty-two!

I listened to "Mean" almost every day when I was in kindergarten. I was new, and behind in school, and started getting bullied. When I listened to that song I imagined myself singing it to that girl who hurt my feelings for no reason. It made me know that people are just going to be mean and I can't let it hurt me.

My mom's favorite Taylor song is "Ours."

My new favorite song is "Shake It Off." I stand in front of the TV and sing the whole song at the top of my lungs. I love jumping up and down with Taylor and trying to copy her moves.

My favorite place to listen to Taylor is in the car.

My favorite lyric is "My ex-man brought his new girlfriend / She's like 'Oh my god!' but I'm just gonna shake / And to the fella over there with the hella good hair / Won't you come on over, baby? We can SHAKE, SHAKE, SHAKE."

When Taylor dances and acts goofy like no one's watching, it makes me so happy.

My mom asked me what I would do if I ever meet Taylor Swift. I would take her to McDonald's for a Happy Meal.

I saw a commercial on TV with Taylor. She was exercising and singing "JUMPMAN JUMPMAN" on a treadmill. She fell down and I said, "Is she okay?!" Everybody was laughing. I didn't know it was a commercial and not real, but it was funny.

One thing I have in common with Taylor is I have blond hair just like her. I used to beg my mom to style my bangs to the side like hers.

If I could do something fun with Taylor I would take her skating, like in her video, and bowling. I love bowling and pizza.

When I'm a grown-up, I hope Taylor is my friend.

"My new favorite song is 'Shake It Off.' I stand in front of the TV and sing the whole song **at the top of my lungs.**"

Taylor Swift

ME

BFF

Carlee♥ Langham 2016

tAYloR · Swift & Me♥

Wonderland

didn't you calm my fears with the cheshire cat smile

too in love to think straight

We both went mad

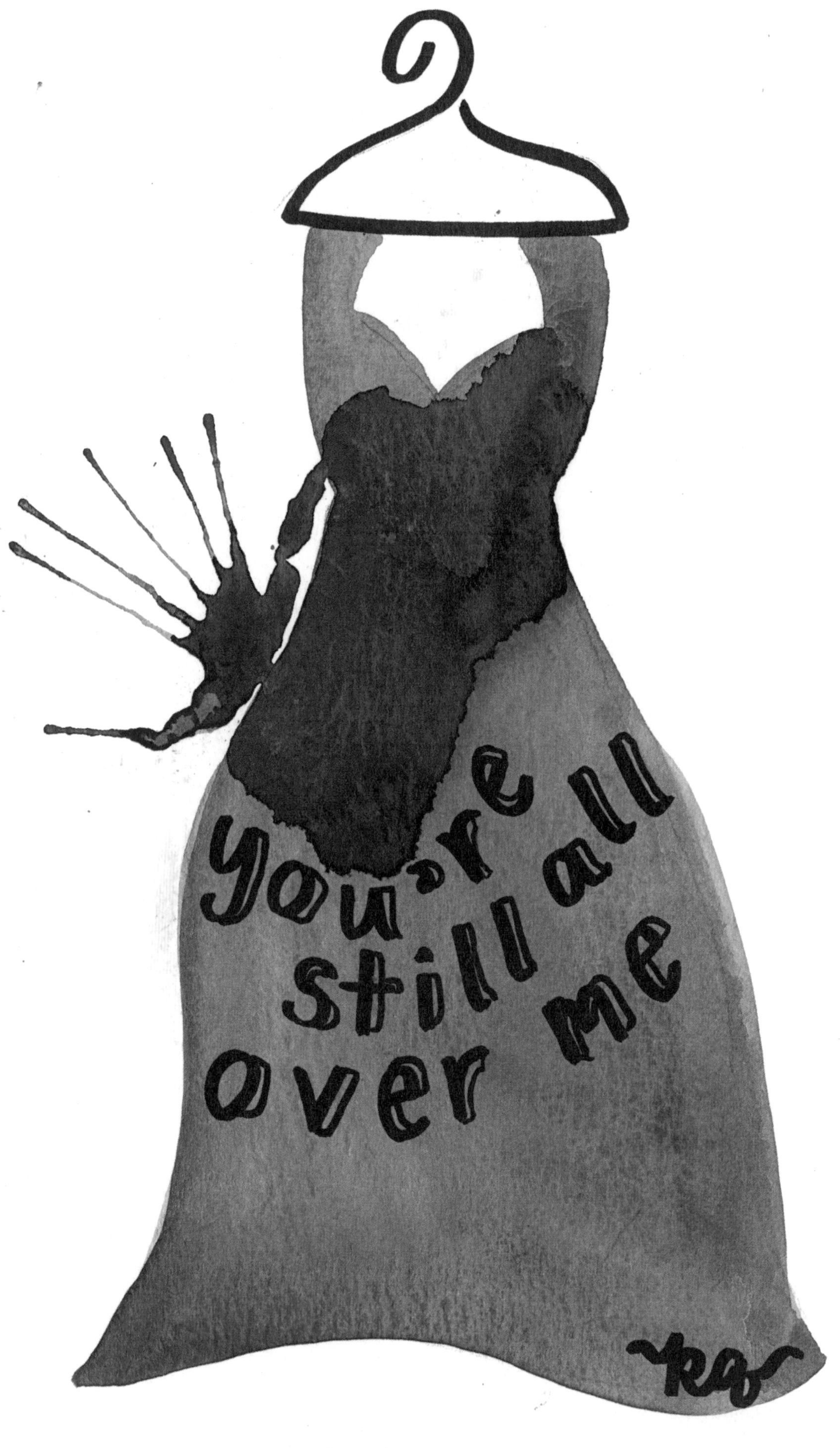
you're all
still
over me
~KA~

A Reasonable Conversation About Taylor Swift's New Album, Which Is the
BEST ALBUM EVER

THE HAIRPIN, **OCTOBER 2014** | JANE HU and JEN VAFIDIS

JEN VAFIDIS: HI JANE. There is a new Taylor Swift album out today, and it is already totally undeniable. The first single is a No. 1 hit, the second single was No. 1 on iTunes within ten minutes of its release, and Taylor has been teasing us via Instagram about these new songs for what seems like years. It's only been a few weeks, but still. I love her, you love her, let's talk about her.

JANE HU: When I tell people that *1989* is going to get me through the rest of 2014, I'm 100 percent not exaggerating. Even though the three prereleases have really sent some MIXED SIGNALS about the feel of the album, T-Swift has never let me down before. I adore this album, but the leading track actually had me a little worried for a moment!

VAF: I hate the first song on this album, and I have a feeling you also don't love it. But maybe I am wrong?

HU: No, I think you're right! This opening track is kind of terrible. Why is this the opening track? Why is this track even on the album? Is the album about New York? NOPE. Also, as someone who has once upon a time fallen HARD for New York, I'm just not sure it captures anything cogent about the experience. It's so repetitive. Do you have anything else to say about this track?

VAF: It's so repetitive. And it's bland, which is something I haven't thought about a Taylor single before, I think. It's so flat and nonspecific that it's about nothing instead of being universal. I have been pretending it doesn't exist, basically. Do you want to skip ahead to the next track, which we both love? I kind of want to do that.

HU: YES, LET'S. "Blank Space"! Where do I even start? This might be my favorite track on the album so far? Though Tay albums are usually slow burns, which is part of why they're amazing.

VAF: Yes. Somehow my favorite song from *Red* is "Holy Ground" now? I don't know when that happened.

HU: There's a general consensus around how unequivocally "poppy" this album is, which I think is basically another vague way of saying that Tay is continuing her departure from country (confessional/narrative) songs toward the more general (vague? repetitive? timeless?) tradition of "pop" lyrics. "Blank Space" is pop, but it's also doing something incredibly interesting vis-à-vis Tay's earlier music; instead of fixating on the end of a relationship (post-breakup) or the burgeoning start of a romance (see half the tracks on *Red*), "Blank Space" is thinking in terms of the whole trajectory of one relationship BEFORE it begins.

VAF: Yes! The narrative has changed from "I'm taking a risk and I don't know how it's going to turn out" to "I can see how this is going to go, and I'm going to do it anyway."

HU: As someone who unabashedly overidentifies with Tay's ability to build deep attachments very quickly—over and over—this feels like a song that I didn't even know I was waiting for. Jon Caramanica describes it as "a meta-narrative about Ms. Swift's reputation as a dating disaster," but it might be more than that? It's meta, certainly, but

it also allows for the possibility of different future outcomes that do not have to repeat Tay's past (whatever that might be). I mean, the song is titled BLANK SPACE. "So it's gonna be forever / Or it's gonna go down in flames." There's a lot of old Tay even in this pop song, by which I mean it's not really about being a disaster, and a lot about being hopeful.

VAF: Right. Call her insane, but she's more than that. She puts extremes side by side to reveal their limitations and to show they can coexist. She's "a nightmare dressed like a daydream." That's such a great reveal: you're the bad boy,

but guess what, I'm worse! And I'm one step ahead of you because I know I'm like this, I've always been like this, and you're only about to find out.

HU: If she's a disaster, she's a very disciplined one: "I can make the bad guys good for a weekend"; "Find out what you want / Be that girl for a month"; Keep you second-guessing like oh my God, / who is she?"

VAF: If it's a game, she's going to win. How about the third song? My first thought, before I realized I loved it anyway, was: someone loved the *Drive* soundtrack, I guess.

HU: And like *Drive*, it's completely invested in CLASSIC HOLLYWOOD TROPES.

VAF: OH GOD, YES. All surfaces. He's driving her around, like the guy from "All Too Well" was upstate, but no one is finding out about anyone's T-ball days in "Style."

HU: Totally. It's so unspecific! Unlike the next track, "Out of the Woods," which has this amazing bridge that is kind of surprisingly specific? "Remember when you hit the brakes too soon? / Twenty stitches in the hospital room."

VAF: Oh Lord, that bridge. It's something, right?

HU: It simultaneously enacts loss AND hope.

VAF: The way she sings "I remember" makes you think that's the most powerful thing a person could say about something so distressing. She's so good at that.

HU: I am pretty breezy about the next track, "All You Had to Do Was Stay." It's just fine for me! What about you?

VAF: Oh man, I love this embarrassing song. It's the most Max Martin–y song on the album, I think? Like, put this song in the hands of a boy band, film them dancing a really literal dance in an airplane hangar, and it wouldn't be too much of a surprise.

HU: My favorite part is definitely the dragged-out "this is what you wanted (ah ah ah-ohh)" bridge. (The bridges on this album are incredible.)

VAF: She's teaching a master class on both pop bridges and uncomplicated (but perfect) rhymes.

HU: Ummmm speaking of: what about the talky bridge in "Shake It Off"? "TO THE FELLA OVER THERE WITH THE HELLA GOOD HAIR"? I think about that line all. The. Time.

VAF: Ahhhh, I meaaaan. I feel like the bridge to "Shake It Off" is unfairly maligned, Jane. UNFAIRLY MALIGNED. It's not cool, it's not good "rapping," but it is somewhat uncanny, right? It's fun, it seeps into your brain. It's just kind of a

fact, I'm used to it now. I also find "Shake It Off" sad, but maybe I'm alone in that. The way she sings, "But I keep cruuuising," makes me sad.

HU: Y'know, the way Tay has to necessarily clamp up a bit in this album in order to be more pop is melancholy in its own way. Or that the trick here is to "shake it off" instead of laying it all out there in the open? Shaking it off is, more often than not, HARD. And perhaps not coincidentally, the track that follows is all about forms of not letting go. The opening line, "It's 2 a.m., in your car"—which later modulates to "It's 2 a.m., in my room"—resists forgetting, and I think that spirit haunts a lot of this album that is often about nostalgia.

VAF: Yeah, one of my favorite Taylor themes is a song's potential to shape someone else's nostalgia. "When you think Tim McGraw / I hope you think my favorite song" being one of the best examples, of course.

HU: Your point about "Tim McGraw" also helps clarify Taylor's move from drawing from a country music legacy to a pop one. "Out of the Woods" sounds like a track from *The Breakfast Club* soundtrack.

VAF: Oh God, it does. Taylor's version of the late '80s / early '90s is pop you'd hear in a dentist's waiting room. I made a Spotify playlist to keep track of the songs/artists I was reminded of while listening to this album, and there are a LOT of Roxette songs on it. There are also some Phil Collins singles, some Amy Grant classics (LOL), and one T'Pau song. Sometimes I thought she was trying to remake *Diamonds and Pearls* without the sex. Like, if

Prince sang "Cream" or "Gett Off" without sounding like he had a painful erection. Which some people might argue is a bad/impossible thing, but I don't know, it makes sense in my head, and it's kind of sweet when it's Taylor. Lots of these songs sound like she's enthusiastically playing air drums in the car. The beginning of "Bad Blood" is some arena rock/ glam thing, and I LOVE it.

HU: "Bad Blood" reminds me of anthemic Queen, in a very endearing way. Its "Hey!"s are far more Brian May than Marcus Mumford. The metaphors are sometimes painfully literal ("Band-Aids don't fix bullet holes"), but they completely work in the context of such instrumentals.

VAF: It's a musical step up from her previous brat anthems ("We Are Never Ever Getting Back Together," e.g.), but the lyrics are still classically junior high. I want to congratulate both of us on not saying who any of these songs are "about," by the way.

HU: We've made it so far!!! Whoever he is, he completely deserves the rhyming designations of "mad love" turned to "bad blood."

VAF: She rhymes "love" with "blood." And "problems" with "solve 'em."

HU: She's a poet. So even while people won't stop comparing "Wildest Dreams" with Lana Del Rey, I actually think the poetic logic is still fundamentally different there.

VAF: Go on! I am lukewarm on this one, mostly because it depresses me. She wants him to remember her, but does he? Probably not. I do love the bridge though.

HU: Part of what's so enabling about Taylor's lyrics are that it's almost irrelevant whether he remembers her or not. His wildest dreams are, first and foremost, hers—I love the privileging of that! Lana Del Rey sings "Summertime Sadness" (the closest relative to "Wildest Dreams"?) largely from a position of what she can communicate to the departed: "I just wanted you to know that, baby, you're the best." But Taylor oversteps this and allows the other to exist ONLY in the context of him desiring her. Does that make any sense, or have I completely lost it?

VAF: It makes perfect sense. She did it on *Red* too, which I think we emailed feverishly about. She says that maybe what they had was a "masterpiece" and "the

only real thing" he's "ever known," and it's way over-the-top and flattering to her and her alone. She might as well be saying, "Oh, maybe I'm amazing, and you're the worst?" Another good Tay theme that comes up on this album is her obsession with vows. Speak now or forever hold your peace: you get the girl, she tells us on "How You Get the Girl," by telling her how you feel AS SOON AS YOU CAN. Meet me in the pouring rain, etc.

HU: "How You Get the Girl" is, for me, a kind of sweeter response to "Blank Space." It's also about the prelude to a relationship, and again, deeply about timing:

> *Say it's been a long six months*
> *And you were too afraid to tell her*
> *what you want*

> *And that's how it works:*
> *It's how you get the girl*

And then, later: "I want you for worse or for better . . . I want you for ever and ever." That's a LOT of commitment to be thinking about for someone who hasn't even asked the girl out yet. It's insane and bold and I love it. It's like, Taylor knows it's inappropriate to ask these things on a first date, but she's still going to FLIRT with the idea of forever. Deeply romantic in retrospect, maybe, but overwhelming and potentially creepy to start? But, I mean, I get it.

VAF: I get it too. It's what we love about her. She's a demanding person.

HU: But demanding with a PURPOSE.

The lyrical implications of the song are kind of buried by the fact that this is basically a disco song? It really reminds me of Rita Ora's "I Will Never Let You Down," which is about forever in a different way. Disco can get away with a lot of feverishly dreamy content.

VAF: Right, because disco operates in the dark, when everything is INTENSE and you say shit you might not mean in the morning.

VAF: I think here is where we mention that there's an excessive cheesiness to Taylor's pop moments that is reminiscent of Dolly Parton's pop moments. Both women like sequins and fringe and silliness. But you know what's sort of not silly and seems to be on a different plane from the rest of the album? "This Love," the eleventh track, is so, so serious. Like Taylor is gunning for having her songs overplayed at every wedding ever.

HU: This is going to reveal the range of pop I listen to, but "This Love" reminds me of Emmy Rossum's "High"?? I think it might be trying to be Annie Lennox but it ends up sounding like over-synthesized classical pop—which, again, not necessarily a bad thing.

VAF: I'd also throw Donna Lewis's "I Love You Always Forever" into that mix.

HU: Ooooooooh yes, totally. "Your touch / my cheek" makes me want to laugh and cry at the same time. "I Know Places" escalates Seriousness one step further, eh?

VAF: I hate "I Know Places." Taylor is the most paranoid singer in pop right now, and it's stifling on this song.

HU: What is happening in that intro!

VAF: NOTHING GOOD, JANE.

HU: I don't think anyone can get away with ending so many phrases with vocal up-slides.

VAF: Not even Taylor.

HU: MAYBE RIHANNA. Maybe Rihanna could get away with it.

VAF: Rihanna could get away with several murders.

HU: Can you imagine ANYONE ELSE singing "Rude Boy"??

VAF: Nope. No one else should sing "Rude Boy," it's a proven fact.

HU: If Taylor Swift is the most paranoid singer in pop, then we just might be the most paranoid readers of her. I have to tell you my theory that the next track, "Clean," actually doubles as a song about the current drought in California. We just had experienced a good bout of rain over the weekend for the first time in tooooo long!

VAF: I'm glad to hear it! I hate this song though, and I don't know why.

HU: You probably hate it because it's just a slightly less slide-y version of "I Know Places."

VAF: Yes, that's probably it. Okay, moving on. THE BONUS TRACKS.

HU: MOVING ON TO "WONDERLAND." OK, can we please discuss the cameo of Mr. Green Eyes? These lyrics: "Didn't you flash your green eyes at me."

VAF: Oh, I didn't notice that!

HU: I sort of want Taylor to be singing about green eyes forever. This song is lilting and lyrical, but I don't find it tired or anything. It kind of moves between angry and dreamy? Even that line about the green eyes is menacing: he FLASHES them at her? This song is torn!

VAF: You mean it's TORN???

HU: "Torn" is such a musical predecessor to Taylor Swift. But I think maybe the song that cites most explicitly from pop music's repertoire is "You Are in Love."

VAF: Yes, that song strongly echoes Bruce's "Secret Garden," which, you might recall, was on the *JERRY MAGUIRE* SOUNDTRACK. How romantic. I bet Taylor does a really good "Dancing in the Dark" at karaoke.

HU: Oh my God. I sort of like to think of this song as the real coda to *1989*, because it thematizes retreat and retraction. Instead of lyrical overtelling or overcompensating, it makes an attempt to mark silences. So first the chorus goes: "You can hear it in the silence (silence) / You can feel it on the way home (way home)." But THEN, she takes out the echoes so that you get this space where you expect / recall the words without actually needing them present. It's sort of how the album works for me in terms of Taylor's entire oeuvre? Like, her prior work is embedded into the work of *1989*, but they can haunt her "pop" songs without her needing to inject it with bio-

graphical details. The clues are there and not there: "You understand now why . . . why I've spent my whole life trying to put it into words." Yes, we do. And now, this song can simply be about that quiet moment when you're "on the way home," just contemplating the beginnings of falling in love. I like that it's allowed to be simple.

VAF: That analysis makes me like this song so much more, Jane! Now the last bonus track seems even less substantial than I thought. But I look forward to having "New Romantics" on my workout playlist for at least a month or two. It seems destined for the trailer of a Garry Marshall holiday movie.

HU: I was thinking, it's an anthem, yes, but it's also kind of a new pop music manifesto??

VAF: Oh, true. I do like how she brags on it. "Mine is better." Also: "the rumors are terrible and cruel / but honey, most of them are true." LOL, you bitch.

HU: LOVE New Pop Bragginess. There are so many delicious details like that in the song that actually make me believe in its message too—who hasn't cried "tears of mascara in the bathroom"?

VAF: I can't say that I haven't!

HU: Cried mascara tears in the bathroom, A+, would do again. "And please take me dancing / And please leave me stranded it's so romantic."

VAF: You know, I was thinking: maybe I'm too jaded for Taylor? But then she proves me wrong. It feels pretty great. ♦

ASHLEY FRIEDMAN

MARKETING, 28, ILLINOIS

My first memory of Taylor is my friend Zac repeatedly telling me that I needed to listen to "that new Tim McGraw song" in 2007. I was confused about why somebody would use his name as their song title, but I finally checked it out and was hooked.

I love her dry sense of humor. She never has to try to be funny. She just is.

I was at the first night of the *Red* tour in Omaha. It was the first time I got to see the opening night of one of her tours, and seeing a show without knowing any spoilers was a priceless experience. That was the first time she ever played "All Too Well" live. Three years later, I'm still not sure I've emotionally recovered.

Meeting her was such a big goal of mine that it literally kept me up at night sometimes.

It happened before the *Red* show in Saint Paul in 2013. I had a bulleted list in my head of the specific talking points I needed to hit and in what order because I knew it would be a short meeting. I somehow managed to get most of them out. But I talked so much that I barely let her get a word in, and I still regret that. Still, just getting to look her in the eye and tell her thank you was all I ever wanted, so it was perfect.

It's not only not weird but *necessary* to see a tour more than once.

It breaks my heart to say this but she can't stay on top of the world forever. The music industry and what's popular changes so fast, and one day she won't be selling as many albums or as many tickets as she does now. She's always said that when that day comes she'll bow out gracefully and probably do something more behind the scenes like songwriting for other people. I think it's better to go out on top than to fight it. I don't see it happening anytime soon, but when it does I know she'll handle it with grace like she does everything.

I was in a car the first time I heard "Love Story." I screamed so loud I think I scared the drivers around me. There's no better feeling than the first time you hear a new song from your favorite artist.

It makes me incredibly happy to imagine Taylor doing an acoustic album. Even after all her achievements, people are so quick to throw around the "she can't sing" criticism. When she does acoustic sets like she did at the Grammy Museum in 2016 the songs sound even better than the album versions. And her acoustic songs on tour are usually my favorite part of the show. I think it's a side of her the world hasn't seen enough of and would be different than what she's done before in the best possible way.

She made me realize that no matter what people are saying about you, you control your own narrative.

Everyone in my life would think I was insane if they saw how much Taylor merchandise I actually own. I only have a handful on display in my apartment. But if you open a drawer or look in a cabinet?

I was so excited when I found out "New Romantics" would be a single. It's such a perfect anthem for going out with your friends or blasting in the car with the windows down. I'm glad she let it out into the world.

If I could snap my fingers and change one thing about Taylor it would be to assure her that she could go away for any length of time and her fans would still be here when she comes back. I can understand why she might feel afraid to go away for too long. But she deserves an actual break. It would only strengthen her popularity and songwriting.

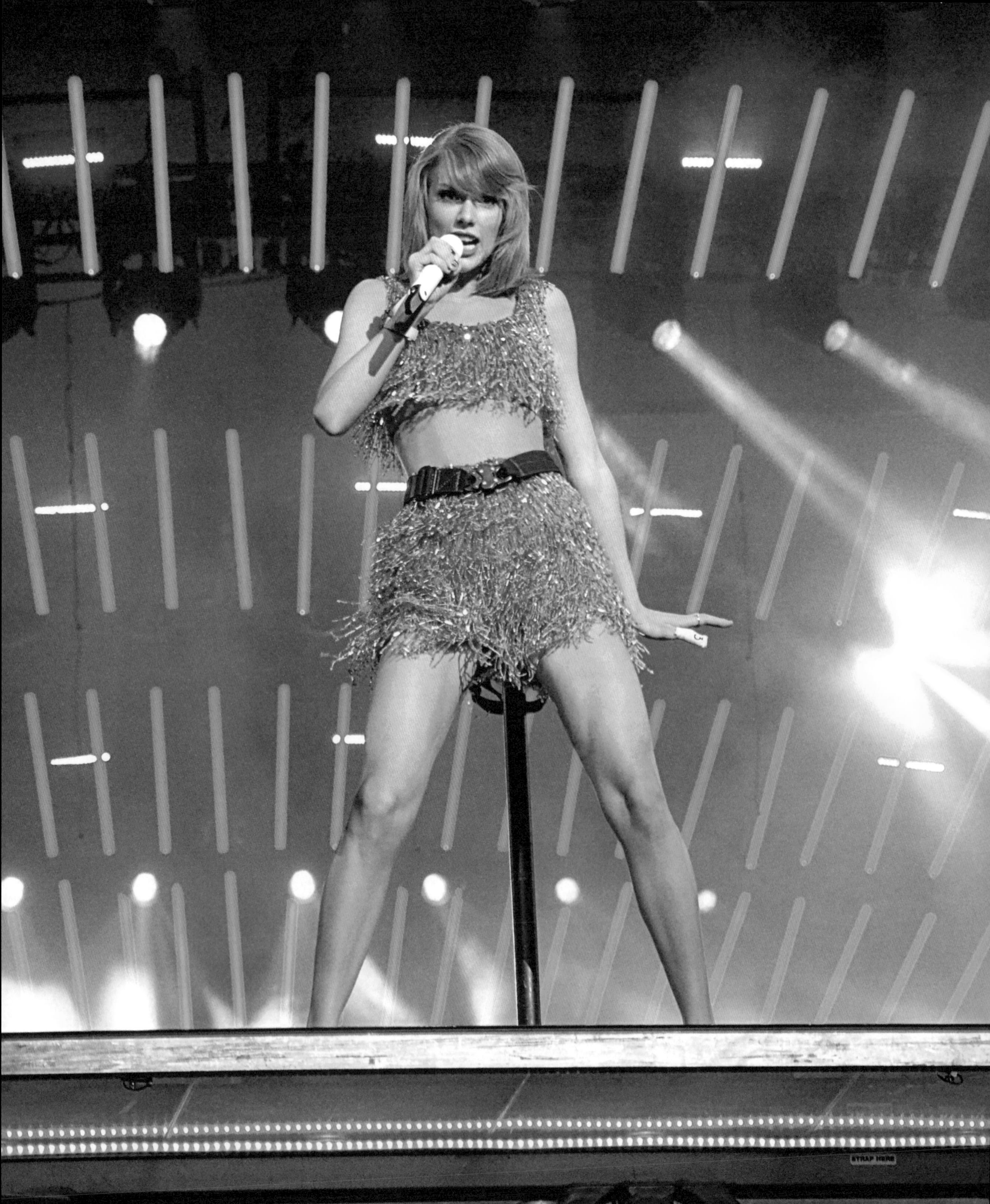

"ANYTHING THAT CONNECTS"

A Conversation with Taylor Swift

ALL THINGS CONSIDERED, OCTOBER 2014 | MELISSA BLOCK

Taylor Swift has had one amazing week. Her new album, released Monday, is on track to eclipse one million sales by Tuesday. The last artist to go platinum in a week was Swift herself with her 2012 album, *Red*. So by the time she arrived at NPR's New York bureau today, she'd earned the right to a little goofiness—in this case, showing up in her Halloween costume, a fuzzy white bodysuit with wings that she described as a Pegasus-unicorn hybrid.

Her new album is titled *1989*. That's the year Swift was born, which means that at just shy of twenty-five years old, she's spent close to half her life in the music industry. In a far-reaching conversation with NPR's Melissa Block, she addressed how things have changed since she began her career a decade ago—not just for her, but for the teenage girls who have always been her primary demographic—as well as how she's reacted to the digital age's effect on media, music, and feminism.

Melissa Block: I enlisted some expert outside counsel for this interview: my twelve-year-old daughter. And I want to start with a question from her. "In your hit song 'Shake It Off,' why'd you address the song to your haters and not your motivators?"

Taylor Swift: That's amazing. With the song "Shake It Off," I really wanted to kind of take back the narrative, and have more of a sense of humor about people who kind of get under my skin—and not let them get under my skin. There's a song that I wrote a couple years ago called "Mean," where I addressed the same issue but I addressed it very differently. I said, "Why you gotta be so mean?" from kind of a victimized perspective, which is how we all approach bullying or gossip when it happens to us for the first time. But in the last few years I've gotten better at just kind of laughing off things that absolutely have no bearing on my real life. I think it's important to be self-aware about what people are saying about you, but even more so, be very aware of who you actually are, and to have that be the main priority.

Here's a related question about the same song, from a seventh grader. She's thinking about the lyrics, and she says, "That sounds a lot like middle school. Do you have anything that you can tell a middle school girl to help 'shake it off'?"

She's exactly right. When I was in middle school, I had this fantasy—and I really thought this was how life worked—that when we were in school, we had to deal with bullying and kids picking on you for no reason, or making you feel like somehow you don't deserve what you want, or you're not what you should be. And I thought that when you grow up and you're not in school anymore, when you're out there in the world with adults, that it's not like that anymore, that people don't attack each other for no reason or try to tear each other down. And I realized when I grew up that it's the same. It's the same dynamics, except we're not walking from classroom to classroom.

It's just interesting how you have to learn how to deal with this at one point or another in your life because people don't necessarily ever grow out of those impulses to pick on each other. Some of us do; some of us realize that's something you do when you're insecure, you try to lash out at someone else. But a lot of people will always do that to other people. So I guess what I try to encourage girls who are in middle school to do is to figure out a way to distract yourself from that negativity. Figure out what kind of art you love to create, or your favorite hobby. Something to throw all of your energy into. And realize that you're gonna have to learn how to cope with this at some point—because it's never going to end, necessarily.

There's definitely a different sound on this new album. You've left country completely behind; this is a really highly produced electronic pop album. But you also say to your fans in the liner notes that "this is a different story line than I've ever told you before." I'm not sure I'm hearing that—so what do you think is new about the story line in these songs?

In the past, I've written mostly about heartbreak or pain that was caused by someone else and felt by me. On this album, I'm writing about more complex relationships, where the blame is kind of split fifty-fifty. I'm writing about looking back on a relationship and feeling a sense of pride even though it didn't work out, reminiscing on something that ended but you still feel good about it, falling in love with a city, falling in love with a feeling rather than a person. And I think there's actually sort of a realism to my new approach to relationships, which is a little more fatalistic than anything I used to think about them. I used to think that, you know, you find "the one." And it's happily ever after, and it's never a struggle after that. You have a few experiences with love and relationships, and you learn that that's not the case at all. Lots of things are gray areas and complicated situations, and even if you find the right situation relationship-wise, it's always going to be a daily struggle to make it work. So those are different themes that I don't think people have really seen in my lyrics before.

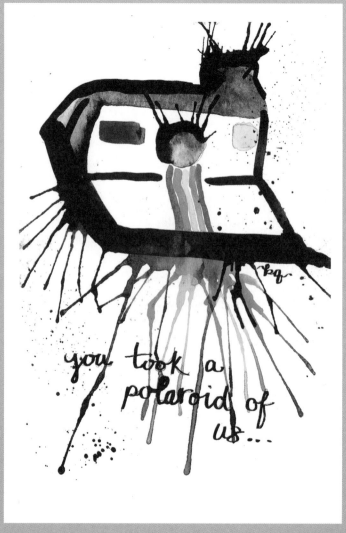

Is the song "Wildest Dreams" maybe an example of that?

That's actually a really good example of the way I go into relationships now. If I meet someone who I feel I have a connection with, the first thought I have is: "When this ends, I hope it ends well. I hope you remember me well." Which is not anything close to the way I used to think about relationships. It's that realization that it's the anomaly if something works out; it's not a given.

Are there new musical influences here? Some music reviewers have been mentioning the influence of Lorde or Lana Del Rey or maybe Robyn in some of your songs. What do you hear?

I hear Peter Gabriel and I hear Annie Lennox. Those were the two artists that I was listening to a lot when I was making this record. What Annie does is so interesting to me, and it's not something you could ever try to duplicate. But the way she conveys a thought, there's something really intense about it. And I think that's something I'll always aspire to.

And what about Peter Gabriel?

With Peter, that's an artist who has such incredible taste and such an incredible finger on the pulse of what would excite people, musically. What he was doing in the '80s was so ahead of its time, because he was playing with a lot of synth-pop sounds, but kind of creating sort of an atmosphere behind what he was singing, rather than a produced track. It was just kind of astonishing how he was able to do that. And then you see him in his later work, when he did that album full of modern-day covers. I mean, I just think that he's remarkable at giving people what they want, but they didn't think they wanted.

I want to ask you about the song "Out of the Woods." There's this intriguing lyric in there about some-

body "hitting the brakes too soon, twenty stitches in a hospital room." What's that about?

That line is in there because it's not only the actual, literal narration of what happened in a particular relationship I was in, it's also a metaphor. "Hit the brakes too soon" could mean the literal sense of, we got in an accident and we had to deal with the aftermath. But also, the relationship ended sooner than it should've because there was a lot of fear involved. And that song touches on a huge sense of anxiety that was, kind of, coursing through that particular relationship, because we really felt the heat of every single person in the media thinking they could draw up the narrative of what we were going through and debate and speculate. I don't think it's ever going to be easy for me to find love and block out all those screaming voices.

Not to ignore the broader metaphor here, but I am curious about the actual event. What happened?

I'll bet you are. That's kind of between us, between the two people who it happened to. I think I put it in the song knowing it was an evocative lyric. And it was almost like this very strange, subtle clue to the media that they don't know everything that happened in that relationship, and they don't know everything that happens in my life, and I can have something really major and traumatic happen to me and they don't know about it.

How rare are those moments? When you feel like you can do something

on your own that nobody will know about if you don't want them to?

It's strange because my life now is really abnormal. I get used to the fact that when I go out, there's gonna be a line of people wanting pictures on their phone, and there's gonna be crowds everywhere, even if there weren't crowds when I walked into a store. I realize the only privacy I'm really entitled to is when I'm in my own apartment or my own home, 'cause everything else is kind of—I'm looked at as sort

of public property. And there's nothing I can do about that perception except control my mental perspective on it, which is, I need to treat people well. I need to be grateful. I need to take pictures with people when they ask for one. So if I'm not in the mood to do that, I don't leave my house.

You also do, in a certain way, make yourself pretty accessible through social media, right? You've been posting Polaroids of your fans hold-

ing your new album on your Twitter feed. And you chose fans to invite over to your various homes to have listening parties for the new album— made them cookies, I think? You do have this funny dynamic of bringing people in a very managed way, in a very calculated way, and then having to figure out where the boundary is.

Well, yeah. I like for them to be in situations where they feel they can be themselves. Places they can't be themselves are when they're being pushed up against a barricade and there are thousands of them outside of a talk show, and they're trying to get a picture but they're screaming and everybody's freaking out. They can't necessarily be themselves when they're in these chaotic situations where fans usually find themselves.

I did this thing called the *1989 Secret Sessions* a few months ago, way before the album came out. I had spent months picking fans on Instagram, Tumblr, Twitter—people who had been so supportive and had tried and tried to meet me, had been to five shows or however many events but had never met me before. And so I picked these people. And in every single one of my houses in the US and my hotel room in London, I would invite eighty-nine people over to my living room, play them the entire album, tell them the stories behind it. And I'd say, you know, you can share your experience, but please keep the secrets about this album a secret. Let's not talk about lyrics before the album comes out. Let's not talk about song titles. And if you see anybody leaking music, please let us know.

We spent four hours together each

night, taking Polaroids and having a great time and giving them a chance to tell me their stories that they wanted to tell in their own time. Not being rushed. Not having to feel panic. And then they went back out into the world, and they kept those promises. They didn't talk about lyrics. They didn't spoil the secret for other fans. Two days before the album came out, it leaked online, and it was the first time I've ever had an album leak without it trending on Twitter—because my fans protected it. Anytime they'd see an illegal post of it, they'd comment, "Why are you doing this? Why don't you respect the value of art? Don't do this. We don't believe in this. This is illegal. This isn't fair. This isn't right." And it was wild seeing that happen.

What do you think other artists could take from that? You are having huge success with this album at a time when a lot of artists can't sell albums to the same extent as they used to.

Well I truly believe in the album. From the start of making one to the time it's finished, I focus on there being a visual theme and emotional DNA to it—including the physical package. I mean there has to be an incentive to go to a store, buy a CD. What people who are forecasting the downfall of the music industry don't think about is that there is still a huge percentage of the country who drive their kids to school every day and play a CD and listen to it with their kids—there's a CD in the CD player in their car. So I understand that the industry's changing and a lot of people are streaming. However, there are a lot of people who aren't, which is what this release

reflects. And so, in the physical CD, we've done an exclusive at Target that has three extra songs. It has three songwriting voice memos from my cell phone that were, you know, the initial rough rough ideas that I had; we put those on the album so people can have insight into the songwriting process. I have five sets of thirteen Polaroids from the album photo shoot that are in an envelope in the CD, and depending on what album they get, they'll get a different set of Polaroids with lyrics written on the

bottom of them. So it's very much an experience that's different than downloading the music itself. It's almost like this kind of collector's edition, the physical copy.

I can imagine other singers listening to this saying, "You know, that's great for Taylor Swift. She has the resources to do all that. It's great marketing, but it's not art—and the rest of us are on a different playing field. We just can't compete with that."

I think that the way that the music industry is changing so quickly, we can learn something from every big release, anything that connects with people. At the end of the day, this is a case-by-case scenario. If some other artist tries to have the same exact marketing campaign, tries to do secret living room sessions, that's great—if it makes a connection with their fans. If it doesn't make a connection with their fans, then it's not gonna work for them. And I think that what we need to start doing is catering our release plans to our own career, to our own fans, and really get in tune with them. I've been on the internet for hours every single night figuring out what these people want from me. And when it came time to put out an album, I knew exactly what to do.

Let's think back to when your first album came out, when you were sixteen. You'd moved to Nashville with your parents to try to make this dream of yours come true. You were writing really personal songs about young love and your broken heart. Can you go back to those songs now? I mean, is there any way you can tap into that sixteen-year-old girl—or even younger, when you wrote them?

I wrote my first album when I was fourteen and fifteen, so now we're going on ten years of making albums right now. The formula has never changed, in that I try to make an album that best represents the last two years of my life. People have essentially gotten to read my diary for the last ten years. I still write personal songs, and sometimes people like to put a very irritating, negative spin on that—as if I'm oversharing, as if it's too much information—when this has been the way I've lived my life and run my career the entire time. So I do think it's really important that I continue to give people an insight into what my life is actually like, even though it comes at a higher cost now.

If you were to go back and perform one of your earliest songs, a song like "Tim McGraw," say, from your first album, could you connect? Could you go back to the girl who wrote that song as a young teenager?

Yes and no. When I do a live show, there are certain songs fans really want to hear, and I'm gonna always play those songs. There's a song called "Love Story" that I wrote when I was seventeen. I'm going to be playing that as long as I'm playing concerts. And I can go back and I can connect to that song—because of the stories I've heard from fans saying, "We walked down the aisle to that song," or how special I feel it was when that was our first No. 1 worldwide hit. But "Tim McGraw," that song I don't really connect to as much. I connect to it in the form of nostalgia, but that was a song about a first love. I'm in a very different place in my life right now, and I think you can only hope to grow so much, emotionally, that you can't necessarily connect to wide-eyed fifteen-year-old ideas of love anymore.

I've been thinking about that song—I was listening to it today—because it feels to me like "Wildest Dreams" is in many ways the ten-years-older version of "Tim McGraw," of telling somebody, "Look back and remember me this way." In that song it's a

black dress and in the new song, I think it's a fancy dress.

Absolutely. I didn't think about that at all. The only difference is that "Tim McGraw," I wrote that song about a relationship that had already ended, hoping that he would remember me well. "Wildest Dreams" is about a relationship that is just beginning and already foreshadowing the ending of it.

Like I said, I am the mother of a twelve-year-old girl, and she loves your music. Her friends love your music. You have a huge platform among a very vulnerable, impressionable set of the population. And I wonder if you think about turning your lens outward, turning it away from the diary page, and sending a broader message to girls who would be really receptive to hearing about big ideas and the big world that's outside.

Like what kind of messages?

Well, other characters. I don't mean to minimize the effect of a love song or a pop song. But do you ever think about writing about other experiences, things that might turn girls away from themselves in a different way?

There's nothing that's gonna turn girls away from themselves at age twelve. I think that it's really important that I speak about things in interviews that I'm passionate about. I have brought feminism up in every single interview I've done because I think it's important that a girl who's twelve years old understands what that means and knows what it is to label yourself a feminist, knows what it is

to be a woman in today's society, in the workplace or in the media or perception. What you should accept from men, what you shouldn't, and how to form your own opinion on that. I think the best thing I can do for them is continue to write songs that do make them think about themselves and analyze how they feel about something and then simplify how they feel. Because, at that age—really at any age, but mostly that age—what can be so overwhelming is that you're feeling so many things at the same time that it's hard to actually understand what those emotions are, so it can turn to anxiety very quickly.

We are dealing with a huge self-esteem crisis. These girls are able to scroll pictures of the highlight reels of other people's lives, and they're stuck with the behind-the-scenes of their own lives. They wake up and they look at their reflection in the mirror, and they compare it to some filtered, beautiful photo of some girl who's really popular and seems like she has it all together. This is not what you and I had to deal with when we were twelve. It's so easy and readily available to compare yourself to others and to feel like you lose.

I'm twenty-four. I still don't feel like it's a priority for me to be cool, edgy, or sexy. When girls feel like they don't fit into those three themes, which are so obnoxiously thrust upon them through the media, I think the best thing I can do for those girls is let them know that this is what my life looks like. I love my life. I've never ever felt edgy, cool, or sexy. Not one time. And that it's not important for them to be those things. It's important for them to be imaginative, intelligent, hardworking, strong, smart, quick-witted, charming. All these things that I think have gone to the bottom of the list of priorities. I think that there are bigger themes I can be explaining to them, and I think I'm trying as hard as I possibly can to do that.

I'm really surprised to hear you say that you never feel cool or edgy or sexy. I mean, you spend a lot of time on red carpets. You go to fashion shows. Those three words don't fit into your view of yourself?

Not at all. I mean, going back to your daughter's age, I think a lot of our self-esteem and self-image is frozen in those formative years. And that was not a time in my life where I felt accepted or invited or like I belonged. And so I've kind of come into my own in that I no longer prioritize feeling those things.

You mentioned earlier you try to talk about feminism. What does feminism mean to you?

I mean, by my basic definition, it means that you hope for equal rights and opportunities for men and women.

And how does that play out in the music world that you're a part of? I mean, do you feel like that's not an issue for you anymore?

It's an issue every day that I read a headline that says, "Careful, guys. She'll write a song about you." Meanwhile, I have best friends who are male musicians and songwriters, who write songs about their girlfriends and their ex-girlfriends, and that joke is never made about them. As women in the public eye, our relationships are tallied up in ways that they aren't for men.

And if men have a lot of relationships that are tallied up, it's thought of as mischievous, cheeky. "Oh he's just out again with another girl." It's somehow done with a wink and a smile. But for us it's supposed to be shameful if we've had a few relationships that haven't worked out. When I open up a magazine and it says, "Who's the hotter mama: J-Lo or Beyoncé?" You don't see, "Who's the hotter dad: Matt Damon or Ben Affleck?" It just doesn't happen. And if we continue this perception that women should be compared to other women and there's a winner and a loser, we're doing ourselves a huge disservice as a society.

Taylor Swift, thanks so much for coming in to talk to us. I appreciate it.

Thank you; it's been good to talk to you, too. Tell your daughter hey for me. ♦

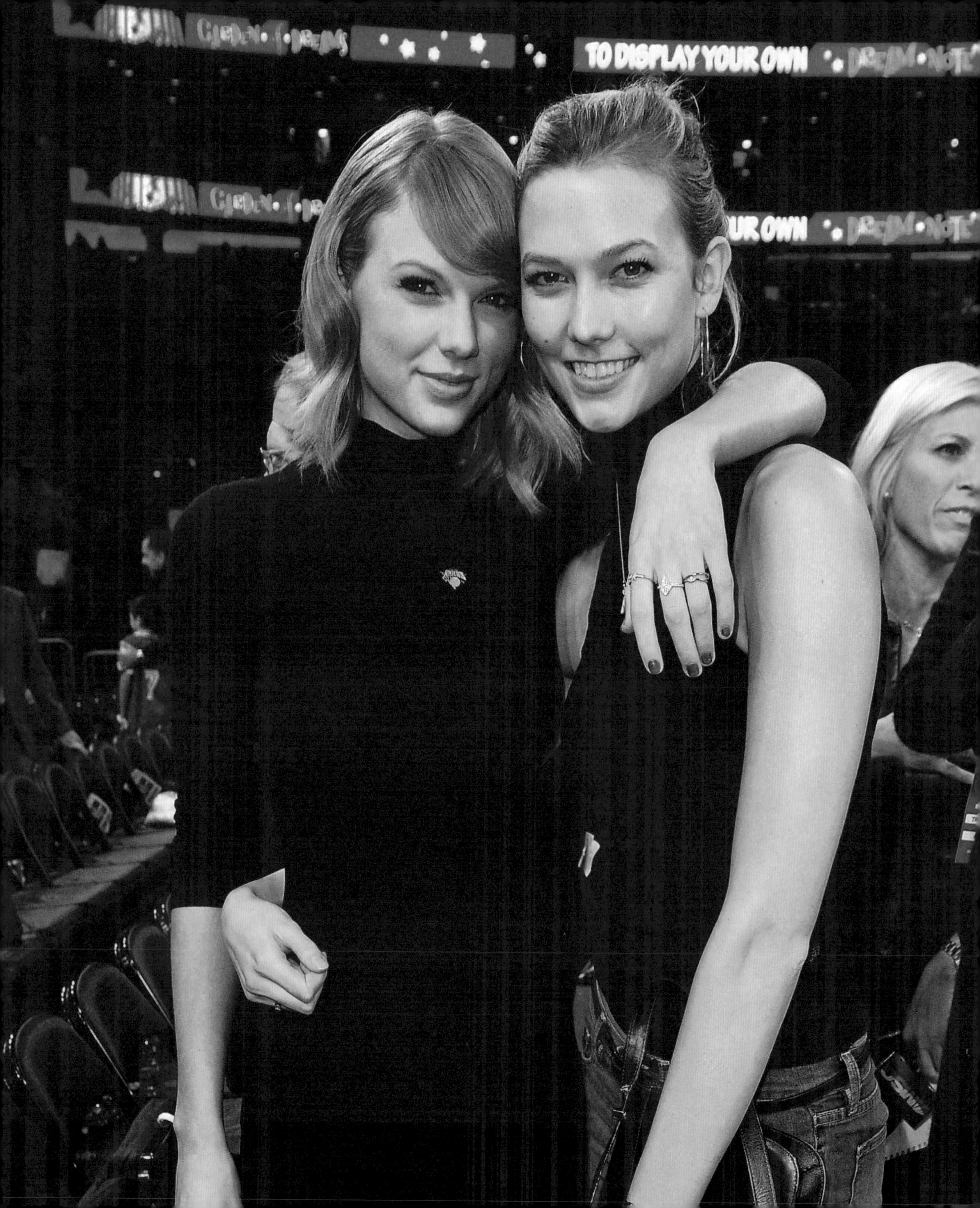
TO DISPLAY YOUR OWN

On the Road with Best Friends
TAYLOR SWIFT and *KARLIE KLOSS*

VOGUE, **FEBRUARY 2015** | JADA YUAN

One of the first things Taylor Swift did after moving from Nashville to her sprawling two-story penthouse in New York's Tribeca was cover a wall of her den with framed, blown-up Polaroids of the most important people in her life. "This is when me and Karlie first met," she says, pointing to a picture of her grinning and hugging model Karlie Kloss backstage at the 2013 Victoria's Secret Fashion Show, where Kloss walked the runway in pink underwear and giant psychedelic wings and Swift performed with Fall Out Boy. The caption, handwritten in Sharpie, reads BEST FRIENDS FOREVER VS2013 and feels rather prescient given how close the two have become over the past year or so, with a road trip to Big Sur (dreamily documented on Instagram), restaurant outings, shopping excursions, sleepovers, texting marathons, ModelFit and SoulCycle sessions, and a second joint VS outing late last year in London, where, as the pair walked side by side down the runway in black lace, they exchanged "Can you believe this?!" grins—two friends on top of the world.

Lena Dunham and Cara Delevingne also make the Polaroid wall, as does Swift's younger brother, Austin, twenty-two, a senior at Notre Dame, standing next to his sister in the matching red plaid adult onesies she bought for her family last Christmas. A Polaroid captioned SQUIRREL INVASION documents the first time Swift met Lorde (whom Swift calls by her given name, Ella), as the two set out for dinner at Shake Shack in Madison Square Park only to

be attacked by rodents. "We were taking these photos, and all of a sudden, like in a horror movie, there were squirrels sitting on our shoulders trying to eat our food," says Swift, reenacting the moment. "Perched, like parrots! They're like, 'We deserve French fries, and we're going to take them from you.'"

Swift click-clacks through her kitchen to her living room in black stiletto Louboutins, plops down on a burnt-orange velvet sofa, wiggles into a slouch, and props

those heels up on a tufted brown-leather ottoman. Everything in the apartment is rendered in velvet, leather, and wood in dark, rich earth and jewel tones, from her rosewood Steinway grand piano to her pool table (where VS models Behati Prinsloo and Lily Aldridge apparently proved themselves to be quite the sharks when they came over earlier in the week).

> "You get these **bursts of inspiration** right at the moment you're not expecting to. You just have to live your life, and hopefully you'll take the right risks."

It's two days before her twenty-fifth birthday, and Swift is brimming with the confidence of a young woman who's come into her own. It's been quite a year: she not only moved to New York, away from her family; she's also taken risks with her sound, stepping back from the world of country to embrace the throwback purity of '80s pop—with amazing success. "Blank Space," a defiant (and impossible-not-to-sing-along-to) response to the media's depiction of her as a crazed

man-eater, enjoyed a seven-week run atop the *Billboard* Hot 100. Swift also became the first female in the chart's fifty-six-year history to replace herself at No. 1 (her earlier single was the now-ubiquitous "Shake It Off"). Both are from her remarkable new album, *1989*, named after the year she was born, which has sold more than six million copies and become, along the way, the fastest-moving record of the past decade. *Saturday Night Live*, meanwhile, aired a parody commercial for Swiftamine, a drug to treat the epidemic of vertigo in adults who suddenly realize how much they love Taylor Swift. "People are finally starting to discuss her artistry—how she's on the level of some of the great all-time songwriters," says Jack Antonoff of the

band fun., who's cowritten several songs with Swift and likens her deeply personal storytelling to new chapters of a book the whole world wants to read. "The other day my grandmother was asking me about *1989*. We're all talking about it. In my lifetime, I haven't experienced that since Michael Jackson—that one artist who stands above and unites us all."

Swift has also remixed her personal life. For starters, the once-hopeless romantic who laid her emotions bare in songs about whirlwind love affairs and their aftermaths, like "We Are Never Ever Getting Back Together" (reportedly about Jake Gyllenhaal) or "I Knew You Were Trouble" and *1989*'s "Out of the Woods" (reportedly about Harry Styles), is push-

ing back at critics who have dismissed her as boy-obsessed. The tongue-in-cheek "Blank Space" video shows her stabbing a heart-shaped cake with a butcher's knife, setting a boyfriend's clothes on fire, and taking a golf club to his gorgeous silver sports car. Kloss, Dunham, and Delevingne, meanwhile, are part of a close-knit group of powerful women friends that Swift has been building over the past few years. Members also include Selena Gomez, whom Swift has known since they were both teenagers dating Jonas brothers; Jaime King, a kind of Earth Mother figure; and the Haim sisters, whom she met last fall. Devoting this much time to her female friendships started out as a reaction, Swift says, "to the way people were overreacting to my life. I was really irritated by the whole serial-dater play that people tried to make about me."

She responded by pulling the plug on her love life. "I just decided I wasn't willing to provide them that kind of entertainment anymore," she says. "I wasn't going to go out on dates and have them be allowed to take pictures and say whatever they wanted about our body language. I wasn't going to sit next to somebody and flirt with them for five minutes, because I know the next day he'll be rumored to be my boyfriend. I just kind of took the narrative back. It's unfortunate I had to do that. And it's unfortunate that now I have this feeling like if I were to open myself up to love, that would be a career weakness." Instead, Swift is emerging as a powerful figure for teenage girls and young women—someone who takes to task critics and bullies and, yes, men who've wronged her, and provides a shining example of a woman shaping her own destiny.

"This last year has felt very different than any other year of my life," Swift tells me. "I've felt more settled and unapologetic about who I am and what I stand for. I think that might be one of those symptoms of growing up and becoming your own person, and depending less on other people's opinions of you. I just hope that keeps going—because I'm liking it."

Swift is describing her philosophy about making friends—basically, wear 'em down till they like you—when Kloss sweeps into the apartment, a six-foot-one beam of sunshine. Though Swift and Kloss have known each other for only a year, their best-friendship, they tell me, was instantaneous. They're a striking pair, particularly now that Kloss's formerly tawny hair is blond. "When I did SNL they both came, and at the after-party it was so confusing to everyone, like these Amazon twins," says Dunham. "Taylor's so tall, Karlie's even taller, and together it's just surreal."

If Swift wears heels and Kloss wears flats, they're the same height. But today, Kloss has messed up the equation by wearing skintight Tamara Mellon leather leggings with boots attached. "All-in-one, baby," she says, showing them off as she walks the floor bearing a tin of her gluten- and dairy-free Karlie's Kookies, from her collaboration with Milk Bar.

"They're kind of the greatest thing I've ever seen," Swift gushes. "You look like Catwoman!" Kloss says they're custom-made, but she can hook Swift up with a pair. "They're pretty good," says Kloss, "but I can't take them back to St. Louis. When I go home, if I have even an ounce of New York attitude, my family's like, 'Nope, nope.' They don't let it happen." "They're like, 'You with your shoe pants, you leave those out-

side!'" says Swift, laughing. "You put on some real pants!"

Though Kloss seems to have a keen awareness of every stitch of fashion she has on her body, when I ask Swift who made her black knit tank dress, she has no idea.

Kloss notices the dress, too. "What is this? Alaïa?"

Swift turns to me for help. "I don't know—do I have a tag in there?" she asks,

lifting up her fluffy fair hair and leaning her back toward me. RVN, the tag reads. "My stylist put it in my closet," she says, burying her face in her hands.

Somehow, though, despite their differing levels of fashion expertise, they often tend to dress the same. "The other night I

came over," says Kloss, "and we were both going someplace from here, and we were both wearing black crop tops and high-waisted skirts. It's kind of getting weird."

"Black tights, hair done the same way," says Swift. "Just like, 'Ugh, be more annoying.' We couldn't possibly be.

"People had been telling us for years we needed to meet," she adds. "I remember makeup artists and hair people going, 'Doesn't she remind you of Karlie? God, she and Karlie would be best friends. They're the same. Karlie's such a good girl. She brings us cookies every time we do a shoot.'"

"Still do," says Kloss. As a teen she made them from scratch. Now she makes them professionally—Karlie's Kookies raises money for charities like FEED, Hurricane Sandy relief, and the CFDA. In addition to the baking venture, Kloss has studied at Harvard Business School (her boyfriend of two years, Joshua Kushner, an early investor in Instagram who recently cofounded the health-care start-up Oscar, is an alumnus) and is now learning computer coding.

A mutual friend, Kloss's fellow VS model Lily Aldridge, introduced her to Swift, "and we were just like, 'You. My friend. Now,'" says Swift. A few months later they saw each other again at an Oscars after-party, and Kloss suggested they do something spontaneous. "I'd been to Big Sur once before, and I was like, 'We should just do it,'" says Swift.

They walked beneath the redwoods, ran on the beach at sunset, took a picture hanging off the state-park sign with Kloss wearing Swift's sweater, the front of which spelled out GENIUS. "It's ironic, clearly," Swift is quick to add.

When I ask what they bonded over,

they shrug. "We're both normal people," says Kloss.

"We're real girls," says Swift, who, as if on cue, drops part of the cookie she's eating on her dress, picks it up, and eats it. "Five-second rule."

Swift is, by all accounts, an amazing person to be friends with. She cooks, she bakes, she does the dishes; she's a fantastic host, she gives great gifts. She has a collection of old-timey nightgowns that she and her friends wear while watching television and—technology aside—pretending they're living in frontier days. (Swift, who shows me a picture on her phone of her, Cara Delevingne, and Kendall Jenner all lying in her bed looking like *Little House on the Prairie*, inspired Dunham to start her own collection.) Every hang, it seems, ends in a dance party in her kitchen. Dunham calls her "the Betty Crocker of friendships" and says she's most impressed by how Swift always has time for the people she loves. "It's amazing to have a friend who's that busy and also so available," says Dunham. "Even if she's in Hong Kong on tour and I'm going through something, if I text her, I get an answer in two seconds. If something good happens to me—say, I get a nomination, or it's my birthday, or the day before my birthday, or my book comes out—I get a text from Taylor way before I get a text from my mom."

Some of Swift's eagerness to make friends probably comes from her having felt like an outcast while growing up. "I have lots of issues from school," she says. "You can tell, probably." Essentially, she left the small Pennsylvania town where she was made fun of for her music and formed a close community where she's now surrounded by people with similar talents and creative ambitions. It's a kind of high school do-over in which she can join whatever clique she wants—or decide to abolish cliques altogether. When I ask Swift which metaphorical lunch table she sits at now, she immediately gets what I'm saying. "I want to make the table as big as possible, and I want everyone to sit with me," she says.

The next day at *Billboard*'s Women in Music Awards luncheon (where Aretha Franklin sings her an impromptu "Happy Birthday" that Swift later tweets will take her decades to recover from), she sings along to every song, from performances to montages—she knows the words to everything. If female musicians are supposed to all be out for one another's blood, it's not happening on Swift's watch.

Every kid in the room who comes up to her, meanwhile, gets not only a selfie but a conversation. "Little children! I must attend to them," she says, apologizing for running off in the middle of a conversation. An eleven-year-old girl sheepishly tells Swift she's from New Jersey. "I spent the summers going down to the Jersey Shore," says Swift and poses for four apparently blurry selfies before gently taking the phone from the girl's hand. "You're really bad at this," Swift jokes, taking the photo herself. The girl is going to be at Z100's Jingle Ball concert, where Swift is the closing performer, that night. "I go on really late," Swift warns her. "Do you drink coffee?" The girl says she drinks Frappuccinos. "Okay," says Swift, "drink a

Frappuccino and you might be able to stay awake long enough to see me."

"New York City, it's good to be home! I'm Taylor," says Swift. It's shortly before midnight, and she's standing onstage at Madison Square Garden addressing a screaming crowd of seventeen thousand as if she's talking to one of her girlfriends on the phone. Dressed in red plaid high-waisted pants and a matching crop top, her hair feathered like Blondie-era Debbie Harry, she blazes through four hits before announcing that she has officially turned twenty-five. "I know why you choose music—it's because you want to escape from haters and frenemies," Swift tells the crowd, instructing us to exchange nods

of solidarity with our neighbors. "This is the last song of the night," she continues. "No one's gonna judge you for how you dance during this song. New York City, are you ready?" The place goes nuts.

Swift returns to her apartment well past midnight, orders sushi, and sets up a makeshift photo booth to host what seems like every famous person in music. She has invited all her fellow performers (Iggy Azalea, Charli XCX, Ariana Grande, Sam Smith, Nick Jonas), along with other friends ranging from Kloss to Abigail Anderson—Swift's best friend since freshman year of high school in suburban Hendersonville, Tennessee—to Justin Timberlake and Jay Z and Beyoncé. "I have, like, twenty different people flying in," Swift had told me the day before. "My friends are staying in every room." Her mother, Andrea, however—who flew in from Nashville earlier laden with decorations now draped over mirrors and mantels, with every window in the place (I lose count at fifteen) garlanded as well—isn't there. "I think a twenty-fifth birthday, no mother should be there," Andrea told me. "You need to know when to step away."

The next time I catch up with Swift, she's still in her PJs at eleven fifteen on a perfect sunny January morning at her house in Beverly Hills. In the month since I saw her turn twenty-five she's become the proud owner of a bejeweled necklace (a birthday gift from Dunham) bearing the image of her kitten Olivia; danced like crazy with Beyoncé and the Haim sisters at a Justin Timberlake concert in Brooklyn; bought the shirt off Hugh Jackman's back (giving $6,000 to the Broadway Cares / Equity Fights AIDS charity in the process) while seeing him perform on Broadway with her family; sent out a large batch of gift packages to her fans, one of which included a Swift painting of flowers and a check for $1,989 to help pay off a student loan; and rung in the New Year onstage in Times Square in front of a million people live and a billion more on TV and the Web. Since she's been out West, though, she's been doing what she can to catch up with friends, including "a lot of cooking nights," hiking with Lorde, and wandering around Catalina Island eating ice cream with her girlfriends and her dad. When Lorde sounded stressed about going to the Golden Globes, Swift showed up in support wearing a bright-yellow dress (in honor of Lorde's

"Real friends are hard to find—and Taylor's a **real friend**. There's nothing better."

nominated song, "Yellow Flicker Beat"). "We just turned it into a girls' night," Swift says over the phone.

For both today and the foreseeable future, though, Swift is going to be all business getting ready for the 1989 world tour, which kicks off May 5 in Tokyo. There's a set list to finalize, and wardrobe and production design to approve, and choreography to learn. She insists she's not nearly as awkward a dancer as she pretends to be in the "Shake It Off" video: "If I get serious about choreography, I will learn it and I'll do it correctly—most of the time," she says.

Looking back on what's been both a tumultuous and momentous time in her life, Swift says she and her family "had a lot of moments where we would look at each other and say, 'Wow—I can't believe people got it.' You only hope for things like this." She's been trying to take it all as it comes. "I don't get so caught up in the work that I don't appreciate the crazy, incredible, astonishing, joyous success that's happened," she says. "Putting pressure on yourself is good, but putting unnecessary stress on yourself is bad—so I don't worry that I haven't started the next record yet. I don't worry that I don't know what it's going to be. I'm not worried that I have absolutely no timetable as to when it needs to be done. It could be two years from now; it could be three, it could be four. Or it could be one. You get these bursts of inspiration right at the moment you're not expecting to. You just have to live your life, and hopefully you'll take the right risks."

Kloss, for her part, has been maintaining the kind of schedule that would seem to require its own air-traffic controller. After a short break back home in St. Louis, she's been back and forth to Paris twice in early January alone as part of her new job as a L'Oréal Paris spokesperson; to the Florida Keys for a Bruce Weber shoot; and to L.A. and Paris again for L'Oréal. Next up: back to L.A. for the Oscars before ramping up for Fashion Weeks in New York, Milan, and Paris. "In moderation it can be really fun," says Kloss, who's cut the sixty shows she used to walk at the start of her career down to a fraction of that. "For me, runway is an opportunity to perform."

She's also practically bursting to tell me some big news: she's been accepted to NYU's Gallatin School of Individualized Study. (NYU alum Christy Turlington Burns wrote her letter of recommendation.) "I was waiting for the mail to arrive every single day," she says. "It's something that I've wanted to do for a very long time." Kloss doesn't yet know what she'll study; for now, she's just excited to be taking classes. "I'll still be working full-time," she says. "I'm incredibly ambitious and have lots of goals within my career that I'm not slowing down on anytime soon."

Swift says she and her friends don't talk much about work. "The fun thing about my friends is that they don't necessarily know a lot about what I do business-wise," she says. The first time Kloss ever saw Swift pick up a guitar and noodle around on it was during the photo shoot for this story. "I'm not one of those singers who's always like, 'Look at me!'" says Swift. "I'm not the person who grabs the guitar at a party and wants all the attention. I have attention on me enough, so I want my friends to just like me because we have things in common rather than me sitting in a corner being like, 'Listen to this song that I wrote about my life!'"

No matter how busy they are, though, Swift and Kloss continue to make time for each other. Swift recently had Kloss over to her place for a night of cooking pasta with model Martha Hunt, stylist Ashley Avignone, and Tavi Gevinson. A few days later that same group went to dinner at Ralph Lauren's restaurant, the Polo Bar, in midtown. ("The French fries were delicious," says Kloss.)

Kloss says that bringing together disparate women from different industries may be Swift's most unsung talent. "I've met a lot of really great girls through Taylor. She's incredible at connecting people who might not normally meet. We're all in different jobs, but we've become strong friends who are there for each other—a sisterhood of girls, a support team. But we're also just normal twenty-something girls, and I think you have to have people that you can be that with. You know, real friends are hard to find—and Taylor's a real friend. There's nothing better." ♦

ZAINUB AMIR

STUDENT, 20, NEW YORK

My first memory of Taylor is from 2008. I heard a radio host introduce her as a new artist and I thought her name was "Taylor Swiss." I kept thinking, "What kind of name is *that*?" Then I came across the "Love Story" video and fell completely and utterly in love with her music and her talent. I was also captivated by the way she talked in interviews. I related to her so much that I knew she'd be an amazing role model.

My favorite show was her first night at Gillette Stadium on the *1989* tour when she brought out Walk the Moon and had the whole crowd jump in unison. A close second was on the *Red* tour at MetLife Stadium in 2013. That was when I got to meet her for the first time. Her mother saw me and took me on a private backstage tour.

I've been running a fan account called @SimplySFans since 2010. Taylor invited me to her last secret session the day the *1989* album came out, and when she saw me in the crowd during "Out of the Woods" she smiled and sang to me and gave me a little head nod like, "You made it."

Afterward, during the actual party, everyone was mingling and she saw me and opened her arms wide and said, "Hey, buddy!" I think I must have looked shocked that she remembered who I was. She said, "Duh, Zainub, I invited everyone here. Of course I know who you are!" Then she took me across the room by the hand and we took a funny photo under a tablecloth where she exclaimed, "Simply S for *sass*!" She also said that she related to my posts on social media and some of the selfies I'd posted.

It's impossible to pick a favorite song. If you made me, I'd probably say "Change." It got me through a lot during my teen years.

I was an outcast for most of middle school and high school. I went through being bullied. I didn't know my place

or who I was meant to be. But I always knew I had a friend in Taylor Swift.

The album I find myself going back to the most is *1989*. That's probably because it's the most recent. But a lot of times I find myself going back to *Red*. It all depends on what I'm going through in life and how I feel. I think that's her most magical quality: you relate so much that you can dive into her diary and go back as if it were your own.

Her most romantic songs are easily "Wildest Dreams" and "You Are in Love." Easily.

My favorite car song is "New Romantics"—but honestly, you can make any moment memorable out of her songs.

My parents think I'm crazy because I'm always ready to defend Taylor on anything. She's become someone I see as a friend, and I'm here for her no matter what.

It makes me incredibly happy to imagine Taylor becoming a leader and a voice for women everywhere—to spark change, to get involved with the world outside her own field just like Audrey Hepburn did and Emma Watson does. To just go out there and use her power to change the world.

She taught me that being kind and genuine goes a long way. She also made me see that you are *not* the opinion of someone who doesn't know you. I went through a lot of different friends (no longer friends) who thought just because I'm kind and optimistic that I had to be fake—that there was something wrong about me because I would never look down on someone or be rude to someone. After I left those people behind, I've started to blossom into the person I'm meant to be, following my passions and achieving so much more than I would have if I still paid attention to the opinions of other people. Thanks, Taylor!

My life would be so much worse if I'd never discovered Taylor Swift.

NO BLANK SPACE, BABY

Taylor Swift Is the Soul of Ryan Adams

NPR, SEPTEMBER 2015 | ANN POWERS

Perhaps the least surprising thing a popular musician can do in 2015 is to interrupt the flow of her own work with a left-field cover song. It's been nearly three decades since art rockers Sonic Youth briefly refashioned itself as a Madonna tribute band, and even longer since those slaphappy nights on the college-bar touring circuit when the Replacements would pull out forbidden gems by Kiss and Aerosmith. Those moves said something about indie music's tendency to self-limit: they revealed the snobbery inherent in subcultural opposition and questioned the scene's authenticity-fetishizing judgments against female-driven mainstream pop or showy classic rock. Risking a reinterpretation of "Into the Groove" or "Black Diamond," these groups reminded young aesthetes that pop pleasure can be as freeing, in its own way, as underground discernment.

Now, pop is critically cool, the mainstream music industry has flattened, and artists use whimsical covers as branding devices, not bold statements. It happens in every corner: country star Sam Hunt covers Mariah Carey to prove his '90s R&B bona fides; divo Sam Smith dares a little Whitney Houston to cement his reputa-tion as a vocal powerhouse. A firmly indie artist like Empress Of turns to Katy Perry's oeuvre, not as a joke, but to show that today's biggest hits are on a continuum with her more experimental efforts. This is a natural progression for a culture whose ruling metaphor is the network, within which every connection is ostensibly equal. It's also reflective of a musical generation that grew up with hip-hop, which puts redeployment of others' music at the heart of the creative act, through sampling and verbal interpolations.

When Ryan Adams first announced his song-for-song reinterpretation of Taylor Swift's mainstream-defining album *1989*, it seemed that this was just another somewhat lighthearted move across today's musical landscape. But an actual listen to the self-directed singer-songwriter's take on the pop queen has a headier impact. The thoroughness of this project, Adams's obvious care for the material, and his clear thinking about how to approach it, have made this *1989* not just another eyebrow-raising stunt, but a means of exposing the ways the old prejudices still hold—even within this poptimist moment. It also hints that to truly counter those prejudices requires deep adjustments to the way we listen.

Adams has made it clear that he considers Swift a peer and has forged a deep emotional connection to her songs. "They're very vulnerable and brave and all the stuff I love about Hüsker Dü and Bob Mould's records," he told *Grantland* music writer Steven Hyden, deliberately comparing the twenty-four-year-old Swift to an irreproachable indie rock elder. Having grown into a complex formalist himself—adept in his home style of alt-country, all varieties of rock, and even with radio-ready pop—Adams came to *1989* to recharge (having previously done so with other inspirations, like the Strokes or Oasis.) His intention matters: it turns him away from cynicism and toward an introspection that can't be laughed off. In the end, though, whatever private need Adams fulfilled by focusing on the versatility of Swift's compositions is less important than how this *1989* causes listeners to realize exactly what still so often defines pop-musical meaningfulness.

It's not necessarily musical innovation—*1989* sparkles with that, though its hooky flourishes only further alienate the haters. Working primarily with producer Max Martin, Swift experimented with all kinds of beats and studio elements in embellishing her conversational composi-

tions. Adams, on the other hand, returns to a relatively tight rock framework, the one that defined the dominance of artists like Bruce Springsteen, Tom Petty, and U2 during the same 1980s blockbuster era that, for Swift, meant the Eurythmics, Phil Collins, and Cher. His version of "Shake It Off" does away with handclaps and kiddie rap, instead mimicking the Boss's moody ballad "I'm on Fire." His cracking tenor on "This Love" is pure contemplative Bono. In a nice contemporary twist, his pulling back on the beat on "I Wish You Would" makes it sound even more like a song by Swift's friends and contemporaries Haim—an all-female band that bends gender by riding on the majestic chemtrails of blockbuster rock. And when Adams invokes his own past, in slightly twangy takes like "Wildest Dreams," he's drawing a thread between rock's modern patriarchs and his own generation, reminding listeners that even upstarts like Mould, Paul Westerberg, and Adams himself benefited from the enduring rock truism that testosterone enables seriousness.

This is the assumption that Adams's 1989 (perhaps unintentionally) feeds and finally complicates. Women artists have, for much of the past decade, defined the face of pop, but they still aren't trusted as custodians of its voice. Key figures like Swift, Beyoncé, Rihanna, and Perry constantly face accusations of not truly governing their own creative processes—of only cowriting their songs, hiring others to determine their images and stage shows, and dwelling in the shallows of romance instead of addressing more serious subjects, the way blockbuster rock's

titans did. (In songs like "Dancing in the Dark," one supposes.) Within what's left of Rock, women are gaining footing. Yet even greats-in-the-making, like Annie Clark of St. Vincent, remain caught within a defined margin: the one female performer on the festival main stage, representing a supposedly limited perspective. The idea that male experience and expression defines our norms, even at the level of basic communication, and the female always enters the conversation as an afterthought, in protest, or as exceptional, remains a buried reality in popular music.

Adams has made it clear that **he considers Swift a peer** and has forged a deep emotional connection to her songs.

In Taylor Swift's songs, though, the female perspective is the rule. She focuses endlessly on the struggle to maintain both personal independence and intimate connections; her language unfurls in the fits and starts of interrupted talk; her songs build to struggled-for climaxes the way a young woman, taught to behave, builds toward speaking her mind. A man singing a Swift song must perform the kind of masquerade that women have done for the entirety of rock: tucking in his privilege and unconsidered bluster, taking on language and an affect that's been endlessly condemned as frivolous and weak. Adams does this not as drag, but to think differently about human experience. Take "Blank Space" and Swift's invocation of a kind of emptiness: Beneath the song's

overt message of romantic need lies a deeper one about how women are expected to let men construct the meaning of their lives. But Swift doesn't do that. She speaks of herself, for herself.

Speaking through Swift's voice, Adams recalls how those other supposedly definitive male rockers also claimed something hidden from the feminine. Bruce Springsteen loves girl groups; he recently wrote two songs for Darlene Love's new album, produced by his longtime guitarist Steven Van Zandt. Tom Petty's whole 1980s output can be viewed as a buried dialogue with his friend and vocal doppelganger Stevie Nicks. Nicks's former lover Don Henley forged the Eagles sound by working with Linda Ronstadt. Yet most histories of rock—and frankly, most fans' own presumptions—place these female figures on a second tier.

Adams's 1989 recognizes a rock lineage born of a woman. He's not legitimizing Swift's work—he's figuring out how her voice can validate and include his. Some critics have derided his arrangements for being overly somber, doing away with the playful inventiveness of Swift and Martin, so fundamental to today's genre-dissolving pop palette. Others have pointed out that Swift, the most successful musical figure of her generation, hardly needs a midlevel rock moptop to lend her gravitas. These are valid criticisms. Yet his execution makes them moot, because whether he intended to do so or not, he always keeps her words, her worldview, her voice at the center. Taylor Swift is not a blank slate that Ryan Adams writes upon. She is his album's defining element. And that is a change that women musicians have deserved for a very long time. ♦

TENAY BARKER

STUDENT, 19, TEXAS

If I ever meet Taylor I'll probably faint. When I fangirl, I fangirl all the way.

My favorite car song is "Shake It Off." Just before I started my senior year of high school, my parents got me a new car. This was no ordinary new car. This was my *dream* car. The first time I took it for a drive, the first song that came on the radio was "Shake It Off."

My favorite album is *Red*. It speaks to me on a spiritual level. I love Taylor's use of the color red to symbolize hatred and anger, love and romance. It's so simple and so complex. You can feel it in every song on the album.

I try to learn as many Taylor songs as I can on my ukulele. The first one I ever learned was "Our Song."

If I were to give her a gift it would be a performance of the mash-up I created of her biggest hits. I don't have Taylor's angelic pipes, but maybe she could sing while I play my ukulele.

I was so disappointed when I didn't get tickets to the *1989* tour when it came to Texas. HOW COOL ARE THOSE FREAKING LIGHT-UP WRISTBANDS EVERYONE GOT!?!?

It makes me mad when people say that Taylor's songs are all about the same thing. Yes, a lot of them are about relationships, but no relationship is the same, and there are so many aspects to love that you can't just write one song about it.

> "If I ever meet Taylor **I'll probably faint.** When I fangirl, I fangirl all the way."

My favorite music video of Taylor's is the one for "Bad Blood." It looks amazing and has a lot of other awesome, fierce women. I think we can all agree that it should be turned into an actual movie.

Taylor's awkward dancing cracks me up. I can relate.

The media's coverage of Taylor annoys me because they always focus on who she's dating instead of what she does. Why aren't there more stories about how she goes to hospitals to visit kids or gives her fans Christmas presents? She is such a humble person and so much more than what the media says about her.

My parents surprised me with tickets to the *Red* tour when I turned sixteen. All of my friends and family were in on the secret but didn't tell me. They were placing bets on whether I would scream or cry first.

That concert was the most magical experience of my life. I'll never forget it. Thanks, Mom. (For the millionth time.)

She's taught me to voice my opinions and not let anyone silence my voice. She's lived her life without conforming to anyone's ideas or desires. That's what I love most about her: "The haters gonna hate, hate, hate, hate, hate / Baby, I'm just gonna shake, shake, shake, shake, shake, I shake it off."

TAYLOR SWIFT on "Bad Blood," Kanye West, and How People Interpret Her Lyrics

GQ, **NOVEMBER 2015** | CHUCK KLOSTERMAN

That's a pap," she says as we leave the restaurant, pointing toward an anonymous gray car that looks like the floor model in an auto dealership specializing in anonymous gray cars. Her security detail suggests that it's probably not a paparazzo because there's no way a paparazzo could find us at such an unglamorous, unassuming establishment. But as with seemingly every other inference she has ever made, Taylor Swift is ultimately proven right. The guy in the gray car is taking her picture. This annoys her, but just barely.

It's August in Southern California. We crawl into the back of a massive Toyota and start driving to Swift's West Coast residence, located in a rural enclave of Beverly Hills. The gray car trails us through Franklin Canyon. Swift whips out her phone and starts showing me images from the video shoot for "Wildest Dreams," including a clip of a giraffe licking her face. She has more photos on her phone than any person I've ever met. "I wanted this video to be about the making of a 1950s movie being filmed on location in Africa," she explains. Swift came up with the concept after reading a book by Ava Gardner and Peter Evans, *The Secret Conversations*. Her premise for the video (costarring Clint Eastwood's son) is that—since social media did not exist in the '50s—it would be impossible for actors not to fall in love if they were isolated together in Africa, since there would be no one else to talk to.

> If you don't take Swift seriously, you don't take **contemporary music** seriously.

We chat a little about Ryan Adams and a little about books. Swift mentions that she wrote a non-autobiographical novel when she was fourteen, titled *A Girl Named Girl*, and that her parents still have it. I ask her what it was about, assuming she will laugh. But her memory of the plot is remarkably detailed. (It's about a mother who wants a son but instead has a girl.) If she released it today, it would immediately be the best-selling YA novel in the nation. When she was about that same age, Swift's family moved from Pennsylvania to Nashville, to jump-start her music career. I ask what she imagines might have happened if they'd never moved and if she'd never become an artist. "I would still be involved with music in my spare time," she says. "But I would have gone to college, and I would probably be involved with a form of business where words and ideas are at the forefront. Such as marketing." She returns to her phone and starts scrolling for an old voice memo she sent to Jack Antonoff of the band Bleachers while they were cowriting songs for *1989*. Antonoff's nickname for Swift is Dead Tooth, a reference to a minor dental mishap. Just as she tells me this, her cell phone rings. The display panel says the incoming call is from J TIMB. "Oh, my God. Justin Timberlake?" Her surprise does not seem artificial. "Can I take this?"

She takes the call. The volume on her phone is loud enough for me to intermittently hear both sides of the conversation. Swift explains that she's driving to her house, but that she can't actually stay there because contractors are renovating almost every room. "Have you ever seen the movie *The Money Pit*?" asks Timberlake. She has not, so Timberlake provides a capsule review. He has a four-month-old baby at home and is constantly tired, yet he can't fall sleep. He asks Swift for advice on sleeping. Swift tells the driver to pull over to the shoulder of the road, since she keeps losing reception as we drive through the canyon. The paparazzo in the gray car casually passes, having not-so-casually followed us for at least five miles.

The conversation lasts almost fifteen minutes (which is a little weird, since I'm just sitting there beside her, openly taking notes). "You're never going to get old," Swift assures Timberlake. "That's scientific fact. That's medical." Even her sarcasm is aspirational. Eventually JT tells her the reason he's calling is because he wants to perform the song "Mirrors" with her on the last night of her upcoming five-date stand at Staples Center. (Late in every concert, Swift brings a surprise guest onstage.) She reacts to this news the way a teenage girl in Nebraska would react if suddenly informed that a paternity test had revealed Taylor Swift was her biological sister.

When she ends the call, Swift looks at me and says, "This is so crazy. This is so crazy." She repeats that phrase four times, each time with ascending volume.

Now, inside my skull, I am thinking one thought: This is not remotely crazy. It actually seems like the opposite of crazy. Why *wouldn't* Justin Timberlake want to perform with the biggest entertainer in America, to an audience of fifteen thousand people who will lose their collective mind the moment he appears? I'd have been much more surprised if he'd called to turn her down. But then I remember that Swift is twenty-five years old, and that her entire ethos is based on experiencing (and interpreting) how her insane life would feel if she were exactly like the type of person who'd buy a ticket to this particular concert. She has more perspective than I do. Every extension of who she is

and how she works is (indeed) "so crazy," and what's even crazier is my inability to recognize just how crazy it is.

So Taylor Swift is right again.

If you don't take Swift seriously, you don't take contemporary music seriously. With the (arguable) exceptions of Kanye West and Beyoncé Knowles, she is the most significant pop artist of the modern age. The scale of her commercial supremacy defies parallel—she's sold one million albums in a week three times, during an era when most major artists are thrilled to move five hundred thousand albums in a year. If a record as comparatively dominant as *1989* had actually existed in the year 1989, it would have surpassed the sales of *Thriller*. There is no demographic she does not tap into, which is obviously rare. But what's even more atypical is how that ubiquity is critically received. Swift gets excellent reviews, particularly from the most significant arbiters of taste. (A 2011 *New Yorker* piece conceded that Swift's reviews are "almost uniformly positive.") She has never gratuitously sexualized her image and seems pathologically averse to controversy. There's simply no antecedent for this kind of career: a cross-genre, youth-oriented, critically acclaimed colossus based entirely on the intuitive songwriting merits of a single female artist. It's as if mid-period Garth Brooks was also early Liz Phair, minus the hat and the swearing. As a phenomenon, it's absolutely new.

And this, somewhat predictably, creates a new set of problems.

Even within the most high-minded considerations of Swift's music, there is inevitably some analysis (or speculation) about her personal life. She's an utterly credible musician who is consumed as a tabloid personality. Very often (and not

without justification), that binary is attributed to ingrained biases against female performers. But it's more complicated than that. Swift writes about her life so directly that the listener is forced to think about her persona in order to fully appreciate what she's doing creatively. This is her greatest power: an ability to combine her art and her life so profoundly that both spheres become more interesting to everyone, regardless of their emotional investment in either.

Swift clearly knows this is happening. But she can't directly admit it, because it's the kind of thing that only works when it seems accidental. She's careful how she describes the process, because you don't become who she is by describing things carelessly.

Even the most serious critics inevitably discuss the more tabloid aspects of your life. Is this valid? Does the fact that you write about yourself in such a confessional style require intelligent people to look at your music through that lens?

I don't feel there is any injustice when people expand beyond my music and speculate on who certain songs might be about. I've never named names, so I feel like I still have a sense of power over what people say—even if that *isn't* true, and even if I don't have any power over what people say about me. The fact that I've never confirmed who those songs are about makes me feel like there is still one card I'm holding. So if you're going to look at your life and say, "I get to play sold-out football stadiums all over the world. I get to call up my favorite artists and ask them to perform with me, and most of the time they say yes. I get to be on the cover of this magazine"—this is all because I write songs about my own life. So I would feel a little strange complaining about how it's covered.

But I'm not asking if it's fair or unfair, or if the downside is worth the upside. I'm asking from an aesthetic perspective: Is thinking about your real life an essential part of appreciating your music? Could your music be enjoyed the same way in a vacuum, even if no one knew anything else about you?

"Shake It Off" is one of my most successful songs, and that has nothing directly, intricately, pointedly personal in it. No one really says I stay out too late. I just thought it sounded good.

Have you ever stopped yourself from writing a fictional lyric because you feared it would be incorrectly applied to your nonfictional life?

No. Some of the things I write about on a song like "Blank Space" are satire. You take your creative license and create things that are larger than life. You can write things like "I get drunk on jealousy but you'll come back each time you leave, 'cause darling I'm a nightmare dressed like a daydream." That is not my approach to relationships. But is it cool to write the narrative of a girl who's crazy but seductive but glamorous but nuts but manipulative? That was the character I felt the media had written for me, and for a long time I felt hurt by it. I took it personally. But as time went by, I realized it was kind of hilarious.

It's impossible for an artist to control how she is perceived. But an artist can anticipate those perceptions, which is almost as good. "A nuanced sense of humor does not translate on a general scale," Swift says,

"and I knew that going in. I knew some people would hear 'Blank Space' and say, 'See, we were right about her.' And at that point, I just figure if you don't get the joke, you don't deserve to get the joke."

There's a long tradition of musicians expressing (or pretending to express) a degree of disinterest in how they are metabolized by the culture. They claim to ignore their own reviews while feigning a lack of discernment about what their audience wants or expects, since these are things that cannot be manipulated. Swift is not like this. She has an extrinsic focus that informs her creative process. From her perspective, not tracking how people view your work feels stranger than the alternative.

"I went through a few years where I just never went online and never looked at blogs," she recalls. "This was around 2013, when the only thing anyone wanted to write about me was about me and some guy. It was really damaging. You're thinking, 'Everybody goes on dates when they're twenty-two. It's fine, right?' Nope. Not when you're in this situation, and everything you do is blown out of proportion and expanded upon. And all of a sudden, there's an overriding opinion that doesn't accurately reflect how you actually live your life. So I didn't go online for a year and a half. I actually forgot my Instagram password. But now I check in and see what's happening. In 2015, that stuff does matter. Because if enough people say the same thing about me, it becomes fact in the general public's

mind. So I monitor what people say about me, and if I see a theme, I know what that means. I've had it happen twice before. In 2010, it was 'She's too young to get all these awards. Look how annoying she is when she wins. Is she even good?' And then in 2013, it was 'She just writes songs about guys to get revenge. She's boy-crazy. She's a problematic person.' It will probably be something else again this year."

How you view this level of consciousness is proportional to how you feel about Swift as a public figure. There is a perpetual sense that nothing about her career is accidental and that nothing about her life is unmediated. These are not unusual thoughts to have about young mainstream stars. But what's different with Swift is her autonomy. There is no Svengali directing her career; there is no stage mother pushing her toward the spotlight. She is in total control of her own constructed reality. If there was a machine that built humans out of positive millennial stereotypes, Swift would be its utopian creation.

"I used to watch *Behind the Music* every day," she says. (Her favorite episode was the one about the Bangles.) "When other kids were watching normal shows, I'd watch *Behind the Music*. And I would see these bands that were doing so well, and I'd wonder what went wrong. I thought about this a lot. And what I established in my brain was that a lack of self-awareness was always the downfall. That was always the catalyst for the loss of relevance and the loss of ambition and the loss of great art. So self-awareness has been such a huge part of what I try to achieve on a daily basis. It's less about reputation management and strategy and vanity than it is about trying to desperately preserve self-awareness, since that seems to be the

first thing to go out the door when people find success."

The advantage of this self-focused fixation is clear. Swift is allowed to make whatever record she wants, based on the reasonable argument that she understands her specific space in the culture more deeply than anyone around her. The making of *1989* is a prime example: She claims everyone at her label (the Nashville-based Big Machine) tried to persuade her not to make a straightforward pop album. She recounts a litany of arguments with various label executives over every possible detail, from how much of her face would appear on the cover to how cowriter Max Martin would be credited in the liner notes.

As far as I can tell, Swift won every one of these debates.

"Even calling this record *1989* was a risk," she says. "I had so many intense conversations where my label really tried to step in. I could tell they'd all gotten together and decided, 'We gotta talk some sense into her. She's had an established, astronomically successful career in country music. To shake that up would be the biggest mistake she ever makes.' But to me, the safest thing I could do was take the biggest risk. I know how to write a song. I'm not confident about a lot of other aspects of my life, but I know how to write a song. I'd read a review of [2012's] *Red* that said it wasn't sonically cohesive. So that was what I wanted on *1989*: an umbrella that would

go over all of these songs, so that they all belonged on the same album. But then I'd go into the label office, and they were like, 'Can we talk about putting a fiddle and a steel-guitar solo on 'Shake It Off' to service country radio?' I was trying to make the most honest record I could possibly make, and they were kind of asking me to be a little disingenuous about it: 'Let's capitalize on both markets.' No, let's not. Let's choose a lane."

Like almost all famous people, Swift has two ways of speaking. The first is the way she talks when she's actively shaping the interview—optimistic, animated, and seemingly rehearsed (even when that's impossible). The second is the way she talks when she cares less about the way the words are presented and more about the message itself (chin slightly down, brow slightly furrowed, timbre slightly deeper). The first way is how she talks when she's on television; the second is unequivocal and less animatronic. But she oscillates between the two styles fluidly, because either (*a*) this dissonance is less intentional than it appears or (*b*) she can tell I'm considerably more interested in anything delivered in the second style.

Late in our lunch, I mention something that happened several years ago: by chance, I'd found myself having dinner with a former acquaintance of Swift's who offhandedly described her as "calculating." This is the only moment during our interview when Swift appears remotely flustered. She really, really hates the word *calculating*. She despises how it has become tethered to her iconography and believes the person I met has been the singular voice regurgitating this categorization. As she explains these things, her

> "You can be accidentally successful for three or four years. Accidents happen. But **careers take hard work.**"

speech does not oscillate from the second mode. "Am I shooting from the hip?" she asks rhetorically. "Would any of this have happened if I was? In that sense, I do think about things before they happen. But here was someone taking a positive thing—the fact that I think about things and that I care about my work—and trying to make that into an insinuation about my personal life. Highly offensive. You can be accidentally successful for three or four years. Accidents happen. But careers take hard work."

Here we see Swift's circuitous dilemma: Any attempt to appear less calculating scans as even more calculated. Because Swift's professional career has unspooled with such precision, it's assumed that her social life is no less premeditated. This even applies to casual, non-romantic relationships. Over the past three years, Swift has built a volunteer army of high-profile friends, many of whom appear in her videos and serve as special guests at her concerts. In almost any other circumstance, this would be seen as a likable trait; Leonardo DiCaprio behaved similarly in the '90s, and everyone thought it was awesome. But it's somehow different when the hub of the wheel is Swift. People get skeptical. Her famous friends are marginalized as acquisitions, selected to occupy specific roles, almost like members of the Justice League ("the ectomorph model," "the inventive indie artist," "the informed third-wave feminist," etc.). Such perceptions perplex Swift, who is genuinely obsessed with these attachments. "I honestly think my lack of female friendships in high school and middle school is why my female friendships are so important now," she says. "Because I always wanted them. It was just hard for me to have friends."

Popular people often claim they were once unpopular, so I ask Swift for a specific

example. She tells a story about middle school, when she called several of her peers on the phone and asked if they wanted to go shopping. Every girl had a different excuse for why she couldn't go. Eventually, Swift's mother agreed to take her to the local mall. When they arrived, Swift saw all of the girls she had called on the phone, goofing around in Victoria's Secret. "I just remember my mom looking at me and saying, 'We're going to King of Prussia Mall.' Which is the big, big mall in Pennsylvania, forty-five minutes away. So we left and went to the better mall. My

mom let me escape from certain things that were too painful to deal with. And we talked about it the whole ride there, and we had a good time shopping."

This incident appears to be the genesis for a verse in her 2008 song "The Best Day," a connection she doesn't note when she tells me the story. A cynical person could read something into this anecdote and turn it into a metaphor about capitalism or parenting or creativity or Pennsylvania. But in the framework of our conversation, it did not seem metaphoric of anything. It just seemed like a (very

real) memory that might be more internally motivating than any simplistic desire for money or power.

So is it unfair to categorize Swift as *calculating*? Maybe, and particularly if you view that term as exclusively pejorative. But calling her *guileless* would be even crazier. Swift views her lyrics as the most important part of her art ("The lyrics are what I want you to focus on," she asserts), so we spend some time parsing specific passages from specific songs. Here is how she dissects the conjecture over "Bad Blood," a single universally assumed to be about Katy Perry.

You never say who your songs are about, but you concede that if enough people believe something, it essentially becomes fact. So by not saying who you're writing about, aren't you allowing public consensus to dictate the meaning of your work? If everyone assumes that "Bad Blood" is about a specific person, aren't you allowing the culture to create a fact about your life?

You're in a *Rolling Stone* interview, and the writer says, "Who is that song about? That sounds like a really intense moment from your life." And you sit there, and you know you're on good terms with your ex-boyfriend, and you don't want him—or his family—to think you're firing shots at him. So you say, "That was about losing a friend." And that's basically all you say. But then people cryptically tweet about what you meant. I never said anything that would point a finger in the specific direction of one specific person, and I can sleep at night knowing that. I knew the song would be assigned to a person, and

the easiest mark was someone who I didn't want to be labeled with this song. It was not a song about heartbreak. It was about the loss of friendship.

But nobody thinks that song is about a guy.

But they would have. So I don't necessarily care who people think it's about. I just needed to divert them away from the easiest target. Listen to the song. It doesn't point to any one person or any one situation. But if you'd listened to my previous four albums, you would think this was about a guy who broke my heart. And nothing could be further from the truth. It

"After ten years, you learn to **appreciate happiness when it happens**, and that happiness is rare and fleeting, and that you're not entitled to it."

was important to show that losing friendships can be just as damaging to a person as losing a romantic relationship.

Now, there are more than a few molecules of bullshit in this response. When Swift says, "And that's basically all you say," she's neglecting to mention that she also told the reporter that the disharmony stemmed from a business conflict, and that the individual in question tried to sabotage an arena tour by hiring away some of her employees. These details dramatically reduce the pool of potential candidates. Yet consider the strategy's larger brilliance: In order to abort the possibility of a rumor she did not want, she propagated the existence of a different rumor

that offered the added value of making the song more interesting.

Swift can manufacture the kind of mythology that used to happen to Carly Simon by accident.

Speaking of accidents, here's some breaking news: They happen to Taylor Swift, too. She believes the most consequential accident of her professional life was when Kanye West famously stormed the stage during her acceptance speech at the 2009 MTV Video Music Awards. I'm surprised when she brings this up unprompted, because she has barely addressed the incident in five years, aside from the (comically undisguised) song "Innocent." But fences have been mended and feelings have been felt. At this summer's VMAs, Swift warmly presented West with the Video Vanguard trophy. She'll probably serve as secretary of the interior when he becomes president.

Swift was lauded for handling West's '09 intrusion with grace and composure, but her personal memories of the event dwell on the bewilderment. When West first jumped onstage, Swift halfway assumed he was about to make a special presentation, honoring her for being the first country artist to ever win a VMA. She truly had no idea what was transpiring. "When the crowd started booing, I thought they were booing because they also believed I didn't deserve the award. That's where the hurt came from. I went backstage and cried, and then I had to stop crying and perform five minutes later. I just told myself I had to perform, and I tried to convince myself that maybe this wasn't that big of a deal. But that was the most happenstance thing to ever happen

in my career. And to now be in a place where Kanye and I respect each other—that's one of my *favorite* things that has happened in my career."

Swift analyzes her friendships so often that I eventually ask what seems like an obvious question: Does she ever feel lonely? She responds by literally talking about *Friends.* "I'm around people so much," she says. "Massive amounts of people. I do a meet and greet every night on the tour, and it's 150 people. Before that, it's a radio meet and greet with forty people. After the show, it's thirty or forty more people. So then when I go home and turn on the TV, and I've got Monica and Chandler and Ross and Rachel and Phoebe and Joey on a *Friends* marathon, I don't feel lonely. I've just been onstage for

two hours, talking to sixty thousand people about my feelings. That's so much social stimulation. When I get home, there is not one part of me that wishes I was around other people."

This is understandable. Still, I note something any musician obsessed with self-awareness would undoubtedly recognize: in the retrospective context of a hypothetical *Behind the Music* episode, this anecdote would be framed as depressing. It would paint the portrait of a super-famous entertainer spending her day emoting to thousands of strangers, only to return home to an empty house and the one-way company of two-dimensional characters.

Does she not see the irony?

Oh, she sees it. But that doesn't mean it's real.

"There is such a thing as having enough," she says in her non-TV voice. "You might think a meet and greet with a hundred and fifty people sounds sad, because maybe you think I'm forced to do it. But you would be surprised. A meaningful conversation doesn't mean that conversation has to last an hour. A meet and greet might sound weird to someone who's never done one, but after ten years, you learn to appreciate happiness when it happens, and that happiness is rare and fleeting, and that you're not entitled to it. You know, during the first few years of your career, the only thing anyone says to you is 'Enjoy this. Just enjoy this.' That's all they ever tell you. And I finally know how to do that."

Taylor Swift is twenty-five. But she's older than you. ◆

I'M SORRY, TAYLOR SWIFT

My one tweet set off a worldwide search for a "missing" pop star from Los Angeles to New Zealand

SALON, **NOVEMBER 2015** | MAGGIE SHIPSTEAD

ould you care to hear a cautionary tale? It's about Twitter, like they all are. It's also about Taylor Swift. And New Zealand.

I'm generally a sporadic and half-hearted tweeter, wary of engaging, reluctant to put myself more in the path of the internet than is strictly necessary. I'm only on Twitter because my publisher asked me to be, so mostly I tweet about upcoming book events, about my dog, about other people's books. If, in life, a political issue turns me into an aspirin-chewing profanity-spewer, I may venture a tentative retweet of the *New York Times*. Once or twice I've publicly pestered customer service at big companies to pay attention to my complaints, which is depressingly effective.

Airports, though, bring out the latent tweeter in me. Maybe it's because I almost always travel alone and there's never a convenient human around to listen to my gripes. For example: people who read over my shoulder on airplanes while I try to work and even go so far as to comment on my writing? I don't like them. The insanely abundant and inescapable flatscreens airing CNN at full volume at every gate in the Atlanta airport? I believe ATL may be a black site for testing new forms of torture. Download the Amazon app or watch an ad in order to access free wifi? I choose death!

Cut to the night of Saturday, November 21. 8:45 p.m. PST. I was at LAX waiting for a flight to Auckland. I'd be gone for a month—ten days working my way southward through New Zealand to the city of Dunedin, from where, on a magazine assignment, I would catch a ship for some windblasted islands halfway to Antarctica. On my way home, I'd spend a few days warming up in the Cook Islands. I'd traveled alone in New Zealand before, blissfully, and was looking forward to repeating the experience.

As I moseyed up and down Tom Bradley International Terminal, I was mulling over whether, perhaps, the people who say not to drink alcohol before or during flights may not have fully considered the fact that I might really want to. Three flights were leaving for Auckland within two hours—sweet, in a way, to think of our little flock of planes playing follow-the-leader over the ocean—and as I passed the gate for the one before mine, my eye snagged on a slight, unadorned young woman in a black sweater. I slowed. Did I know her? No. Or—yes. It was Taylor Swift.

The gate area was almost empty. Final boarding had already been called. She was standing with a small clump of people (her team, I supposed) and appeared to be signing an autograph for someone, maybe the gate agent. Not wanting to be rude, I looked away and continued on. In L.A., where I live, celebrity sightings are common. At my neighborhood coffee shop, just in the month or so before I left for New Zealand, I'd seen Mark Duplass, Alia Shawkat, the red-haired guy from *Modern Family*, and someone who kept his sunglasses on inside and I was like 40 percent sure was Jon Hamm.

I texted a few friends. Saw Taylor Swift in the airport!

Cool, they said. Gotta be a good omen.

Perusing neck pillows, I considered how difficult it must be for Taylor (if I may) to move through public spaces. Probably it was a pretty good strategy for her to hide out in a lounge somewhere until the very last minute, then beeline through the terminal and into first class with her entourage, unseen by the hundreds of people back in economy who could definitely not be trusted to be cool and let her sleep. Last on, first off. Special ops precision.

A friend texted:

That seemed right, right? Sure. I sat on the floor by the big window at my gate. Outside, the pilot was walking around our 777, aiming a flashlight at the landing gear. I picked up my phone.

My tweet, as *The Guardian* would eventually report, was innocuous:

> **Maggie Shipstead**
> @MaggieShipstead
>
> It's like the old saying goes: when you see a Taylor Swift at the airport, you will have a pleasant flight to New Zealand.
>
> 11/22/15, 18:07
>
> ||| VIEW TWEET ACTIVITY
>
> **33 RETWEETS 58 LIKES**

You'll notice I didn't actually say *Taylor* was going to New Zealand. I said *I* was. True, I was reasonably confident she'd been getting on that Auckland flight, but I hadn't stuck around long enough to gawk her onto the jetway. Also, even though I assumed she was on her way to do a show or something else well-publicized, I didn't want to be one of those people who publicly announce the whereabouts of celebrities, steering gaggles

of paparazzi and superfans across the surface of the earth like armies in Risk.

I boarded, and my excitement over Taylor was immediately dwarfed by my excitement at having an empty seat next to me. For more than twelve hours, we were in the air. As the sun rose and breakfast was served, I watched an anonymous Pacific island pass under the wing. Were there people there? I didn't know.

We landed in Auckland around 7 a.m. on November 23, having crossed the international date line and lost a day. I had a couple hours before I had to catch a connection to Wellington. I passed through customs and let a biosecurity officer examine the bottoms of my hiking shoes. I bought a coffee. I logged onto the airport Wi-Fi. I checked my e-mail. I checked Instagram. I checked Twitter.

Something . . . was happening.

This was alarming. I hadn't hashtagged Taylor, but I also hadn't taken into account the people who continuously scour Twitter for her name and certainly not the small subset of that group who are hoping against hope she will someday be mentioned in the same sentence as New Zealand. When I failed to respond (being on an airplane and all) they began to confer among themselves, crowdsourcing the Taylorverse to see if *anyone* knew *anything* about where she was.

As I absorbed the frantic intensity of their intelligence-gathering, I began to wonder: *was* I legit? *Had* I seen Taylor Swift? How sure was I? Not so sure that anyone should fly to Auckland to hunt for her, I knew that much. What if I'd just seen some non–Taylor Swift person? I thought I'd glimpsed her signing an autograph, but what if I'd been mistaken? *Would* she have flown commercial? What did I really know about the range of private jets?

I tried a few experimental searches. "Taylor Swift Auckland concert November 2015." No. "Taylor Swift New Zealand." Nothing recent. In fact, Taylor seemed to be expected to appear at the American Music Awards back in L.A. that very night, and a few fans were upset I was suggesting she might be skipping out. If she *did* show up at the AMAs, my goose was cooked, unless her pre–awards show routine involved flying to New Zealand and then immediately back again.

I was starting to feel like someone who has confidently picked a suspect out of a police lineup, only to be confronted with exonerating evidence later. Maybe I'd had a strong subconscious desire, until now undetected, to glimpse Taylor Swift in real life, and my brain had cooked up a fun hallucination. And if I had seen Taylor, as I still thought I had, and she was trying to travel under the radar, I felt guilty for having carelessly exposed her. I would have guessed that lots of people would have seen her, that nothing she did could remain a secret, but apparently all it took was one bozo with a Twitter account to ruin everything.

There was one voice of reason amid my new correspondents:

kate / 36 @maggiegreenes 4d
okay what why are any of you saying she's in new zealand this tweet says the person is going to nz not taylor

Maggie Shipstead @MaggieShipstead
It's like the old saying goes: when you see a Taylor Swift at the airport, you will have a pleasant flight to New Zealand.

That's right. The person *hadn't* said Taylor was coming to Auckland. Maybe it wasn't too late for the person to weasel out of this.

Maggie Shipstead
@MaggieShipstead

@Emmaa_1989 @TSwiftNZ I don't know! I was going to NZ, but I don't know where she was going. Sorry!

11/23/15, 15:57

Problem: solved. Situation: neutralized. Taylor: somewhere in the universe. I didn't actually care where. Godspeed, Taylor.

In Wellington, my friend Dave picked me up at the airport. We got coffee. We ran an errand. We had lunch. Dave lives with his wife, Kelli, and their two sons in a beach town forty minutes outside the city, and by the time we arrived and I got back on Wi-Fi, the situation had escalated.

The frenzy I'd triggered among Taylor's fans had spread to New Zealand's online media. "Where in the world is TayTay?" read one headline. "Where in the world is Taylor Swift right now?" beseeched another. A Kiwi comedian had tweeted that she'd seen Taylor at the Auckland airport that morning, then later said she'd just made up the sighting to see if she could get on the *New Zealand Herald*'s website. Well, she did. Along with me. Kelli sat at her laptop and laughed, listing the New Zealand news and gossip sites I was showing up on.

One brief and disorienting Google search later, I'd seen myself described variously as a U.S. author, a Los Angeles–based comedian (clearly I was some kind of joker), and an "eager fan" of Taylor's. Screenshots of my tweet were everywhere.

A consensus seemed to have evolved that Taylor Swift being in New Zealand was so profoundly unlikely that the only logical explanation was that I was a big meanie who'd taken it upon myself to prank a sovereign nation. Others had joined in on my hilarious bit. Auckland comedians made inside jokes about Auckland and the mundane activities Taylor had been spotted doing there:

James Roque
@jamesroque

Taylor Swift is driving around Westfield
St Lukes trying to find a park

11/23/15, 16:34

Sam Smith
@ReelBigSmith

I saw @TaylorSwift13 doing the tactile
maze at the bottom of SkyCity Metro
#EDGETaylorSwiftWatch

11/23/15, 16:37

Several radio hosts reported that a customs official had seen Taylor at the airport and that multiple sources said she was filming a music video in the city, but everyone assumed they were full of it.

A reporter, Hayden Donnell, sent me a Facebook message:

> Hi Maggie, wondering whether you know that your tweet about Taylor set off a reasonably epic bout of Twitter trolling, including from one of our most popular radio shows, and ended up spawning stories in our two biggest news websites?
>
> I work for a website that does a lot of more comical/pop culture articles. Wondering whether you'd be happy to give a few quotes about how you didn't mean for this to happen, and how this is weird in general?

It certainly was weird and, no, I had not meant for this to happen. I wrote back and told my little narrative and also said I wasn't really looking to prolong things by contributing quotes.

He responded that he understood my wariness. However, he'd been accumulating more and more tips that Taylor was *indeed* in New Zealand, and while he'd expected to be writing about how I was at the center of a massive fake story, it looked like instead I was at the center of a real, if slightly silly one.

"This is a good intro to the New Zealand psyche," he wrote. "We can't believe she's visiting us." If her presence was confirmed, could he quote me?

Sure, I said.

So then Taylor didn't show up at the AMAs. A kiwi soap opera actor, Ido Drent, said he'd been in first class on her flight (NZ3, the one I'd seen! Fist pump! Yes!) and had chatted with her outside the lavatory. I started to see tweets saying that Universal Music had confirmed Taylor was filming a music video in New Zealand, although at first I wasn't sure if they were legit. All of this had personal significance for me in a way that, twenty-four hours previously, I could not have imagined. I wasn't a troll! I was a loudmouth prophet! As such, I was immediately quoted by my new friend Donnell.

The next day, *The Guardian*, wearily amused, entered the fray with the air of settling things once and for all:

Taylor Swift

Taylor Swift is definitely in New Zealand, media in New Zealand determines

The possibility that Taylor Swift might be in New Zealand sent the news media and Swift fans on a 'wild goose chase all over South Auckland'

Taylor Swift performing in Shanghai, China, in November. The singer is now in a slightly smaller and less populated country. Photograph: ChinaFotoPress via Getty Images

of Afghanistan. I couldn't figure out which one he was. "Hello Ms Shipstead," read the entirety of a message not long ago. The sender lived in Zambia. His profile picture showed a skinny, shirtless man standing in a corrugated hut. I contemplated his image for a long time. How had he found his way to my page? What were his hopes for our correspondence?

Or there's this guy:

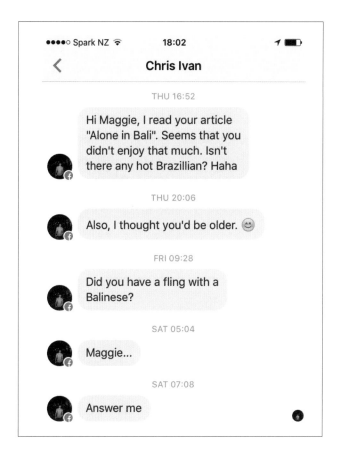

And so, after that, once the mystery was semi-solved, the story began to die out. I listened to pop radio while driving around the South Island and didn't hear myself mentioned, which was honestly kind of disappointing. Taylor moved on to Australia, then presumably onward from there and onward again, as pop stars do.

Where is the caution in this cautionary tale? I'm not sure. Definitely don't disclose the locations or travel plans of celebrities online. Although I didn't actually do that, I came too close. Maybe don't mention celebrities at all unless you genuinely want to be involved in a larger conversation? Maybe. I don't know. Everyone wants something different from the internet. Just as I have a puny Twitter account, I have a puny Facebook author page, and for some reason, probably some algorithm, most of my recent likes are from men in the Middle East, Central Asia, and Africa. Sometimes I look through them. One of my likers has only posted photos of groups of bearded, turbaned men in the mountains

What does he want? I kind of know but kind of don't. Clearly his idea of me (easily flattered, playful, eager to flirt) is nothing like the reality (prickly, solitary). Maybe we're all at cross-purposes with one another most of the time anyway, and the internet has only made our irreconcilable agendas and our impossible demands more visible. How many people on the internet ask Taylor Swift for something in a day? In a year? Right now, how many people are projecting their hopes and aspirations and longings and frustrations and rages onto that young woman in the black sweater? Or onto a flickering, shifting idea of her? Answer me. What does the world want from Taylor Swift?

And, by the way, where exactly is she? Does anyone know? ♦

DAN GIBSON

STUDENT, 24, BRITISH COLUMBIA

I didn't grow up in a wealthy family. I think that's why we valued music so much. It was a critical part of our day-to-day lives.

My first memory of Taylor was hearing "Love Story" during a school assembly in 2008. I was in the tenth grade. There was a girl I really fancied that year and I couldn't help fantasizing about running away with her.

I'm a nostalgic at heart. I find myself going back to Taylor's early work because it takes me to a place that I miss. A time when things were less complicated.

I've battled mental illness all of my life, including OCD, depression, and anxiety.

Fighting mental illness is like fighting any other type of physical illness. I've learned that everyone is dealing with something in their lives. No one is immune to difficulties, not even Taylor Swift. The key is to try to appreciate every moment you have.

My favorite place to listen to Taylor's music is by the ocean. There's something about staring out at the seemingly endless tide while listening to "Last Kiss" that puts life in perspective.

There's a difference between listening to Taylor's music and hearing it. Listening to it can change your life.

I had a dream that Taylor and I were at her apartment in New York City together. We were both wearing all white and she encouraged me to sing for her. Suddenly I looked down and I had a guitar in my hands and I was singing "Broken Wings" to Taylor Swift. When I woke up I laughed because I don't play any musical instruments, I wear black 99 percent of the time, and I don't listen to Mr. Mister.

If I ever actually meet Taylor, I'll probably ask her to marry me.

My favorite television show of all time is *The Walking Dead.* I'd love to see Taylor play a walker.

I've always idolized my grandfather. His attitude is that every day you have to try to keep progressing in your life. There is a lot of overlap between his traits and Taylor's.

My hope for Taylor is that she's able to live her most authentic life, whatever she determines that to be. If she continues to find joy in entertaining her fans, I'll be in the front row. If she decides that she wants to get out of the business and live off the grid in rural Maine, I'll support that too. I think after all she's given her fans, she deserves to be happy.

Taylor's greatest accomplishments will never be visible to her. She won't see them in the form of awards on a shelf or dollar figures in her bank account. She won't even be able to hear them on the radio. They will not be recognizable to her as she passes them on a busy street because they live within her fans. Her greatest accomplishments will be measured in the number of lives she's touched, in the hearts she's mended, and in the spirits she's lifted. And to me, that's a damn impressive legacy to leave behind.

> "There's something about staring out at the seemingly endless tide while listening to 'Last Kiss' that **puts life in perspective.**"

Taylor Swift

AS YOU'VE NEVER SEEN HER BEFORE

VOGUE, **APRIL 2016** | JASON GAY

By now you know that the past few years have been extraordinary ones in the life of Taylor Swift. Even if you have only casual knowledge of Swift's music—there may be six or seven souls left on the planet who can't sing all the words to "Shake It Off"—you're aware that Swift has become not only one of the most successful recording artists ever, but also an unrivaled power broker who has prevailed in a volatile media economy and brought today's music overlords to heel. Swift's 2015 stare-down of Apple—she declined to put her hit album *1989* on Apple's nascent streaming-music service when the company said it would not pay artists during its initial launch; Apple changed its policy immediately and paid everyone—was a seismic example of a single artist's toppling corporate might. At twenty-six, Swift is world-famous, wealthy, critically celebrated, a style influencer, and a cultural movement unto herself, recognizable everywhere she goes. She also has two awesome cats.

And yet today, in this chapel atop a hill in Reading, Pennsylvania, Swift is none of those things. She is the maid of honor at the wedding of her childhood friend Britany Maack. Swift and Maack have known each other since Swift was ten days old and have stayed close—there are grainy home videos of the two romping around a crib together and, more recently, photos of them sitting side by side at the 2014 Grammys. Last spring, after Swift accepted Britany's invitation to be maid of honor via Instagram—kids today!—she took Maack

---

The Christmas-tree farm is real. She showed me herself.

---

to Reem Acra, where Britany got fitted for her custom hand-embroidered silk-taffeta wedding gown and Taylor for the blush-pink, cap-sleeved chiffon maid-of-honor dress that she has on today (the fitting was also Instagrammed, naturally). Swift has even known the groom, Benjamin La-Manna, since kindergarten—she admits to having had a little crush on Ben way back then, when he was "that kid who sat next to me in class with the bowl cut and the Lego lunch box."

Swift hasn't been to Reading in more than a decade; she was fourteen when she moved with her family to Nashville, on her way to becoming a celebrated country singer-songwriter and later blossoming into one of the biggest pop acts in music history. Returning to the place where you grew up can be a bit of a mind-bender for anyone, and Swift is no different. During a car ride earlier in the day, she excitedly pointed out landmarks: the creek where she and Britany used to play as kids; a weathered tree house in the front yard of the former Maack family home; the piney woods she and her friends used to think were haunted.

"It's such a surreal, emotional thing," Swift says. "When you're a little kid, you're riding the same roads to school every single day, hundreds of times. When you come back, you snap into that strange nostalgia."

And the church! There are nuns here at Sacred Heart Chapel who taught Swift in kindergarten. Many of the wedding guests have known her for just as long. To them, Swift is not the superstar who, a handful of days ago, stood on a stage in Los Angeles and accepted a Grammy Award for Album of the Year, the first woman to win that prize twice. No, that maid of honor, currently fussing over and straightening out the train of the bride's gown, is Taylor—Scott and Andrea Swift's older kid, Austin's big sister, who grew up barely a five-minute drive away and used to go for ice cream at the Friendly's down the street.

To be clear: I'm not saying the people in this church aren't aware that Scott and Andrea's kid turned into, you know, *Taylor Freakin' Swift*—it's hilarious to watch the flower girls try to keep it together, and the nuns seem pretty jazzed, too—but that's not the story today. Britany and Ben are. And the only evidence that the maid of honor is you-know-who is the paparazzi who have gathered at the bottom of the hill, hoping to snag a photo with their long lenses.

We need to talk about the Christmas-tree farm.

A treasured footnote to the Taylor Swift backstory is that she spent much of her childhood being raised at, of all places, a Christmas-tree nursery called Pine Ridge Farm. It is the kind of quaint, Norman Rockwell–ian detail that sounds a bit too precious, too good to be true. Weren't her parents in finance? Didn't she grow up in the burbs? How was this possibly real? Come on.

The Christmas-tree farm is real. She showed me herself.

It's the morning of the wedding, and I am riding in an SUV with Swift and her mother, Andrea. Andrea is powering down the road, and Swift, dressed in a caramel-colored Reformation jacket and a pair of black jeans, is sitting passenger side. This area around Reading and its adjacent town, Wyomissing, is rich with

pastoral roads marked by open fields and stone homes, and the kind of rolling countryside that makes you want to saddle up and ride a horse—which Swift did as a child.

"That was kind of my mom's thing," Taylor says. "She really wanted me to be a horseback rider, and I did it competitively until I worked up the nerve at age twelve to tell her I didn't really love it like she loved it."

"I just wanted to make music and do theater," she says. "So I've been a big disappointment."

"I've gotten over the bitterness, finally," Andrea says sarcastically.

Soon we arrive at a clearing with a barn and a small farmhouse. This is the place, they tell me. Taylor and Andrea have not made any calls or arrangements about visiting. It's going to be a random drop-in from a pop star, like the Taylor Swift Publishers Clearing House Sweepstakes or something.

Taylor notices a man stepping into his car in the driveway. We pull up alongside, and Andrea rolls down her window. Taylor

leans over. "I used to live here," she says brightly.

The man immediately gives what can only be described as a Holy crap–it's–Taylor Swift look. "I know," he says, as if on cue.

Everyone laughs. The man's name is Dave Schaeffer, and he has lived here with his wife, Debbie, for about six years. He invites us to have a look around, and we all pile out.

"This must really bring back some memories," Dave says.

"Yeah, this is crazy," Taylor says. She surveys the fields behind the driveway, which include a small grove of pine trees her parents once planted. They now look tall enough for Christmas at Rockefeller Center. "It's beautiful."

This is where, Andrea tells me, Taylor Swift was brought home from the hospital in, well, 1989—I guess everyone knows the year of Taylor's birth by now. The split-rail fence that's still standing—Scott and Andrea built that themselves. Scott, a stockbroker, actually purchased and lived on the property before he'd met Andrea; on their first date, she came to a party he hosted in the farmhouse.

Debbie comes outside and introduces herself. "I always thought you might want to stop by," she says. "But I never wanted to bother you." The Schaeffers confess they lived here for a while before they learned about the famous former resident. "The pizza guy told us," Debbie says. "We had no idea."

She invites everyone inside. As we step into the cozy two-floor home, Taylor takes out her phone and starts filming. There's the living room where the Swifts put their family Christmas tree. There's where they once put the piano.

Casey, Dave and Debbie's daughter, arrives. She actually owns the house with her husband and lives nearby. She's thrilled but also beside herself that her two daughters are away skiing for the day.

"You want to see your room?" Debbie asks Taylor.

We go upstairs into a small corner room where a tiny Taylor used to demand three books and five songs every night. Taylor gathers the family together to make a quick video for the Schaeffers' grand-daughters, Siena and Tarah.

"Hi, Siena and Tarah," Taylor says cheerily. "This used to be my room. We wish you were here so bad."

I can't lie: all I can think of is Siena and Tarah returning from their ski trip to learn that Taylor Swift was hanging out at their grandparents' house, and decid-ing right then they will never go skiing ever again.

On the ride back, Andrea and Taylor sound almost overcome by what has just happened—by the sweet and polite and utterly un–freaked out mood of the whole experience. "My faith in humanity is restored," Taylor says.

And then she turns her head quickly away from the window: paparazzi.

Yes: I should note that when we ar-rived at the farm, we were informed by a couple of Swift's security people that there were at least a trio of uninvited pho-tographers who had followed us to the lo-cation to catch some hot, sexy farm-visit action. To Swift, this is about as surpris-ing as . . . what is the exact opposite of surprise? This is her constant state. She lives with it, adapts to it. Just a few years back, Swift was so excited about relocat-ing to New York City—it was the creative basis for *1989*—but when she's in the city now, within a couple of days, there is a circus of photographers outside her apart-ment building.

"But that kind of happens every-where," she says. The wedding ceremony has finished—Britany and Ben made it official to applause—and Swift and I have huddled downstairs at the church during a break before the reception.

I ask her: When was the last time you were in a place where nobody in the press had any idea you were there—no report-ers, no photographers?

"Mmmm, Colorado's good," she says. "If I go somewhere and stay in a house, nobody knows."

"She's the biggest, but a lot of people have been the biggest. Not a lot of people have been the biggest and the best, and she is."
—Jack Antonoff

Swift says she is ready to lie a little low. After the wedding, she will go to New York, where she will be spotted dining with her friend Lena Dunham, and then be seen a week later in Los Angeles with her brother, Austin, and her friend Lorde at the *Vanity Fair* Oscar party. As for future plans . . . who knows? For the first time in years, Swift is not sure exactly what is next. She is very much okay with this.

So what the hell are you going to do with the rest of your life, Taylor Swift?

"I have no idea," she says, with a sigh that's more blissful than anxious. "This is the first time in ten years that I haven't known. I just decided that after the past year, with all of the unbelievable things that happened . . . I decided I was going to live my life a little bit without the pressure on myself to create something."

Do not freak: Swift is not abandoning making music. Those who know her know this is chemically impossible. ("Her not being creative is one of the last things I'd ever worry about," the musician and pro-ducer Jack Antonoff tells me later.)

"I'm always going to be writing songs," Swift says. "The thing is, with me, I could very well come up with three things in the next two weeks and then jump back into the studio, and all of a sudden the next record is started. That's an option, too."

But probably not for the moment. "I would really like to take a little time to learn things," Swift says. "I have lots of short-term goals."

Such as?

"I want to be a well-rounded person who can make a good drink." (I can confirm from the wedding's cocktail gather-ing that Taylor Swift enjoys an old-fashioned and knows how to make one.)

Anything else?

"To be able to save somebody if they're drowning," she says. She's completely se-rious. "So CPR, all the various kinds of chest compressions. People tell you little tips, but that's different from actually tak-ing a class and getting certified."

Can you change a tire?

"No. I should probably know how to do that.

"I do things like this," Swift says. Once, "I got it in my head that I couldn't do a split, and I was really upset about it. And so I stretched every single day for a year until I could do a split. Somehow I feel better knowing that I can."

I ask her if she'd ever consider launch-ing a fashion line.

"Theoretically, yes," she says. "But I would want it to be something that was relatable and accessible and everyday. I don't see it being couture. I would want it to be reflective of my style. And a lot of things I wear are not highly expensive."

In May, Swift will cochair the Metropolitan Museum of Art Costume Institute's 2016 gala, for the exhibition "Manus x Machina: Fashion in an Age of Technology." It is a topic Swift—easily one of the biggest style icons of the social-media era—understands better than most, from technology's ability to shape trends to its growing influence on creativity and design.

Swift's personal style has, not surprisingly, matured over the course of her career, migrating from the early days of sundresses and, as she describes them, "bedazzled cowboy boots" to the vintage '50s vibe of a few years ago to the sleeker, street-conscious look she favors now. "I can look back at an old photo and tell you roughly what year it's from," Swift says. "Going through different phases is one of my favorite things about fashion. I love how it can mark the passage of time. It's similar to my songs in that way—it all helps identify where I was at in different points of my life."

Her style has never been deliberately provocative or fad-chasing—on the contrary, there's always been a kind of effortless appropriateness to Swift, a quality she shares with her friend the Midwest-raised model Karlie Kloss—and yet it's easy to see a curiosity about new things. Recently Swift cut her hair into a sharp bob, and she's been seen strutting in a pair of gothy, over-the-ankle Vetements boots that look stolen from the closet of Siouxsie Sioux. As usual, the changes are small, recognizable—a genius of Swift's, from music to everything else, is experimentation without alienation. Swift's style never tries too hard or appears publicity-craving; everyone's already paying attention, anyway.

Because I'm a hopeless cheeseball, I can't help asking: Being part of this wedding, does it make Swift think about being married some day? For the past year, she has been seeing the Scottish DJ-producer Calvin Harris. Harris is not here with her, but in early March, he and Swift will post cutesy notices on social media—his on Snapchat; hers on Instagram—commemorating the one-year status of their relationship. Soon after, both will post photographs of an idyllic, whereabouts-unknown vacation in the tropics, with TS + AW written in the sand. (Harris's given name is Adam Wiles.)

"I'm just taking things as they come," Swift says. "I'm in a magical relationship right now. And of course I want it to be ours, and low-key . . . this is the one thing that's been mine about my personal life."

Swift's friend Lorde thinks that Swift can only withdraw from music for so long. "We talk about this—in order to do good work, write these deeply personal records, we're constantly in a place of metacognition. Sometimes it can feel like you're a scholar writing a thesis about your own brain," Lorde says. "So I think she's going to try to pick up some new skills, maybe take courses in something. Tay is a big fan of taking time off until about month two—and then she gets this look in her eyes, and I know all the *Dateline* and frozen yogurt and mooching around is about to go out the window."

Here on a basement floor of the country club, where the bride is adjusting her gown, Swift and I hear the cocktail party gaining steam. A pair of bridesmaids stroll by. Swift gives them high fives.

"Honestly, I never relax, and I'm excited about being able to relax for the first time in ten years," she says.

Swift takes a sip of her old-fashioned. "I feel relaxed right now."

Just a few days before, Swift had been in the thick of it. In her Grammy acceptance speech for Album of the Year, she'd offered stirring words to women in the audience, but also made what was presumed to be a less-than-veiled reply to Kanye West, who'd released a new song in which he'd bragged he'd made Swift famous and tackily theorized the pair would one day have sex. The story pinged around on social media for the next seventy-two hours and generally made me want to put a metal pail on my head and bang it loudly against a wall.

Hadn't this whole Kanye vs. Taylor nonsense—which began, of course, seven years ago, when West barged into Swift's MTV Video Music Awards acceptance speech to argue that Beyoncé should have won—been declared over? Taylor Nation was aghast. Austin Swift posted an Instagram video in which he casually tossed a pair of West's Adidas Yeezy sneakers into the garbage.

I tell Swift the whole thing reminded me of Al Pacino's famous line as the aging Mafia don Michael Corleone in *The Godfather Part III*.

" '*I thought I was out . . .* '"

Swift knows exactly where I am going and finishes it: " '*They pull me back in!*'"

"I think the world is so bored with the saga," she goes on. "I don't want to add anything to it, because then there's just more."

I get why Swift would not want to fuel the dispute, but it's not hard to see a connection between West's credit-taking and the long tradition of men being dismissive—actively as well as subconsciously mansplainy—of

the hard work and success of women. This is something Swift has become hardened to, having spent much of her early years being mainly recognized not for her songwriting gifts (which just about everyone now agrees are rare and special) but for who she was dating, her fame distilled into what Swift calls "my incredibly sexist Men–of–Taylor Swift slideshows."

"You know, I went out on a normal amount of dates in my early twenties, and I got absolutely slaughtered for it," she says. "And it took a lot of hard work and altering my decision-making. I didn't date for two and a half years. Should I have had to do that? No.

"I guess what I wanted to call attention to in my speech at the Grammys was how it's going to be difficult if you're a woman who wants to achieve something in her life—no matter what," she adds.

The day after the awards, Swift went shopping at Barneys in Beverly Hills—"I was like, 'I'm going to buy some nice shoes today'"—and says she was approached by a number of women, mothers in particular, who thanked her. "Their response was really beautiful. You never know what anyone's response is going to be. So when it's good, it's really nice."

Swift has reached a level of fame at which unsolicited drama just finds her. The Men–of–Taylor Swift slideshows have calmed down, but she now takes grief for her "squad" of celebrity female friends, who, depending on the jab, are either too glam or too phony or some combination of the two.

"Ugh," Swift says when I bring it up. "I've had people say really hurtful things about me, and so I've kind of learned how to gauge it: 'This is, like, low-to-medium-level hurtful.'

"There are a lot of really easy ways to dispel rumors," she explains. "If they say you are pregnant, all you have to do is continue to not be pregnant and not have a baby. If the rumor is that you have fake friendships, all you have to do is continue to be there for each other. And when we're all friends in fifteen years and raising our kids together, maybe somebody will look back and go, 'That was kind of ridiculous what we said about Taylor and her friends.'"

It's as if Swift has become so big, so enticing a target, that she is no longer a mere person but a cultural symbol from which anything can be demanded. Jack Antonoff describes Swift's status as "almost like being president." He adds, "She's the biggest, but a lot of people have been the biggest. Not a lot of people have been the biggest and the best, and she is."

All of that feels a million light-years away, here, back home, among friends, at Britany's wedding. Before we part, Swift makes a request: she needs to practice her maid-of-honor speech. Now.

And so, in a basement corridor at the country club, Swift recites her maid-of-honor speech, which she has memorized.

I don't have to tell you that Taylor Swift's maid-of-honor speech is great. Of course it's great.

Here's one other thing about this wedding: Britany and Ben made the brilliant decision, which apparently is becoming a bit of a thing with twenty-first-century nuptials, to politely ask their guests to not bring their phones. So from the ceremony to the receptions and the toasts, people actually paid attention to the bride and groom—they focused, laughed, existed in the now. "All of our guests were present," Britany tells me later. "I truly attribute this to everyone unplugging from distractions and enjoying the moment."

When the time comes, Swift grabs the mic and delivers her maid-of-honor address with the unperturbed calm of someone who does this kind of thing before fifty thousand people. She tells the story of having a crush on kindergarten-era Ben with his bowl cut and Lego lunch box. She talks about how, as toddlers, Britany was the physical one, and she was the verbal one. "Essentially what you had were these two babies who each made up for what the other lacked," Swift says. "One couldn't really walk. One couldn't really talk. And interestingly enough, we assume those exact personas to this day when we are drunk . . . give us an hour."

The room goes crazy.

A few beats later, Swift has everyone teary when she talks about the "real love" she sees between Britany and Ben. "Real love doesn't mess with your head," she says. "Real love just is. Real love just endures. Real love maintains. Real love takes it page by page."

(I told you it was a good speech.)

Later on, there will be cake. Later on, there will be dancing, those flower girls getting a story that is going to totally blow their classmates' minds at school on Monday. Later on, the wedding band will entice Swift to the stage, where she will sing "Shake It Off" for her childhood friend on her wedding night and an audience that for the first time in history isn't waving ten thousand smartphones in her face. The night—the whole weekend—is storybook warm. You know the old Thomas Wolfe novel *You Can't Go Home Again?* Sometimes it's really true.

But Taylor Swift did. ◆

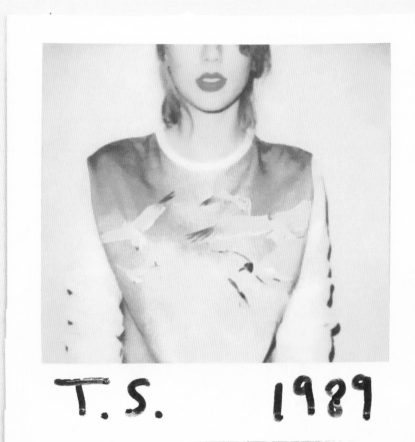

T.S. 1989

Taylor, thank you for those countless nights I'd take the long way home so I could listen to that one song one more time. Thank you for that lump in my throat right before you come on stage because I can't believe how <u>happy</u> I'm about to be for the next two hours. Thank you for continuing to write, brave girl. Thank you for understanding me always and helping me understand my worth. Thank you for all those dark room stereo feels on my bedroom floor. People haven't always been there for me, but your music has.

Thank you Taylor.

Crossword Puzzle Solutions

Solution to "Taylor Swift" (Page 7)

Solution to "65-Across" (Page 33)

Solution to "Speak Now" (Page 89)

Solution to "Red" (Page 115)

Solution to "1989" (Page 209)

Acknowledgments

This book was born out of two seemingly contradictory emotions—love and exasperation. The first emotion is simple enough: We love Taylor Swift's work more than that of any other contemporary musician. (We also love the uniquely positive example she sets for millions of girls and young women around the world.) The exasperation part is also straightforward: As literary types, we found it absurd that there was no great book about this great artist—a woman who, more than anything, is a terrific *writer*. Think of all the books that have been published about Bob Dylan or Bruce Springsteen, for instance. The fact that not a single serious book about Taylor existed came to seem like a failure of our entire profession. It *bothered* us.

We'd long been in the habit of sending mash notes to Taylor's management. Our hope, then and now, was that she will eventually decide to write books of her own. Her manager always seemed happy to answer our emails and explain that the time just wasn't right, which made sense. Taylor had the music world to rule, not the literary one. But with the ten-year anniversary of her career on the horizon, we began to think: What if, while we waited for the time to be right, we went ahead and created a book of our own to celebrate the first decade of Taylor's reign?

From there, the project evolved in beautiful and spontaneous ways. We asked ourselves: What Would Taylor Do? We soon realized that the only proper way to honor Taylor and her legacy (so far) would be to involve the people she loves the most: the fans. We thought of all the times she's invited us backstage, sent us presents, responded to our messages, and made it known she cared. Wouldn't she want all of us involved in something like this? Wouldn't she sponsor fun, inclusive contests to decide the book's title, design its cover, and be its honorary author? Wouldn't she invite fans to submit their favorite photos and artwork for use in the book? Wouldn't she ask other fans to dream up crossword puzzles, adult coloring pages, and other Swift-themed elements to include? Wouldn't she invite thirteen other superfans to become advisers/ambassadors on the project? (And, crucially, wouldn't she insist on *paying* all of the fans who contributed to the book for their work, as we've done?) We thought so, and came to think of the book as the ultimate group effort to show Taylor how much she has meant to all of us over the past ten years. A *very* elaborate mash note, if you will.

So we built a website, sent out a press release, and held our breath. Happily, we didn't have to hold it for long: Our fellow Swifties responded with instant and overwhelming enthusiasm. Within hours we were swimming in contest entries, emails, ideas, and the best kind of collaborative energy, ultimately receiving more than ten thousand submissions from fans from Los Angeles to New Zealand and everywhere in between. (A favorite far-flung video entry came from Ruth in Dubai. Look it up.)

It's only appropriate, then, that our first thank-you goes out to the thousands of Swifties who embraced the project and proved, again and again and again, that Taylor Swift has the most passionate, creative, engaged, and caring fans of any artist on the planet.

Special thanks go to the fans who emerged as the book's core group of advisers and advocates, all of whom contributed in ways large and small and literally shaped the book into the amazing object you hold in your hands. We've been making books for a long time, and this has been one of the most inspiring experiences of our careers, thanks to you. Much love and gratitude to contest winners Tyler Conroy (honorary author), Tenay Barker (who titled the book), and Shanna Canarini (who designed the cover), and to ambassadors Zainub Amir, Mallory Arnold, Taylor Compton, Emma Dugan, Kelsey Eihausen, Ashley Friedman, Dan Gibson, Livia Jahn, Carlee Langham, Anna Perillo, Kelsey Quitschau, Mikayla Scanlan-Cubbege, and Alyssa Walters. Thanks also to cool-parents Jennifer Dugan, Pam and Russ Eihausen, Kristy Jahn, and Sarah Langham for signing off on participation.

The book would not exist without the ridiculously talented group of writers, critics, artists, puzzlers, and others whose work we are grateful for permission to include. Thanks to Jeremy Carroll, Rick Bell, Kelsey Quitschau, Tony Orbach, Jon Caramanica, Sasha Frere-Jones, Robert Christgau, Aimee Lucido, George Hatza, Austin Scaggs, Vanessa Grigoriadis, Rob Sheffield, Chris Willman, Finn Vigeland, Lizzie Widdicombe, Erik Agard, Brad Nelson, Brian Hiatt, Tavi Gevinson, Tony Millionaire, Jason Polan, Jody Rosen, Larissa Zageris, Kitty Curran, Hermione Hoby, Francis Heaney, Brendan Emmett Quigley, Jared Smith, Jane Hu, Jen Vafidis, Melissa Block, Jada Yuan, Ann Powers, Chuck Klosterman, Maggie Shipstead, Jason Gay, Caitlin Buckvold, Richie Wentworth, Megan Romero, Ryan Murphy, Becky Sullivan, and Christian Santillo.

Thanks to the following for their essential help behind the scenes: Harry Deitz and Bill Uhrich of the *Reading Eagle*; Jeff Remz of *Country Standard Time*; Lachlan McLean, Valerie McFaddin Fitch, Amanda Murphy, Calvin Gilbert, and Jason Hill of Viacom/MTV; Maria Barrera of PARS International; Kyle Tannler and Deanna Scopino of Condé Naste; Sarah Lazin of Sarah Lazin Books; Rex Parker; Benjamin Tausig of American Values Club crossword; Debbie Paitchel of Wenner Media; David Bressler of *New York* magazine; Andi Winnette of *The Believer*; Steve Gevinson; Marya Spence of Janklow & Nesbit; Choire Sicha; Jenna Meade of National Public Radio; Amy Trombetta of Wright's Media; David Daley of *Salon*; Rebecca Gradinger and Veronica Goldstein of Fletcher & Company; Debbie Chitwood at the Borough of Wyomissing; Lieutenant Tom Endy of the Wyomissing Police Department; Michelle Butnick-Press of Getty Images; and Matthew Lutts of the Associated Press.

To borrow a phrase from another Simon & Schuster author, it takes a village to publish a book, and the citizens of S&S embraced this project wholeheartedly and made it better at every turn. Love and thanks to Jonathan Karp, Richard Rhorer, Julia Prosser, Dana Trocker, Elizabeth Breeden, Jackie Seow, Kristen Lemire, Allison Har-zvi, Lisa Erwin, Paul Dippolito, Jane Archer, Chelsea Cohen, Felice Javit, Emily Remes, Adam Rothberg, Cary Goldstein, Allison Fitzpatrick, Jeff Wilson, Marie Florio, Ben Loehnen, Erin Reback, Elizabeth Gay, Rakesh Satyal, Emily Graff, Zack Knoll, Amar Deol, Megan Hogan, Johanna Li, Kaitlin Olson, Eloy Bleifuss, Sydney Morris, Mark Speer, Craig Dean, Mick Wieland, Kevin Weaver, Stephen Bedford, Abigail Bergstrom, Brit Hvide, Megan Reid, Kelsey Donohue, and Lindsay Means. And we want to offer a special word of thanks to Jessie Chasan-Taber, our editorial intern in the fall of 2015 who did brilliant, and crucial, early work on the project. Thank you, Jessie!

Many thanks to the team at 13 Management for tolerating our regular mash notes with such warmth and good cheer: Robert Allen, Jay Schaudies, and Tree Paine. Obviously, we hope to work with you when the time is right. To Andrea, Scott, and Austin Swift: thank you for raising and supporting such an incredible woman, and for sharing her with all of us.

And, finally, the words *thank you* don't seem big enough to convey the magnitude of our gratitude to Taylor Swift for everything your work has given us over the past decade. So we made a book, collectively, to try—an attempt to "capture it, remember it." It's imperfect, surely. But it's a sincere effort, and it's a start. On behalf of all your fans: Thank you, Taylor.

Text Credits

Jeremy Carroll, "Twelve-Year-Old Performs at 76ers Game," *The Reading Eagle*, April 19, 2002. Used by permission of *The Reading Eagle*.

Rick Bell, "A Review of *Taylor Swift*," *Country Standard Time*, Fall 2006. Used by permission of the publisher.

"20 Questions with Taylor Swift," CMT.com, November 2007. Used by permission of CMT.com.

Jon Caramanica, "My Music, MySpace, My Life," From *The New York Times*, November 2008. © 2008. *The New York Times*. All rights reserved. Used by permission and protected by the Copyright Laws of the United States. The printing, copying, redistribution, or retransmission of this Content without express written permission is prohibited.

Sasha Frere-Jones, "Prodigy: The Rise of Taylor Swift," *The New Yorker*, November 2008. Used by permission of the author.

Robert Christgau, "A Review of *Fearless*," 2008. Used by permission of the author.

George Hatza, "Taylor Swift: Growing into Superstardom," *The Reading Eagle*, December 2008. Used by permission of *The Reading Eagle*.

Austin Scaggs, "The Unabridged Taylor Swift," *Rolling Stone*, November 27, 2008. Copyright © 2008 Rolling Stone LLC. All Rights Reserved. Used by permission of Wenner Media.

Vanessa Grigoriadis, "The Very Pink, Very Perfect Life of Taylor Swift," *Rolling Stone*, March 5, 2009, Copyright © 2009 Rolling Stone LLC. All Rights Reserved. Used by permission of Wenner Media.

Rob Sheffield, "A Review of *Speak Now*," *Rolling Stone*, November 11, 2010. Copyright © 2010 Rolling Stone LLC. All Rights Reserved. Used with permission of Wenner Media.

Chris Willman, "Princess Crossover," *New York*, October 2010. Used by permission of the author.

Robert Christgau, "A Review of *Speak Now*," 2010. Used by permission of the author.

Lizzie Widdicombe, "You Belong with Me," *The New Yorker*, October 10, 2011. Used by permission of Condé Nast Publications.

Robert Christgau, "A Review of *Red*," 2012. Used by permission of the author.

Brad Nelson, "If You Listen Closely, Taylor Swift is Kind of Like Leonard Cohen," *The Atlantic*, November 2012. Used by permission of the author.

Brian Hiatt, "Taylor Swift in Wonderland," *Rolling Stone*, October 25, 2012, Copyright © 2012 Rolling Stone LLC. All Rights Reserved. Used by Permission of Wenner Media.

Tavi Gevinson, "Just Kidding, Love Sucks," *The Believer*, July/August 2013. Used by permission of the author.

Jody Rosen, "Platinum Underdog: Why Taylor Swift is the Biggest Pop Star in the World," *New York*, November 2013. Used by permission of *New York*.

Larissa Zageris and Kitty Curran, excerpt from *Taylor Swift: Girl Detective and the Secrets of the Starbucks Lovers*, July 2016. Used by permission of the authors.

Image Credits

Kelsey Quitschau
Art on pages x, 10–11, 53, 96–97, 194–195, 214–215, 228–229, 272
All coloring pages
Photographs and art on pages 40–41

Richie Wentworth
Art on pages 28–29, 95

Megan Romero
Art on pages 122–123

Caitlin Buckvold
Art on page 279

Ben Tausig
All crossword puzzles

Tyler Conroy
Photographs on pages xi–xv

Christian Santillo
Photographs on pages xi–xii, 126, 260

Becky Sullivan
Photographs on pages xiii–ix, 1, 128–129, 226

Livia Jahn
Photographs on pages 14–15

Ryan Murphy
Photographs on pages 16 and 262

Mikayla Scanlan-Cubbege
Photographs on pages 22–23

Mallory Arnold
Photographs on pages 62–63

Taylor Compton
Photographs on pages 84–85

Emma Dugan
Photographs on pages 110–111

Alyssa Walters
Photographs on pages 124–125

Tony Millionaire and Jason Polan
Illustrations on pages 140–147

Anna Perillo
Photographs on pages 148–149

Kelsey Eihausen
Photographs on pages 204–205

Sarah Langham
Photographs on pages 212–213

Ashley Friedman
Photographs on pages 224–225

Zainub Amir
Photographs on pages 242–243

Tenay Barker
Photographs on pages 248–249

Dan Gibson
Photographs on pages 270–271

Getty Images
Endpaper One—Jason Squires
Title Page—Fred Lee
Dedication Page—Christopher Polk/TAS
Endpaper Two—Sascha Schuermann
Page 2—Jesse D. Garrabrant
Page 12—Kevin Winter/ACMA
Pages 20, 21—Ethan Miller
Page 24—Rusty Russell
Page 26—Ethan Miller
Page 27—Larry Busacca
Pages 44, 45—John Mabangalo-Pool
Page 48—Ed Rode (far left), Rick Eglinton (second from left)
Page 49—Kevin Mazur (second from right), John Shearer/LP5 (far right)
Pages 50, 51—Rusty Jarrett
Page 76—Kevin Mazur
Page 80—Rick Diamond
Page 83—Jeff Kravitz
Page 90—Rick Diamond
Page 92—Rahav Segev
Page 93—Rob Verhorst
Page 94—Bryan Bedder (top), Rick Diamond (bottom)
Pages 98, 99—Ethan Miller

About the Contest Winners

Tyler Conroy (who is the honorary author) has been a Swiftie since Taylor Swift's tour bus almost ran him over in 2008. Born in Conway, Massachusetts, he began taking guitar lessons at age fifteen just so he could learn every song on *Fearless*. Since then, he has ugly cried at nineteen Swift shows, met her three times, put on an entire Taylor Swift musical, been invited to her NYC loft, and gotten the word *fearless* in her handwriting tattooed on his left foot. "I am so proud to be the honorary author of this book," he says. "Taylor made being different cool and, for all of us who see ourselves as different, she's given us a reason to stay fearless." Tyler may be contacted on Twitter at @tyvid5.

Tenay Barker (who titled the book) is a freshman at Stephen F. Austin State University in Nacogdoches, Texas. She is studying computer science and hopes to be as great a role model as Taylor is someday. "I have always been a fan of Taylor Swift," Barker says. "My title tries to express the way that Taylor and her fans have grown as one over the course of her incredible journey. She has been so dedicated to us, and we have been so dedicated to her, and I am so ecstatic that we can to do something for her tenth anniversary by creating this book." Tenay may be contacted on Twitter at @tenaybarker.

Shanna Canarini (who designed the book's cover) grew up in Lowell, Indiana, and graduated from the American Academy of Art in 2015 with a bachelor's degree specializing in graphic design. Canarini has seen Swift in concert twelve times, and she got to meet the artist at the 2010 CMA Festival. "I always knew I wanted to be an artist," Canarini says, "but Taylor was the one who influenced my decision to become a graphic designer. My biggest dream would be getting to work with her to design tour merchandise, album art, or promotional material." Commenting on her winning cover design for *Taylor Swift: This Is Our Song*, Canarini says, "I wanted to capture as much as I possibly could from each era, pulling from everything Taylor's put out there for us and really showcasing each era as a sort of puzzle piece to the much larger picture that is not only Taylor but the last ten years we as fans have spent together with her." Shanna may be contacted on Twitter at @scanarini.